THE LONELY PLANET TRAVEL ANTHOLOGY

EDITED BY DON GEORGE

Published in 2016 by Lonely Planet Global Limited
CRN 554153
www.lonelyplanet.com
ISBN 978 1 7865 7196 0 (pbk)
© Lonely Planet 2016
Printed in China
10 9 8 7 6 5 4 3 2 1

Managing Director, Publishing Piers Pickard
Associate Publisher Robin Barton
Commissioning Editor Don George
Editor Karyn Noble
Art Direction & Design Dan Di Paolo
Typesetting Palimpsest Book Production
Cover design Hayley Warnham
Print production Larissa Frost, Nigel Longuet

STAY IN TOUCH
lonelyplanet.com/contact

AUSTRALIA
The Malt Store, Level 3, 551 Swanston St,
Carlton, Victoria 3053 03 8379 8000

IRELAND
Unit E, Digital Court, The Digital Hub,
Rainsford St, Dublin 8

USA
150 Linden St, Oakland, CA 94607
510 250 6400

UK
240 Blackfriars Rd, London SE1 8NW
020 3771 5100

Paper in this book is certified against the Forest Stewardship Council™ standards. FSC™ promotes environmentally responsible, socially beneficial and economically viable management of the world's forests.

CONTENTS

INTRODUCTION

BY DON GEORGE

This book represents two milestones for me: it's the 10th literary anthology I've edited for Lonely Planet, and its publication marks my 40th year as a travel writer and editor. Contemplating these connected milestones as I complete this collection, I've realized that they share a fundamental truth: every LP anthology is a new journey, and just as with all my worldly journeys, each of these word-journeys teaches me something new and precious about the planet too.

To begin this year's literary journey, I reached out to a wide range of celebrated essayists, novelists, mystery writers, journalists, and travel writers, asking if they would like to write about a travel experience that had exerted a particularly profound and lasting influence on their lives. Despite daunting deadlines and demanding schedules, two dozen of these responded with impassioned tales. Humbled and heartened by their enthusiastic response, I posted a call for submissions online, inviting writers around the world to submit tales of travels that had in some way changed their lives. I received hundreds of stories, many of them exceptionally eloquent and compelling.

From these rich pieces I composed the collection you hold in your hands: 34 stories representing a world-spanning spectrum of themes, styles and settings.

Some of these stories present youthful adventures that bestowed indelible lessons. On her first trip to the US, Jan Morris discovers the quintessence of America in a moment of Wisconsin wonder. Inspired by a cologne commercial, teenager Elizabeth George sojourns in Swinging London on a school program – and falls under the spell of a subject and setting that will become the focus of her life's work. In his mid-twenties, Alexander McCall Smith tastes triumph and tragedy on an odyssey around a momentarily idyllic Ireland, and on her first trip overseas, Blane Bachelor courts disaster by turning an eight-hour airport layover into an innocent exploration of downtown Bangkok.

In some of these stories, travel sows the seeds of love, as it does for Ann Patchett when she misses a flight to Vienna, then puts her ticket to much better use one year later, and for Francine Prose in Oaxaca, where the theft of her family's passports and plane tickets delivers an unexpected, life-threading reward. TC Boyle settles uneasily into an isolated Irish farmhouse for three and a half months, and unexpectedly makes lifelong friends. And Shannon Leone Fowler experiences love and loss of the most profound kind, as she and her boyfriend explore the far reaches of China – and each other.

Sometimes our travels confer unexpected connections. Suzanne Joinson is enchanted by the jasmine-scented mysteries and marvels of Damascus, Porochista Khakpour finds an unfamiliar sense of belonging on her first visit to Indonesia, Natalie Baszile follows her heart into the home of an unconventional Louisiana family, and James Michael Dorsey communes with his ancestors – and plays a crucial, unwitting role – on a hunting expedition with a Stone Age tribe in Tanzania.

Sometimes we are at a turning point in our lives when we travel, and our journey becomes both compass and balm: Mridu Khullar Relph conjures the resolve to overcome intimidation in Ghana, Carissa Kasper finds herself via sickness and salt flats in Bolivia, Maggie Downs unloads her grief with strangers-become-family in Egypt, and Bridget Crocker navigates uncharted waters – literally and emotionally – on a remote river in India.

And sometimes travel bestows endlessly rippling life-lessons, as it does for Jeff Greenwald tracking the divergent trails of love from

Introduction

Greece to Nepal to California; Pico Iyer trying to foresee the future in Kathmandu and Kyoto; and Tahir Shah following the teachings of a seed into the mountains of Morocco.

These are just some of the stories herein. All of the pieces in this extraordinary collection are equally moving and inspiring tales of life-changing adventures. I have felt honored and privileged to edit them, and I want to thank all the authors for their evocative, poignant and courageous contributions.

———————

These days I spend much of my time teaching and speaking around the world, and one question I'm invariably asked is: what is the point of travel writing? I usually answer that, for me, travel writing is an attempt to record and share my experiences away from home – to evoke the cultures, landscapes, and people that I've encountered, and to share the challenges and revelations these encounters have bestowed.

But now, as I contemplate this collection of tales, I realize that even more fundamentally, the point of travel writing is simply to make sense of the world – the world outside and the world inside, and the sacred place where they intersect. Travel writing is an attempt to impose order and meaning on the chaos of experience, and in this, it taps deeply into the rich and ancient vein of human storytelling.

In this sense, the tales in this book hearken back to travel writing's distant roots, but they also have great contemporary significance, for as the landscape of publishing has transformed over the past few years, some critics have predicted the death of travel writing, opining that vividly written and deeply reflected accounts would give way to superficial blog posts and insipid prose-selfies. As the stories collected here resonantly attest, great travel writing – transporting travel storytelling – is alive and well in 2016.

Another heartening gift I take from this collection is the illustration of how important travel is to our planet. It's important to each of us as individuals. And it's important to us collectively too.

Forty years ago, on a balmy spring night in Athens, I sat in the moonlight reflecting on the first of my own life-changing travel experiences: I had spent the year after college living in Paris and Athens, and traveling to Italy, Austria, Switzerland, Germany, Turkey, and Egypt; in a month I would leave for Kenya and Tanzania. I took out the tattered, wine-spattered journal that had accompanied me throughout these adventures and wrote, 'These travels have expanded and enriched my world view more than I can comprehend. The more I travel, the more I see, the bigger the world becomes. And the more cultures and peoples I encounter, the more I am awed and fascinated by the incredibly intricate and beautiful tapestry of humanity that covers this small globe.'

I didn't know then that I would become a travel writer, and that I would spend the next four decades of my life wandering the world and trying to make sense of my adventures. But now, looking back on that wide-eyed young man, I can see that the life-map I would follow was already being drawn.

Recently I sat in the California moonlight writing the introduction to an anthology of my own travel writing from the past 40 years. Reflecting on the meaning of travel for me, I wrote, 'As I have learned over and over, travel teaches us about the vast and varied differences that enrich the global mosaic, in landscape, creation, custom, and belief, and about the importance of each and every piece in that mosaic. Travel teaches us to embrace our vulnerability and to have faith that whatever energy we put into the world will come back to us a hundredfold. Travel teaches us to approach unfamiliar cultures and peoples with curiosity and respect, and to realize that the great majority of people around the world, whatever their differences in background and belief, care for their fellow human beings. And ultimately, travel teaches us about love. It teaches us that the very best we can do with our lives is to embrace the peoples, places, and cultures we meet with all our mind, heart, and soul, to live as fully as possible in every moment, every day. And it teaches us that this embrace is simultaneously a way of becoming whole and letting go.'

Introduction

Reading these words now, I'm struck by how deeply these same themes weave through the stories in this anthology. The tales presented here show how, at its best, travel is a profoundly surprising experience, one that opens our eyes, minds, and hearts to the wonders of the world. They show how travel tests us and teaches us – that we are not alone, that we are resilient, that we can overcome the greatest challenges and forge paths through even the most daunting mountains and deserts, literal and metaphorical. And they show us that the way to find and forge these paths – and to complete the connections they make possible – is by pouring our love into the world.

That's the final, most precious lesson this collection affirms for me: if we follow the compass of the heart, we will always find our way.

Thank you for taking this book into your life. As you travel through these pages, may your mind be widened, your spirit enlivened, and your own path illuminated by these worldly word-journeys.

LONG DISTANCE
BY TORRE DEROCHE

(Names have been changed.)

It's a well-known fact that teenagers can't see long distance. They can only see as far as the back corner of a sports oval, where the cool kids are smoking cigarettes and making out with mouths bracketed by zits. Beyond that point, the world obscures into vague, peripheral irrelevance. Whateverland. It therefore seemed odd that my high school would arrange for a busload of fifteen-year-olds to travel to the very centre of irrelevance, a mindboggling 2380 kilometres from our normal seeing range and into the blank void of the Australian outback.

What do you pack for a journey into barren nothingness? Well, in my case, everything I could stuff into a duffle bag only marginally smaller than a Mini Cooper, including most of my wardrobe, a pair of black Dr Marten boots for hiking, John Lennon sunglasses, a disposable camera, a Walkman and mixtapes, a journal with a lock and key, my favourite stuffed toy, my favourite padded bra, zit cream and a huge feather comforter patterned with lions and tigers (to keep the monsters out at night).

We were headed towards the country's red centre, to the world's largest monolith, Uluru, but of course we didn't care about enormous rocks or monumental deserts or the fact that, in the outback, you can see a zillion burning suns on the ceiling of night, a shooting star a second. We cared only about the fact that, for three delicious weeks, our days would be spent pressed up against forty other teens in the small and breathy space of a moving vehicle – without parental supervision.

We knew we'd left the suburbs when we saw a truck fly past with a bloodied kangaroo tangled in its bumper, little paws angled in haphazard directions, guts woven through the steel grill like a macabre cross-stitch. 'Ewwww!' everyone on the bus chorused in disgusted delight. The outback roadside was littered with a hodgepodge of dead wildlife, each with its own halo of blowflies. You don't often see death in the suburbs, and seeing so many lifeless mammals was like witnessing something illicit. But what was going on outside the windows was not nearly as exciting as what was going on inside the bus....

In the seat next to mine, there was Marike: an exceptional artist, the coolest girl in school, and as stylish as she was self-assured. I was in love with her, platonically speaking, though I wasn't sure if I wanted to be friends with her so much as drape myself in her like a wolf-skin coat so I could navigate the world inside that much chutzpah. She had a mean streak in her too, but we were best friends, so I was never the target of her bite. I was safe next to this big, bad, beautiful wolf – protected, even.

Then there was Kurt. He was new to our school and darkly mysterious, like Christian Slater in *Heathers*, and so, of course, when he spoke to me, each and every hair on my body stood to attention. When he accidentally brushed past me one time, electric currents ran through my bones. Strategising ways to sit closer to him consumed most of my mental energies.

There was Carolina, who'd been my friend since we were wide-eyed and clear-skinned. She taught me how to shoplift and carve a bong from an apple at a time when I was still memorising all the lyrics to Disney songs. She was way cooler than me, luminous and magnetic, quirky and pixie-like, which is why Kurt couldn't take his eyes off her.

There was Lars, with his shock of white-blonde hair, tanned skin, chiselled cheeks, and blue eyes that gazed with the kind of disquieting intensity that makes jelly out of knees. He had a knack for making me laugh by poking me in the ribs and saying 'Boop!' He loved me; I knew it. The only trouble was: Lars loved every girl on the bus. My Plan B love interest was a grade A player.

And then there was me: twig-skinny, giraffe-tall, naively trusting, and offbeat by accident. While all the girls had turned into hourglasses, pears, apple bottoms, and other soft, exquisite shapes of femininity, I was still angled and pointy. Any day, I expected my curves to pop too. It was like waiting for Christmas to come.

Three weeks. I was to have three glorious weeks with these people, during which time anything at all could happen. The bus passed another mangled roo on the roadside, his body a crimson smear on black tarmac wobbling with heat. 'Ewwwwww!' we chimed.

This was looking like it was going to be the best time of my life.

Seventy percent of the Australian mainland is classified as semi-arid, arid, or desert, and so you'd think I would've known what most of my country looked like. I didn't. The sight of the desert surprised me. I'd always pictured Sahara-like rolling dunes of golden, shifting sand, but this was all red dirt and spiky spinifex from horizon to horizon, for days and days. The flatness was astounding. I'd never seen so far into the distance before.

Sometimes we slept on the bus while it sped northwest in a dead straight line. Sometimes we stopped and camped in the desert. The nights dipped to freezing and the mornings were fresh for a few hours before the heat of the day arrived. One morning, we emerged from our tents groggy and puffy-faced to find our teachers gathered around looking stressed and angry. They called a meeting. We gathered in a semi-circle, all forty of us.

Long Distance

One of the teachers held up a square foil packet, torn at its perforation. My first thought was that it was some kind of snack that I'd never seen before. Ooh, is that chocolate? I wondered. Chocolate for breakfast!

'Whose condom packet is this?' the teacher said.

A condom? People my age were having sex?

Nobody said a word.

The dirt at our feet became very interesting to us all, and it was then that I noticed Dr Marten boots paired with my twiggy legs made me look like a newborn giraffe who had joined the military. Idiot.

'Well?' the teachers prompted.

More silence.

In the beats of that silence, I grew overwhelmingly sad. My idea of fun at fifteen was watching Warner Bros. cartoons on Saturday mornings with my little sister sleepy-eyed beside me, my mum in the kitchen cooking waffles. I worried that sex might change this, that I would outgrow my little sister. I worried that it would end the waffles. But more than anything, I worried that everyone else was speeding along a fast, straight road towards adulthood while I was still a twig with a washboard chest and Disney songs resounding joyously in my head.

'Is anyone going to own up to this?' the teacher prompted.

No doubt our eyes became impossibly wide and glassy as we shape-shifted into the most puppyish version of ourselves – a superpower that only teens have – until the teachers hesitated, unsure of how to proceed. They gathered heads and whispered among themselves, likely discussing whether it was more important to punish teenagers for hooking up on a school camp or to celebrate the fact they did so safely.

The issue was dropped.

I still hoped there'd somehow be chocolate.

Uluru first came into sight in the Pitjantjatjara tribal lands, looking like a pimple that had budged from the horizon. As we neared, we dug deep into our juvenile vocabularies to describe what we were seeing, exchanging such riveting dialogue as:

'Oh, wow, it really is big.'

'Yes, it's massive.'

'Way more massive than I thought.'

'Oh my god, you guys, it's soooo big!'

We quickly ran out of adjectives and grew listless. We'd travelled such a long way to get here and our excitement turned to impatience, impatience to indifference, so that when we finally got off the bus at the rock we were complaining of hunger and tiredness, and the relentless nuisance of flies.

The Australian flag will tell you that the British own the country, while history and due respect indicate that it belongs to the indigenous people. Actually, it's flies that own the continent. They're ruthless dictators who help themselves to the corners of your eyes, drinking from tear ducts and gathering in great armies to loop-the-loop around your face in infuriating black clouds that can't be shooed away by even the most enthusiastic jazz hands. There is no swear word in the English language that can adequately express the frustration felt as a result of non-stop fly harassment. Perhaps the Aboriginals have one, I don't know. Either way, the flies could've been the reason we all began unravelling, or maybe it was the heat and the storms, the broken sleeps, or the fact that we were a fizzing, noxious hormone cocktail – on wheels.

We pitched our tents for the night in the campground closest to the rock. A torrential rain began without warning, and leaked into the tent canvas to form a waterfall over my bed. Marike dashed into the tent to move her stuff out of the way, and, anxious, I yelled, 'Move my blankets! Move my blankets!'

She glared at me with her green wolf eyes and said, 'Grow up, bitch!' I wasn't immune from Marike's bite after all, wasn't protected alongside this big, bad, beautiful wolf.

Outside the tent, I cried until I coughed and choked. Behind me, a rock nine kilometres in circumference shone brilliant copper against the silver of passing rainclouds, but who cares about staggeringly beautiful geological anomalies when life is rushing forward at breakneck speed and you're being left behind.

My favourite teacher, Miss Michaels, asked me if I wanted to go for a walk with her to talk it over, and we left the campsite to follow train tracks into the colourless and disturbing emptiness of the desert, as lonely as Mars. The tracks were covered in dry bones in both directions – femurs and ribs, jaws and teeth, and I wondered how so many bones had ended up in one place. The only logical reason for this, I decided, is that once upon a time, an unfortunate animal was sitting on the tracks when a train came along and squashed it. The meat of that dead thing attracted a hungry dingo, who then got killed by a train, who then attracted another dingo, who then got killed by a train... until it became a museum of fatal mishaps. This seemed slapstick hilarious, like a Warner Bros cartoon, but I was too involved with choking on tears to switch out to a giggle.

Miss Michaels listened while I ranted and wept. Her motherly attention opened my floodgates, and from my skinny body poured the great burden of being a 15-year-old girl, only without either the perspective or eloquence that comes with time and maturity. 'Like, she's being mean to me for no reason, and, like, she can be such a bitch sometimes and...' Flies gathered on my teary face for a drink. I shooed them with two hands. Fuck you, flies. Fuck you, Marike.

Miss Michaels pulled a white carton of cigarettes out of her handbag. 'Want one?' she said.

My jaw dropped like a train-struck dingo. I didn't know how to respond. I wasn't a smoker – she'd mistaken me for one of the cool kids, but I considered taking it up on the spot so as not to leave her hanging.

'Um... thank you,' I said, 'but... I don't... actually... smoke.'

She shrugged and lit the cigarette for herself, her cheeks caving into her jaw as she sucked hard on the filter. I noticed her face was pockmarked and weathered, ravaged by both puberty and time, her hair frizzy and dry. She was so old. 30? 35? Fuck you, Miss Michaels.

We continued to walk along the tracks, crunching dry dust, bones and tussock grass beneath our feet, our earlier ease now strained.

Maybe I should've taken the cigarette. I bet Marike would've taken the cigarette. Carolina would've taken two cigarettes – one for her lips, one to stick behind her ear – and then she would've taught Miss Michaels how to make a bong from a dead dingo's skull.

On the tracks I spotted a dingo's jawbone with two clean rows of intact teeth and not a flay of skin or tuft of fur remaining. I picked it up to take home as a souvenir. The trip would be coming to an end soon. This was looking like it was going to be the worst time of my life.

While the morning was still fresh from the previous night's freeze, we set out to climb King's Canyon, a rocky interruption to the desert plain. I broke away from the group on 'Heartbreak Hill' and dashed ahead, traversing cliffs and waterholes, gorges and sandstone domes. 'It's not a race!' cried a teacher from behind me, but I kept racing, because I craved air.

To my advantage, I had the body and athleticism of a boy. I rounded corner after corner, my feet stepping over rocks and ruts in a dance, until I could no longer hear a chorus of gossiping teens behind me. I was alone. Though it would take me eighteen more years to stop being terrified of it, what I didn't know then was that aloneness would become a sanctuary to me – be it on a plane to somewhere new, a hotel room for one, or under the ocean's waves drawing oxygen from a tank. What other people call loneliness would become my Church, its silence my God.

From a rocky outcrop with a panoramic view, I looked out over the middle of my country. The landscape stretched out flat in every direction, placing me at the centre of a distance so unfamiliar that I had no language in my fifteen-year-old mind to articulate it. When I'd return from the journey, my dad would say, 'So tell me about your trip,' and I would summarise all this stunning, perplexing largeness into a monotone 'It was okay.' (That I'd grow up to become a writer would surprise us both.)

Long Distance

So distant was the horizon that I felt I should've been able to see the whole world from that vantage point – only this, unbelievably, was but a small portion of it. These wide sweeping spaces were not just names to be memorized for geography tests, not just a collection of tonal areas on the gridded spinning globe my dad kept in his office – they were actual places made up of dizzying spaces. This could only mean that the blue regions on the maps marked in cursive lettering with Pacific and Atlantic were also harrowing volumes of space, not to mention the endless stretch of universe overhead. I was but a dot on this giant blue ball, a grain of desert sand, and just as irrelevant too. It was a thought so surreal that it was difficult to hold for longer than seconds. But in those sweet seconds, I could breathe.

The sun rose higher, saturating the grey morning light with a spectrum of colours. Nothingness was not nothing at all; it was packed full of somethings. Who knew the colour brown could come in so many different shades? The carpet of spinifex turned a lustrous beige-green as the sun angled over it just so, the shadows taupe, the dirt a rich ochre against the blue of day. With my eyes fixed into the far distance, I watched the beauty of an ancient land being changed by the turning sun.

EIGHT HOURS IN BANGKOK

BY BLANE BACHELOR

'Please don't leave the airport.'

It was an order more than a request, my mom's worry transmitting loud and clear over the thousands of miles of fiber optic from Florida to a pay phone in the Rome airport, where I sat fiddling with the cord. A beep cut through the line, warning that there was one minute left on my prepaid card.

'Ok, Mom, I gotta go now – my time is up on the phone and my flight is leaving soon.'

But she was insistent. 'Promise me you won't leave the airport.'

We were talking about the upcoming leg of my current journey, quite literally, around the world. After stopping for week-long visits with friends in London and then Italy, I – a newly turned 22-year-old with a newly acquired passport – was headed for a couple of weeks Down Under, where my dad was working temporarily in Canberra, Australia. One of the conditions of my relatively cheap round-the-world ticket was nightmarish connections and layovers, including the one my mom was pleading with me about now: eight solid hours in Bangkok.

I sighed and slung my carry-on corduroy bag over my shoulder. 'Ok, Mom, I promise I won't leave the airport.'

She thanked me, said she loved me, and we hung up. I felt only a slight pang of guilt as I scanned the boards for my departure gate to Bangkok. This was a prime opportunity to snag another stamp for the almost bare pages of my passport, my first time ever to set foot on the Asian continent, and a chance to explore – albeit briefly – one of the most exotic-sounding cities I'd ever heard of.

Of course I was leaving the airport.

By that point, I had been traveling for about two weeks. The original plan had been to head straight to Australia. But then I remembered I had a high-school friend in London and a high-school sweetheart in Italy. Both extended warm invites. I got an extended leave from the newspaper where I was working, got my passport, and started planning my itinerary: London, Italy, then Australia. By the time I would head back to Tampa via Los Angeles some five weeks later, I'd have flown around the globe.

This was my first time in London since my family had lived there when I was a wee little thing, and the city was as wondrous as an adult as I remembered from my childhood days. I'd never been to Italy, though, and my former flame and I made the most of our time there. My trip coincided with his return to the States, and we spent his last couple of days on a farm stay near Sienna working hard in the field by day, and gorging on amazing pasta dinners at night. I turned 22 in that tiny town – how worldly I imagined myself, shedding the clichéd debauchery of my 21st year in one of Europe's most romantic countries.

We hit Florence after that, and then Rome. But by then the glorious Mediterranean sunshine had turned to endless rain, bringing a depressing gray pallor to the grand city. I was depressed, too: a little homesick, still smarting from a devastating heartbreak prior to my trip, and sad that my high-school love, moodier than I'd ever remembered him, seemed to have zero interest in rekindling the flame. We went our separate ways in the Rome airport, him heading back home, me continuing my journey. I had at least 24 hours of traveling ahead.

I couldn't wait to see Australia, but exploring Canberra – a city an Aussie friend had warned me wasn't exactly brimming with excitement – with my dear old dad wasn't exactly going to scratch the adventurous itch I'd been feeling throughout my trip. But Bangkok! I couldn't get the song out of my head: '*One night in Bangkok makes a hard man humble....*' Surely, a few hours there could make me, an eager but inexperienced traveler, more wise in the ways of the world.

Our flight touched town early, around 9am on a Sunday morning. I flagged down a flight attendant and asked for her advice: Did an eight-hour layover allow enough time to do some exploring in the city? Yes, she told me, but only because there was much less traffic on a Sunday. As the plane emptied out, several other flight attendants hovered around me like a cloud of butterflies, their long purple dresses fluttering. They wrote the name of a market on a slip of paper and, as politely as they could, issued words of advice: 'Only go this market – nowhere else!' 'Bangkok traffic very very bad sometimes – come back airport early!' 'Don't lose passport!' 'Be careful what eat!' 'Don't miss flight!' Yikes. This all sounded alarmingly similar to what my mom had said. But I thanked them all and smiled graciously, pushing those thoughts aside as I gathered my stuff and left the plane. How hard could this really be?

I made my way through the airport, the unfamiliar rhythms of Thai chattering all around me. I found a currency booth and exchanged $US75 – until that moment, I had no idea that baht was the national currency of the country. There was no line in customs, but the thrill over acquiring my third passport stamp was offset by the stern look on the official's face as he handed it back to me. How suspicious would it look when I returned just a few hours later? I started to sweat in my wool jacket, doubts about the sanity of my plan creeping in again.

I walked through the sliding glass doors to the taxi line and a cloud of men in suits swarmed around me, buzzing offers: 'Taxi for the lady?' 'Good rate!' 'We drive you!' I must have looked like an incredibly easy target wearing a heavy coat in such oppressive humidity and mustard-yellow sneakers that had seemed so cool when I bought them in London but now felt like clown shoes, and struggling with a bulky corduroy bag full of souvenirs from England and Italy that I was already cursing myself for buying.

I picked out a man wearing a wrinkled sport coat and tie, the most respectable-looking one of the bunch, looked him right in the eye, and handed him the slip of paper with the market's name on it. Round-trip to the market and back would cost 800 baht, he told me, about US$20. I told him I'd pay half up front and half when he picked me up. He agreed, and we shook hands. I couldn't help but gloat a little over my cleverness. I may have looked like an ugly American, but I was no idiot.

My taxi driver was a balding, frail fellow with glasses who appeared about sixty. He sat on a massage-type seat cover made of small wooden spheres. A tangle of beads, jade, and a round metal symbol inscribed with Thai dangled from the rearview mirror, swaying back and forth as we hurtled down the highway. He spoke no English, and I, of course, no Thai, so we rode along in silence.

Once at the market, he maneuvered to a curb and we agreed on a pickup time – 1.30pm – through a series of hand signals and pointing at our watches. And then I had another thought: what if I could leave my huge heavy carry-on in his trunk? I gestured, he nodded, and it was settled. I stuffed my passport and money into a small purse and left everything else – my travel souvenirs, wool jacket, Discman and CDs – in the bag and shut the trunk, knowing that if I never saw them again, at least I wouldn't have to schlep them around all day in the oppressive heat. The driver smiled and nodded before driving off. I watched the beads sway from the rearview mirror as the traffic engulfed him.

The market, too, was an overwhelming crush of humanity: throngs swarming about in all different directions, no rhyme or reason to the flow; vendors shouting to prospective buyers; rancid, meaty smells wafting through the humidity. The hodgepodge of stalls burst with a cornucopia of food and goods: children's clothes, shoes, CDs, sweets. I couldn't take my eyes off the whole poultry dangling from hooks – ducks, perhaps? – skinned and dripping with sizzling grease.

This was nothing like the Bangkok I had imagined, full of temples, monks in flowing robes, and friendly locals. I felt the weight of infinite eyes on me, the only solo female – and Westerner – in all directions, wandering about helplessly, pushed and pulled by relentless crowds who had things to do, places to go, people to see. I wanted to take some photos, but I was afraid that pulling out my camera would only make me stand out even more, a gawking tourist amid these busy locals just trying to get their shopping done.

I suddenly lurched forward, nearly tripping over something on the ground. It was a man with no legs, rags falling off his frail torso, propped up on a blanket, moaning and waving a tin cup in the air. I was so stunned – I'd never before seen a human in such wretched conditions – and so embarrassed for almost having fallen on him that I didn't even have the wherewithal to dig into my purse for some money. I glanced back as I walked away to see the crowd flowing around him once again, like he was a rock in a roaring river.

I continued through the market. I bought an entire carton of Marlboro Lights (overkill indeed for the occasional cigarette I thought made me look cool, but they were so cheap). Some weird gummy candy. A handful of postcards. Some underwear and a pale green T-shirt with a bunny on it to change into back at the airport, plus a toothbrush and toothpaste.

Eventually, the crowds and endless stalls started to wear on me. I found my way to the edge of the market to figure out my next move, and a youngish boy, a teenager perhaps, rolled up on a pedicab. 'Tour?' he asked. 'Good price!'

Drenched in sweat and tired of walking, I agreed. I hopped onto the back seat – thankfully, it was protected from the sun by a red awning cover – and we were off. We rode for quite some time, the boy pointing out things here and there in his broken English. I couldn't understand much, but I smiled and nodded anyway as we rolled through the shanty towns along a small creek. Their corrugated metal roofs shone brightly in the sun, colorful laundry strung outside. Chickens scratched about in the dirt patches next to the water. I'd never seen such poverty first-hand, and I couldn't help but stare. Occasionally, a small child would stare back at me as we passed.

Eventually, the boy pedaled to some small shops. 'You shop?' he asked, stopping. I didn't feel like buying anything else, but I felt obliged to at least go inside, not even thinking that he may have gotten a kickback from the store owner. Chimes tinkled as I opened the door, the smell of musty incense overwhelming. On the stained red carpet, I noticed a small tray of food: an offering, maybe, with fruit, nuts, and a small, glistening mound of what looked like intestines. My stomach did a somersault.

I slowly browsed the aisles of the stuffy shop, crammed with a little bit of everything: chips and snacks, trinkets, statues shaped like temples. The owner, an unsmiling middle-aged woman, stared at me from the cash register as I picked up a small maroon Buddha, turning it over in my hand before putting it back on the shelf. This did not please her. 'You no buy, you leave!' she shouted at me.

'Um, ok,' I stammered, trying not to look at the innards on my way out.

'Let's go back to the market,' I told the pedicab driver. I was over all of this: the heat, the crowds, this unfriendly shop owner, and feeling so far from home and so glaringly out of place. I checked my watch: thankfully, I had only about an hour before the cab driver would pick me up.

Back at the market, the crowds had become even thicker. I didn't have the energy to battle them, so I found a small cafe and bought a huge bottle of water. The fact that it was ice cold felt like my first victory of the day.

Thirst quenched, I pulled out the postcards I'd bought. A lump formed in my throat as I wrote one to my grandmother in Alabama. I would have given anything to be in her cosy kitchen at that very moment, plowing through a plate of her buttermilk fried chicken and mashed potatoes, accompanied by a glass of iced tea. But I didn't write that. Instead, I scribbled snippets of my trip so far and how much fun I was having.

At about 1.15pm, I made my way to the designated pick-up spot. Like the market, the nonstop whirl of vehicles around the traffic circle seemed more frantic now, too. I couldn't imagine what it would have been like on a weekday. I looked for my driver, and quickly realized what a task it would be to distinguish his cab from the dozens of others that buzzed past. That is, if he was coming back. For all I knew, he was back at home, showering his grandkids with crisps from England, an Italian scarf, and a secondhand CD player brought right from America. I didn't think to write down his license plate number or a phone number for the cab company – not that I could communicate with someone, anyway.

Minutes ticked by. I frantically scanned the roaring maelstrom of taxis, small trucks, motorbikes with mask-covered drivers. My mind started to race with alarming thoughts. I had carefully saved enough baht for the return trip I'd already negotiated, but what if that wasn't enough to get me back with another cab driver? Where in the world would I go to exchange more money? My beloved CD player – my savior on long, crowded flights – how was I supposed to survive the next 20 hours of travel without it? And, most disturbing of all, what kind of moron trusts a stranger to come back to pick her up after she's voluntarily left her stuff in the trunk of his cab?

Standing at the edge of that traffic circle, cars and vehicles maniacally zooming past, I fought back tears. My mom was right: I should never have left the airport. I was surely going to miss my flight, screwing up the rest of my itinerary and endlessly worrying my poor folks. Maybe I wouldn't even be able to get to Australia. So much for a grand adventure that I could brag about later: in just a few hours, Bangkok had beaten me, and beaten me badly.

I sighed deeply and tried to clear my head. It was now 1.45pm, and my next flight would depart at 5pm. I needed to figure out another plan – quickly. I started looking around to see where I could catch another cab, and then, out of the corner of my eye, I caught a glimpse of something familiar: the mass of beads and jade hanging from my driver's rear-view mirror. My heart leapt: had he really come back?

I blinked my eyes as the cab rolled up to the corner, almost weeping with relief when I realized that, yes, it was him: the same frail, balding driver from before. Now, however, he seemed downright heroic. He smiled slightly and nodded, just like he'd done when he'd dropped me off. I wanted to throw my arms around him in a giant bear hug, but instead, I just smiled back and climbed into the cab. Unprompted, he then opened the trunk and loaded my carry-on bag into the back seat with me. I didn't even check inside to make sure everything was there. I knew it would be.

He hit the gas and we chugged back into the sea of Bangkok's infamous traffic. We again rode in silence, the dangling beads and jade swaying gently and hypnotically, lulling my eyes to close.

Hours later on my Australia-bound flight, relishing the feel of a fresh pair of underwear and T-shirt, I reflected on my long layover. Maybe Bangkok hadn't beaten me after all. Instead, this vast, unrelenting, irreverent, unnerving, stifling city had revealed a lifelong truth about travel: that if you take a leap of faith, more often than not a net will appear in the form of a good, honest, trustworthy soul who will save the day in one way or another, sometimes simply by showing up.

And that, I told my mom years later while finally 'fessing up about my layover in Bangkok, is a lesson best learned by getting out into the world – and, most certainly, out of the airport.

SMALL LIGHTS IN LARGE DARKNESS

BY REBECCA DINERSTEIN

My third voyage on the Hurtigruten was the first taken by night: a season earlier I'd crossed Norway's Vestfjord on this boat under staggering daylight. Now, the Arctic's Polar Night had become as dominant as the Midnight Sun had been, and as I waited for the boat to pull away from the shore, the water before us lay black. I could hear bells ringing on distant boats I couldn't see. I sat on the observation deck in my down coat and fur-lined hat. The air was cleaner than any I'd breathed before – its impurities had frozen away. I breathed, and the bells rang. I couldn't argue with that total darkness, I could only admire it; I could only rest within it and look out toward the invisible horizon at the far end of the fjord.

I arrived on Little Christmas Eve. Growing up Jewish in New York City, I'd never celebrated regular Christmas Eve, let alone Little, so the Nordic embellishment of 23rd December enchanted me. In the home of a friend, I found the table set for a grand dinner, and the tree raised. Under the tree lay boxes of icicle ornaments, tiny paper Norwegian flags, and presents bearing every name in the family, including mine. I'd never seen my name under a Christmas tree before. This house sat on an island not far from the North Pole, and these presents struck me as the genuine offerings of elves. We can lose twenty years in ten

seconds when presented with delight this pure; I became a child. I sat at
the foot of the tree. I touched the green needles. I touched the blue
ribbon that held my gift shut. The hills outside my friend's windows
were as dark as the fjord had been, but illuminated with glowing
houses, each house full of its own tree. For the first time, I understood
the holidays as light-oriented, as Pagan in the sense of being rustic and
unaffiliated and merry. This was a time of celebration, no longer of
obligation, a time of rest, not of strain.

In the morning we walked to the graveyard. The graves lay under
thick snow and the tombstones bore elegant, Scandinavian names with
patronymic suffixes: -son, -datter. When you subtracted the birthdates
from the death dates, the difference often approached a hundred years.
Like the air, these lives had frozen their impurities away, had been
preserved, had lasted. The trees rising behind the graveyard were pink
because it was midday and the sun was both rising and setting. The
snow was blue. As Mr Lockwood does at the conclusion of *Wuthering
Heights*, I 'wondered how anyone could ever imagine unquiet slumbers
for the sleepers in that quiet earth.' My friend wished her mormor
(mother-mother, a perfectly simple construction for 'grandmother') a
God Jul, a Merry Christmas.

At home again, we watched Donald Duck, Mickey Mouse, and
Goofy celebrate Christmas in their own colorful homes – a Disney
series that has aired every Christmas in Norway for the past sixty years.
We drank Julebrus, a crimson-colored soda that tasted like pears and
cinnamon. Elaborate gothic font ran over the bottle's label, forming the
words EVENTYR BRUS (FAIRYTALE SODA) over an illustration of a
panicked white goat butting a menacing troll. The fine print read:

FAIRYTALE SODA
THE THREE BILLYGOATS GRUFF
'Now I'm coming to get you,' screamed the Troll. 'Yes, you just
try! I have two horns, with them shall I gore your eyes out! I
have two battle stones, with them shall I crush both marrow

and bone,' said the biggest goat. He attacked the troll, put out
his eyes, beat out both marrow and bone and butted him over
the waterfall. All the goats went to their summer house.'

The holiday season in New York had been essentially competitive –
a choice between endless options, gatherings, sales. In the Arctic, it felt
merely essential, singular. The house was our one, small, true shelter.
The landscape around the house proceeded with its brutal winter
regardless of our festivities and did not ask anything of us. With
nowhere else to be, nothing else to do, and complete darkness around
us, we felt permitted to create boundless, reckless light.

Christmas ended and winter remained. I left my friend's home and
returned to my own: a large empty building on a nearby island. I had
come to write a book of poems and it was time to get back to work after
so much Mickey Mouse. I hadn't decorated every windowsill of my
building with miniature elf figurines, but someone had. These
creatures, called *nisser*, dominated every Norwegian household from
November through February. I sat among the *nisser* and opened my
miniature travel laptop, entering into an undersized realm balanced
only by the enormity of the local weather: Arctic storms howled and
threw the trees against my window.

Every day, for two hours, the darkness would recede. It would be
replaced by pastel colors that washed the sky and snow indiscriminately
until both land and heaven turned the same purple. When the darkness
returned, I knew what fields and what mountains I wasn't seeing – I
learned to see beauty where it was and where it wasn't. I learned to see
beauty where it had been, and where it would appear again when the
sun next came to town.

This winter taught me how to brighten. I learned that a small flame
makes a wide glow. I learned that even night can be visually
scintillating, and that a landscape can communicate a lot of personality
when no other persons are near. For lack of distraction, I worked hard
that winter and finished my poems. Many of them examined the

darkness I'd inhabited, and celebrated the sources of light I'd uncovered. On my final evening in the Arctic, I saw the Aurora Borealis for the first time. It arrived, green, to the patch of sky directly outside my window. Anne, a neighbor in a nearby house, came up to my door. It was two in the morning, I was packing up to leave in a few hours, and, miraculously, Anne had just baked an apple cake. We ate the warm cake in the green snow and thanked winter for its bounty.

EGGS IS DONE!
BY JAN MORRIS

Driving somewhere in Wisconsin 70-odd years ago, near the start of my very first visit to the United States, I stopped off after dark at some simple lodgings by the highway (for I was short of cash, and it was before the time of the ubiquitous motel). I was bemused in those first American days by everything I saw and did – everything was new to me, everything was enthralling – so next morning while my breakfast was being prepared I took a cup of coffee and strolled out to the porch to contemplate the scene outside. It proved a climactic moment of my life.

I remember my responses vividly to this day. Across the highway was a railway track, and beyond that rolled a river. I say 'rolled', because it did not seem to be simply flowing, like the rivers of home, but moving with an altogether different sense of purpose and self-esteem. Rolling was the word for it, and I dare say there came into my mind even then a lyric to go with it – 'Away, you rolling river!' – for 5000 miles away in Britain I had grown up in the haunting presence of Shenandoah, without ever knowing where or quite what it was. There were fishermen out there that morning, in small black boats, and clusters of islands, and somewhere on a distant building the Stars and Stripes were flying.

Eggs Is Done!

Well, it wasn't the Shenandoah River, but it was the young Mississippi, rolling silently down to the Gulf of Mexico, and it caught at my emotions as no other river ever had, and seemed to speak to me of dimensions I had never contemplated. Ever since then the idea of the mighty American rivers has bewitched me, and I have come to think of the greatest of all Americans, Abraham Lincoln, as a sort of American river himself.

I am not making this up, not entirely – I took notes at the time, and have them beside me to prod my impressions. While I marvelled there at the river, as if on cue in an allegorical pageant there came erratically into my line of vision an all-American urchin. He was riding a bicycle along the road, but sort of halfheartedly, lolling sideways on it, hardly bothering to steer the thing, idling his way down the road with an almost arrogant ease. Was he whistling? He may well have been. Was he chewing gum? Of course. Did he have a wodge of newspapers under his arm, ready to be thrown to people's front doors? He surely did, because of course he was conforming to an archetypical figure of my American imaginings, familiar to me already from movies and cartoons and Huckleberry Finn, and here, I thought, most satisfyingly fulfilling the concept.

Where is he now? I suspect he exists no more, in particular or in kind. He himself must be pushing 80, and I suspect he has no successors in his news-round, but he meant a lot to me that day. He was all I wanted of American insouciance, American chutzpah, American youth, riding away there so cheerfully brazen, chewing his gum, chucking his newspapers, I suspect, with perfect accuracy at the thresholds of his clientele, and seeming to me a late and heartening example of what the Frenchman Jean de Crèvecœur long ago called that New Man, the American!

On a shack nearby an election notice was pinned, inviting passers-by to continue their support for an incumbent local sheriff, and engagingly adding YOUR VOTE WILL BE GREATLY APPRECIATED – and oh! how greatly I appreciated that addendum!

I knew very little about American politics, and the style of this approach seemed to me reassuringly domestic, as it were, intimately and comfortingly down to earth. I was soon to learn that it was hardly characteristic of American hustings, but as I copied it into my notebook I thought it hinted at a fundamental, underlying kindness to the American way of life – and as a matter of fact, I think so still….

Now you must believe me – I perhaps make the most of my experiences, but I don't lie. Hardly had that newsboy gone wayward on his rounds, hardly had I scribbled down the sheriff's endearing message, when there appeared on my stage out there one of the supreme symbols of the American drama. Did I really hear a whistle sound? Well, perhaps not, but there is no denying that with a mighty rumble and a rush there swept past me that morning the Great Northern Railway's Empire Builder, bound for Seattle out of Chicago. It is lodged in my memory now with all the other great American trains I was later to encounter, but in my fancy at least it stormed by me then with a colossal splendour of silver coaches, a terrific whirling of wheels, a glimpse of white napkins and, yes, that unforgettable sad wail of the whistle that was to become in my mind a very essential of the American ethos, 1950s style.

Like rivers, like urchins, like country politics, the Empire Builder stamped upon my mind profound conclusions about the meaning of America, as I stood there so wonderingly that Wisconsin morning, and very soon a text of the occasion, too, was imprinted once and for all upon my consciousness. It was not something from Walt Whitman, not a snatch of the Gettysburg address nor even a ditty from Glenn Miller's Chattanooga Choo Choo, but it has remained in my memory from that day to this with a truly poetical clarity. It sang out to me from the cook-house behind my back, and what it said was this:

'Eggs is done!'

THIS BLESSED PLOT, THIS EARTH, THIS REALM

BY ELIZABETH GEORGE

Although I'm an American, I have spent my entire career writing crime novels that are set in Great Britain and that feature a cast comprising nearly all English characters. This is hardly unusual now, but when I started out more than thirty years ago, there was only one other American writer who was using Great Britain as a setting. Unlike me, she was working in mystery fiction – different from crime – and at the time she was rather slapdash in her terminology and her facts. For my part, I set a different course, and I was determined to do well by it.

Since people are often surprised to discover, after reading one of my novels, that neither am I British nor have I ever lived in Britain, they want to know why. Why write novels set in England? Why do it when you've never even lived there? Why go to the trouble that this must cause you? Why compete with genuine British crime writers, who are obviously the real article? Why? Why? Why?

I've come up with a variety of answers to these questions through the years because early on I discovered that answering them in an identical way was quite tedious and possibly the route to madness. So sometimes my reply has to do with my enduring love of Shakespeare. Sometimes it has to do with my exposure to pop culture in the '60s, which was influenced greatly by British films, a crowd of brand new

British actors, British music, and British fashion. Sometimes I tell the story of my friendship with a thirteen-year-old girl from Manchester, England, who came to join my eighth-grade class at St Joseph's Grammar School in Mountain View, California. More often than not, I add that since my background as an English major largely revolved around English and Irish and not American literature, I was naturally drawn to the place, as I'd read so much about it. But I have never told the real story, and I have never touched upon the real reason. It is this: the entire direction of my life was altered by a television commercial.

I can see it even now. Worse, I can hear the little song accompanying it. (As it was quite pretty, I am loath to call it a jingle.) I know exactly what it was advertising: a cologne made by Yardley.

The year was probably 1965. I would be lying if I were to say that at that time I was not a fan of the Beatles. I'd discovered them prior to their coming to America, seeing them on a film that Jack Parr had run as a bit of a laugh on the *Tonight Show*. Little did he know whom he mocked for their hairstyles that evening. A few months later, the Fab Four alighted from that plane in New York City, and the rest is pop music history. But as for me, I was already committed by the time they arrived.

Pop culture historians of that period know the term Swinging London. Indeed, I would venture to guess that anyone alive during that period knows the term. But how many of them remember that Yardley commercial? And of those who remember it, how many could say that their lives were turned upside down by viewing it?

The product was called Eau de London. Or it might have been called Oh! De London. That part of my story I must admit has faded with time. But the advertisement has not faded: a long-haired girl (suitably blonde, as I recall) wears a yellow mackintosh and boots, which were probably white vinyl. She carries an umbrella. She's on a street the pavements (what the English call sidewalks) of which feature pools of water being speckled by the rain. As she walks (she might sashay, or bounce, or jump over puddles, another detail which has faded, I'm afraid), a woman's voice sings: 'Oh jasmine, oh spring kisses, oh summer romance, oh de London!'

On a scale measuring embarrassment, I'm up there when admitting all this. I was a changed individual because of a television commercial. I purchased it all: the yellow mackintosh, the white vinyl boots, the umbrella, and of course, the cologne. The cologne turned out to be only mildly repugnant and, as I am not generally a wearer of what the British call scent, it probably evaporated over time or perhaps I simply threw it away. I don't recall. Years passed, however, before I could bear to part with it.

In 1966, I had an opportunity to go to this place of spring kisses and summer romance. A foolhardy lay teacher from my Catholic girls' school decided to put together a trip to England to study Shakespeare for six weeks. This trip would begin with a few days not too far from Versailles in some sort of dormitory near the Rambouillet Forest, after which we would take the train to Calais then the ferry to London, which would be the headquarters for our proposed studying.

I didn't come from a wealthy family by any means, and I had exactly $170 in my savings account. So I summoned up my courage and asked my parents if they would fork over the necessary cash to allow me this international experience. I'd never even been on an airplane since we'd never been able to afford such a luxury and our family vacations took us to any place we could reach within a day's drive, preferably with a camping site.

Now, my father was a man who hated to deny his children anything. This was largely the reason that I'd only ever asked for one item: a Patti Playpal doll for Christmas one year. I knew that we had little money, I knew my mother was a chronic worrier about this, and I also knew that because I so rarely asked for a thing, my dad would move a mountain or two to make it happen.

So when I asked, he said yes. My mother was in the room, but I didn't look at her. I didn't want to be forced through Catholic guilt to say, 'It's okay, never mind, I don't really want to go' for the simple reason that I really, really wanted to go.

This Blessed Plot, This Earth, This Realm

In those days, it was impossible to fly directly to England from California. One had to stop somewhere for the plane to refuel, and when flying a charter airline as we did, the choice of stop was Iceland or…Iceland. Stopping made the journey over twenty hours long, since we were going to Paris from which we would head to the Rambouillet Forest and our first stop. From this part of the trip, I remember only being exhausted, having the most rip-roaring case of jet lag I have ever had, sharing a room with the redoubtable Pender twins, and discovering the local boys had an excellent view of the girls' showers at night and were making the most of it. I also recall that the food was ghastly, that Bastille Day turned out to be one enormous military parade in Paris, and that my friend Sue Richey did not, unfortunately, speak French as well as she'd declared she spoke it.

But I survived as did everyone else, and soon enough we were dragging our suitcases (there were no wheeled suitcases in those days) from the train in Calais onto the ferry, and from the debarkation point at Dover onto the buses that would, at last, take us into Swinging London.

The trip became magical from that moment on. Along narrow roads that sided a rich green countryside where paddocks sheltered the grazing sheep, our bus trundled us through villages and towns made enchanting by their constantly changing structures: the wattle and daub of cottages, the red brick of Georgian townhouses, the half-timber of Elizabethan farmhouses. Ultimately, as we drew nearer to London, the suburbs rose before us with their lines of Victorian terrace homes, and their pebble-dash houses backing onto the railway. And then…the great city itself and our destination: Fitzroy Square where we clambered off the bus and blinked up at the filthy building that was to be our home for the next five weeks.

I'm sure that our chaperones must have been horrified at what they saw. I'm sure that they were horrified by what they continued to see as the days progressed. For in those days of 1966, the Londoners were still rebuilding after World War II, and they were concentrating first on the areas most hard hit by the Blitz: the East End, the City, and the South

Bank. As for the rest of the town (London is, unusually, always called the town as the word city refers to the ancient walled part of London which is now the booming financial district), it would have to wait, and part of this rest of the town was Fitzroy Square.

Inside the place, a bare stairway climbed up the center of the building, six flights of uncarpeted stairs with rooms deposited along the way. From the bottom of them you could see all the way to a grime-encrusted skylight at the top. If you were lucky, you realized, you would end up with a room that did not require a hike – with luggage in tow – any higher than floor number three. Once again I found myself the room-mate of the Pender twins. We were joined this time by my pal Sue Richey who, it turned out, had been massaging relationships via mail with two different London boys.

I remember that our meals were taken in a dingy basement and that the first meal that evening of our arrival was boiled chicken. Our Shakespeare class was taught in the vicinity of Gower St where London University afforded us a classroom that otherwise appeared to be used for chemistry lectures, if the many charts of the periodic tables were anything to go by. I remember our instructor, too, a rotund balding man with glasses who wasn't quite sure what to do with a classroom of sixty-five high school students. He lectured. We pretended to take notes. But mostly what we did was plan the adventure we would have when class ended for the day.

We were given an utterly free rein. Aside from forbidding us from going into Soho at night (a stricture that Sue and I happily ignored when one of her two pen pals took us on a double date with a friend of his who deposited us at a dark-walled underground nightclub where the music of The Kinks was played at maximum volume, the cigarette smoke made a statement about lung cancer, and for the first time ever, I saw girls dancing together), we could go any other place we liked. All we needed was money for the Tube.

Imagine it. Imagine too that these were the days before Great Britain had given up its wonderfully complex systems of money. In order to use the underground, ride a bus, or buy anything, one first had to master how many pence added up to a shilling, how many shillings made up a pound, what a half crown was worth, what tuppence looked like as compared to thruppence, and above all what it meant when the cost of an item was marked as 1d/6. And imagine the triumph of learning this and understanding it. We strutted down Tottenham Court Rd to Oxford St, we rode the Tube across to Marble Arch, we watched the Sunday soapbox arguers at Speakers' Corner, we explored Hyde Park.

We also went on excursions aplenty: Startford-upon-Avon, Banbury, Canterbury, Richmond Castle, Runnymede, and every iconic sight in London. In those days, a way to clean the great buildings of London had not yet been developed. So instead of what they look like now – pristine in their Portland stone facings – they were all of them streaked black with grime from centuries of coal fires, from the smoke of wood fires, from diesel exhausts, and from car exhausts. So each of them was a wildly atmospheric presence upon the landscape: the Houses of Parliament brooding over the River Thames, Westminster Abbey holding the promise of a hundred hauntings within its Royal Burial Chamber, St Paul's Cathedral blackly raising its great Christopher Wren dome into a blue sky. Whitehall was far from that color. Number 10 Downing St looked like a place of final refuge before the End, which was surely Nigh. Even Admiral Nelson high above Trafalgar Square was a sensational object of utter filth.

I loved it. All of it. Here was a place so absolutely unlike any that I had ever seen – my most extensive excursion so far having been Disneyland in Anaheim, California – that it enchanted me. I felt as if my life were being taken over by the spirits of everyone from Samuel Johnson to Emmeline Pankhurst.

Then we moved. Not my family, but we sixty-five students. Our chaperones, having experienced firsthand the general awfulness of our abode in Fitzroy Square, informed us that we would be going across town to South Kensington, where Chelsea Institute of Science and

Technology awaited us and where we would each have our own room and where the food promised to be more advanced than that which was boiled or stewed.

And thus I found myself in the place that ultimately became my second home as well as the home of my imagination. I speak not of Chelsea Institute of Science and Technology, where we were housed in a tall building with an elevator that regularly became stuck between floors, but of South Kensington. I speak of Cheyne Row, where – good Catholic girl that I was – I found the local church for my daily visitations at mass time. I also found the place where, years later, I would locate the home of three of my many English characters: Simon St James, his wife Deborah, and his father-in-law Joseph Cotter. There on the corner of Cheyne Row and Lordship Place stood a magnificent brick townhouse that called to me. A short distance from it, the home of Thomas Carlyle allowed me to see what the inside of St. James's house could be. But all of that – Simon St James and everyone else who has come to be part of my professional life – was years later and years in the making. Then, when I was just seventeen years old, what was important was being there, seeing it, recognizing how different it was from everything familiar to me, and knowing that I would return because the place called to me in ways that no other place ever has or probably ever will.

I made my second trip to England in 1971. From that point forward I went time and again, nearly every year. Each visit to the country brought a new experience for me. And when I decided that I would indeed do what I had long known I was meant to do – be a writer – there was simply no question in my mind where I would set my novels. As I began to do so and continued to do so, London became more and more familiar to me. I saw it from the top of double-decker buses; I wandered through it on a thousand and one pavements; I witnessed its ordinary citizens going to and fro on the underground; I became, as my British editor once told me, a topographical gumshoe in pursuit of the details that would make London live for my readers.

This Blessed Plot, This Earth, This Realm

I've been many places since then: in the US, in Europe, in Ireland, in Asia, and across Great Britain to more locations than I can even recall. But nothing will probably ever touch me as did that first trip in 1966. England grabbed my heart and gobbled up my soul. England defined what I do today. I am ever the richer for it.

ON THE ROAD TO MATERIAL

BY JANE HAMILTON

In May of 1978 I got it into my head to take a bus north from Edinburgh, where I was a student, to visit a Traveler, as they are now called, named Belle Stewart. (Back then, those of us studying Scottish culture blithely used the politically incorrect term tinkers or gypsies for the Travelers without imagining we were offending anyone.) Belle had been famous for some time in folk singing circles, she'd been on a tour of America, she'd made records and performed at the Edinburgh festival on many occasions.

In the winter she'd come to my class at the School of Scottish Studies, all of us eager to see the singer who'd had a difficult life, yes, but a life filled with what seemed like romantic and even magical incident. The Travelers were known for their psychic powers, and I couldn't help conflating her with the characters she sang about in her ballads, a woman who'd have visitations from the fairies, who might walk along the road and be snatched away to the underworld. She'd grown up in a community that was despised by the outer world, a girl who'd lived in a tent for part of her childhood, whose family now and again were pearl fishers, a girl who'd gone to ceilidhs to sing and learn ballads that had been passed down time out of mind. In 1981 she received the British Empire Medal, an honor she may have felt belonged to all the Travelers.

That winter she came to our class she was in her early seventies but she seemed much older. Her face was deeply lined and she walked with the slow, uneven gait of someone who is in pain. Even before she'd sunk herself into the armchair, she had a weariness that made us feel stupidly, irredeemably young and undeserving of her time. But with the gentle encouragement of our teacher, the poet Hamish Henderson, she fired up her powers and began to flirt. She was by turns brash and fond, tough and generous, her remarkably thick accent the thrilling real thing, an accent we foreigners had come to Scotland to hear. A genuine tinker in our classroom! Before she left, she closed her eyes and sang 'Tam Lin', a ballad of extreme true love where Janet rescues her elfin beau who is in the clutches of the Queen of the Fairies; in order for him to assume his human shape, Janet has to do a Wonder Woman feat of holding fast to him while he changes from one terrifying beast to another. Even though the song was meant to be shared with an audience, the music was so much of Belle, of her breath, her throat, her mouth, that we felt we were watching something private.

I was twenty and had been abroad for some time, and I was as lonely as I've ever been, and wanted to have – if not love, for love seemed out of my reach – then Experiences. Hamish Henderson had said at one point that his students dropped in at Belle's house regularly, she never turned anyone away, always serving them a cup of tea and if they were lucky she'd sing. I didn't actively want to visit Belle Stewart. I wanted, rather, to have visited her, to have a story to tell about being in her living room, to have had an adventure. But that spring was my chance and so I had to take it. I rode the bus to Blairgowrie, about sixty miles from the city, I found the house, and after some hand-wringing, I went to the door and knocked. She answered, the legend herself. I said I was a student of Hamish Henderson, she nodded and led me into the living room, a room in the style of her countrywomen, with floral wallpaper, curio-cabinets stacked up with china, heavily upholstered sofas and chairs, a doily-centric realm. She muttered to her son, who lurked, a phrase which I understood to mean 'another goddamn one.' I was instantly ashamed.

She sat me down in front of the fire and disappeared into the kitchen to fix tea and a tray of biscuits. I wanted to flee but did not know how. When she returned she told me a story, as she felt she must. Five years earlier, she said, she was sitting in front of this very fire when all at once the scene of her husband's (or maybe brother or uncle's) impending death, which she described in some detail, appeared in the flames. I had little to say or ask, nothing to offer, and after she'd finished her set-piece I got out of there.

I'd had my experience! Hadn't it taken bravery to gawk at Belle Stewart? Belle, the Queen of the Heather, had served me tea and told me a terrific story. It was impossible, however, to fake enthusiasm for long. I wasn't to the end of the street when I was again overtaken by shame, abject at being the voyeur, of presuming I'd be welcome – the arrogance of the privileged! – as well as being so young as to be blank. When I got back to Edinburgh I told no one about my trip.

Not long after, I went to the Isle of Raasay, a small island east of Skye, population 152, a place with the lonely splendor that seems particular to the Hebrides: windswept mountains and bluffs and moor, a ruin or two, one road in a loop. Soon after my arrival at the youth hostel, the rains began, a lashing that went on for several days. I had planned on staying only one night, but ferry service was suspended until the all-clear.

There were six of us, strangers to each other, who were stranded. The two girls from Aberdeen immediately bonded over their hatred of Americans. It would have done no good to say that I understood their feeling. The German woman, Gisela, was shy and didn't speak much English. Her short blond hair was nearly white, she was five feet tall, her thick glasses made her colorless lashes look like the cilia you'd observe under a microscope, her oversized fisherman's sweater, greasy with wear, rendered her formless. The Australian, Peter, was tall, quietly cheerful, decency radiating from his lovely face.

On the Road to Material

There was also, by order of the hostel law, the warden. She was probably in her mid-forties. Her long brown braids were at odds with her old lady skin, her face no doubt weathered by the wind and certainly by the cigarettes she chain-smoked. You could tell she wasn't thrilled to be introducing yet another group of young people to the rules and regs of the Raasay International Youth Hostel.

As I remember it, the hostel was a long, rough-hewn cabin. I recall there being a woods surrounding the building, but in the pictures I've pulled up on the Web, the tidy stone and clapboard house is near the water, the terrain a rocky outcropping, a species of stubborn grass having taken hold. Maybe I think there were woods because it was dark not only through the night but during the day as well. The rain did not let up. In the small communal room, heated by a stove that burned peat, with candles for light, the Scottish girls whispered and tittered and read. Gisela initially knitted and looked out the window. By the end of the first evening it had become clear that Peter meant to practice his German with her. She was patient, he was determined. I think they both had sketchpads, that drawing was involved.

That left me with the warden. For a reason which escapes me, on day two I told her I wanted to be a writer. 'Ahhh,' she said ominously. She then challenged me to a game of Scrabble. The rain beat on the windows, the candles flickered, Gisela and Peter were at their lesson, giggling – over the subjunctive, the passive voice? The Scottish girls napped. It turned out the warden actually was a writer, vocationally and professionally. She'd taken the job on Raasay in order to have time to do her work.

During the days that we played Scrabble, days in which the warden trounced me time and time again, repeatedly proving her point that I had no facility for language, Gisela grew more beautiful, the flush in her cheeks, etc., Peter more cheerful. The warden and I noted the hour-by-hour transformation without once mentioning the story unfolding by the window. Despite the wind, the two would disappear into the howling and return some time later, drenched, shivering, speaking of their adventure as lovers will, a sentence in low tones that brings back the happiness. In any language little must be said to recall certain joys.

I learned over the Scrabble board that the warden wrote romance novels in her spare time, that her pulp fiction, as well as the hostel job, supported her real life, that is to say her literary life. Our keenest interest through those days wasn't our endless games, however, or our mutual love of books, but the progress of Gisela and Peter, which as I said we did not discuss. He was an obvious catch, she less so, and yet he was the one who was smitten. As a couple they were so wonderfully unlikely, and all that time out in the rain? They must have found a cave or some freakishly dry patch of ground nearby. You would not go out into a tempest without certainty of reward.

The warden had already proven to me that I ought to give up on the idea of being a writer but she was making another point, too, not in words, but through her scorching gaze. She beamed to me that whatever happened in the confines of the hostel, and even on Raasay, and maybe in all of Scotland was not my material. Hands off, sweetheart. These goods, whether or not I use them, are mine by birthright and otherwise. How did I know this? I just did. The warden by some unfathomable means had drained me of any possible future authority.

This was well before the talk that preoccupies many chatrooms, fierce debate over who owns the story, who may authentically assume control of the narrative. It wasn't as if there was necessarily any great tale to be told and yet on the island I felt it must be so because of the warden's prohibition. Nonetheless, I understood that as an outsider the place was off limits to me in every way, including and especially in my imagination.

The storm ended, the ferry service resumed. It was with great relief that I got to the mainland to take the train to Inverness. In the railway car I sat across from a Danish man about my age. He was delicately and Nordically attractive. Like Peter, kindness and decency seemed part of his high cheek-boned and blond haired architecture. We spoke only occasionally, both of us reading our books, his John Le Carré in

Danish, mine a novel, probably Victorian. It was as if we had an understanding; we could consider ourselves companionable while being mostly silent. In the middle of the journey the train came to a halt for well over an hour out in the dark Highlands. We continued reading.

When we pulled into Inverness we discovered that we were both planning to bunk down at the hostel. We walked together along the empty streets only because we were going to the same place. Surely, even though it was past the hostel curfew, we would be let in; the train being late wasn't our fault. But the heavy door was as if barricaded, a NO ENTRY sign posted. All at once the quality of our affinity changed. It was midnight, and although summer, it was cold. No matter how hard the Dane beat on the door or how loudly we both shouted, the warden was not going to wake up. We set off again, our footsteps in sync.

Every B&B proprietor we managed to rouse had no room at the inn, until we got to the last house, of course, the house at the outer limits. The woman answered, she had one room remaining, a room with a double bed. We looked at each other, my Dane and me. Okay, thank you, we would take it. We climbed the stairs. Once we were in the room, he again said, 'Okay,' in his quiet, gung-ho way. With his back to me, he stripped to his underwear – I turned out the light. I kept my clothes on, we got into bed, we said, 'Goodnight!'

Did we as much as keep each other warm, one body gently providing heat for the other? Yes, maybe a little as we cleaved to our own side. At a suitable hour we woke at the same time. 'Good morning!' Sipping our tea in the breakfast room we talked of this and that, we looked out the window, we fell silent, we spoke again. It was as if we'd been together for decades, a fond couple who had long since gotten over their rapture. When we parted I think we both felt we should exchange addresses but somehow we didn't. We shook hands.

That was good material, I realized many years later: a night with a beautiful man in which nothing and yet somehow a great deal occurs. It clearly wasn't material for a ballad or a pulpy romance, the sleep in

Inverness more Henry Jamesian than EL Jamesy.

It took years, too, for the sorcery of the warden to wear off, to come to the conclusion that no one owns the raw material of experience. It is now dangerously politically incorrect to say so but here it is: I don't believe you have to suffer in the particular way of someone else's interest group or tribe to understand suffering. The warden of Raasay, that variety of wicked queen – *c'est moi*. Belle Stewart, weary old singer with visions, check.

As for the story of the Dane – that's certainly my material, and therefore it not only has a keen specificity, it now has scope: I can see how the event radiated into my future. In truth, however, it could be anyone's material. My story is merely a shape, a structure which can hold infinite variety. Young man and woman thrust together for a night. Insert a vampire if you must, or a selkie, or – as if it's a simple thing – explore the awkwardness of two kids who don't yet know themselves. Stare hard into the fire for awhile. See what happens.

JOURNEY 'ROUND A WAR

BY ALEXANDER MCCALL SMITH

I don't remember the exact route of a journey that I made back in May 1974 as a young man in my mid-twenties. But I do remember the friends with whom I travelled. I remember the weather at the time; I remember the smell of the gorse we passed on a hillside. I remember the music we listened to. I remember being happy on that journey and I remember the tragedy that was unfolding as we drove along those empty side-roads of Ireland. I remember thinking at the end of it that I would never again feel as I felt on that trip and now, all these years later, I know that I was right.

As I think about it now, this recollection that I have never before committed to paper, I feel an extraordinary sense of loss. In the heart of each of us, I think, is a room of that nature in which a memory of this sort resides, behind a door that we never open, even if we know that it is there. What loss exactly? It is difficult to define: nostalgia is a common emotion, and all of us can be nostalgic about a time when we were younger, or happier, or only beginning to discover the world. The warm glow that surrounds our early years grows warmer, perhaps, with every year that passes. A journey taken as a twenty-year-old seems very different from a journey taken forty years later. But pry beneath the surface of this nostalgia and you may find real reasons for feeling as you do – reasons that are to do with growing up and with the growth of understanding.

I had gone the year before to live in Northern Ireland, leaving Edinburgh and Scotland behind me. It was my first proper job, teaching law in a junior capacity at the university in Belfast. I was a callow young man, ignorant of all the things that young men are ignorant of, with only the sketchiest knowledge of the difficult and often tragic history of Ireland. It was a history that cast a long shadow, and the early 1970s were the latest episode of what the Irish call the Troubles, a euphemism for the various uprisings that had flared up on the island in the course of the twentieth century. These went even further back, of course, to the root cause of Ireland's difficulties – its complex and unhappy relationship with its larger and territorially ambitious neighbour, Britain.

If the situation in the south of Ireland – in the Irish Republic – was complicated, it was even more so in the north, where, as a result of the compromise reached in 1921, the six northern counties of Ulster remained part of the United Kingdom. This was the part of Ireland with the largest Protestant population – a population that tended to marginalize the Catholic, more republican-minded people of the province, thus building up a potent mixture of resentment and Irish nationalism. This erupted from time to time, and in 1968 this happened again. Now there arose a low-grade civil war, with the Irish Republican Army (IRA), which favoured the reunification of Ireland, being pitted against the British Army and the majority in the north who wanted to remain linked with Britain. It was a horrible, brutal little war, with terrorist groups on both sides callously resorting to bloodshed to achieve their goals and to settle scores.

I found myself living in Belfast at exactly the time that this conflict was getting to one of its most bitter points. Bombs placed in hotels, pubs, and outside police stations exploded regularly. Windows rattled with the explosions; occasionally gunfire cracked out over the rooftops and echoed against the Black Mountain that overlooked the city. At night the streets were already deserted and if you went out you had to know exactly where you were going. Those who forgot their social geography and who found themselves in territory controlled by extremists of either side could be in very serious trouble. As in all such conflicts, the innocent were frequently the victims.

And then something remarkable happened. At long last the political log-jam moved and the two sides sat down to hammer out a power-sharing arrangement. This was the Sunningdale Agreement, which provide for the formation of a government that represented both Republicans (mainly Catholic) and Loyalists (mainly Protestants). A Council of Ireland was created to give Dublin a say in the governing of Northern Ireland.

I remember the euphoria that many felt over this development. Here was a solution that recognised the aspirations of the two warring communities. Both could see themselves represented in those who wielded power. This, at last, provided a chance to heal the rift between the two communities.

I could hardly believe it had happened. I had been afforded glimpses of just how tragic the conflict was; I remember in particular one of my students coming to see me to explain his absence from class. His brother, a bank clerk, had been murdered by the IRA. He showed remarkably little bitterness; even in such circumstances there were those who were prepared to forgive, who saw no reason to perpetuate the blood-feuds that such conflicts can spawn. And alongside these tragedies, there was much that was positive. I found myself entranced by Northern Ireland, by its liveliness, its literature, and by the spirit and feel of the country that lay to the south – the Republic of Ireland. I wanted to find out more about that place – about Dublin, Cork, Galway, places that were not much more than names to me at that point.

I had close friends in Scotland, a couple I had known before their marriage who were at that time probably the closest friends I had. They suggested that they should come over to Northern Ireland and we should do a trip together to the south. We had no idea of exactly where we would go, but we could start off in Dublin and then head over to the west. I thought this a good idea.

But things were not going well for the new government in the north. There was a substantial body of Loyalist opinion that did not accept the Sunningdale Agreement and were not prepared to allow the Government of the Republic of Ireland to have any say in the affairs of the North. These people decided to bring the system down and planned a strike to do so. They formed a body called the Ulster Workers' Council, a body that had close links with various Loyalist paramilitary groups. Roadblocks were set up by the strikers and the paramilitaries. Men in balaclava helmets patrolled these and prevented people from getting to work or travelling freely. The atmosphere of fear, already present for years, intensified. Now the Loyalists struck back at the Republic of Ireland, which they argued had been indifferent to the suffering they had experienced at the hands of the IRA. Car bombs were exploded in the republic without any warning being given. One in Dublin killed 26 people and injured hundreds of others. We have become more used to indiscriminate bomb attacks with recent outrages, but in those days the callousness of the random blowing-up of innocent passersby seemed something new and abhorrent. I suppose each generation discovers about human perversity afresh.

My friends and I decided to go ahead with our trip. The road to Dublin was clear and what was the point of sitting about in Belfast when ordinary life was being so restricted by the tightening grip of the strike and by all the tension that entailed. And when you are in your twenties you do not think too much about why you cannot do things; you go where the spirit compels. Caution comes slowly in this life. By the onset of middle age we are concerned by the prospects of something unpleasant happening when we travel; but before that, unpleasant things are what happen to others. And who would have it otherwise?

We set off in my friends' car, one of those peculiar French cars known as 2CVs (*deux chevaux-vapeur*, two horsepower). We headed south, leaving behind us the grey skies of troubled Ulster. The memory plays tricks: a *paysage moralisé* is a rare thing, but I felt we were travelling into the sunshine.

I forget exactly which towns we went to, other than Dublin, of course. I think we were in Tipperary and Galway, but cannot be sure; we were certainly in County Kerry, which is as far as we got before we turned back. As we travelled we listened in the car to a tape I had acquired of an Irish traditional band called Na Fili. They used the instruments of Irish folk music, the uilleann pipes, fiddles, and penny whistles, and their songs, in Irish, spoke to all the romance and sadness of Celtic music. I could not understand Irish, but the sentiment of the songs on the tape seemed clear enough: loss and joy in equal measure, hope, yearning. We watched a sunset in County Kerry to the accompaniment of one of these tunes, a soulful melody accompanied by long drawn-out notes, and even today, as I listen to that tune, I see the touching of the sea and land with gold.

We reached a place called Dingle, a small harbour town on the peninsula of the same name. It was early evening and after we parked the car we looked for somewhere to eat. We chanced upon a group of three nuns taking a stroll and asked them for a recommendation. They knew where to send us: Doyle's Seafood Restaurant, they said, was just the place. And they were right. Doyle's knew how to cook seafood, and prepared a meal that I remember still. Most of us, I think, are likely to be able to bring to mind only a handful of great meals we have had over the years. This is one of mine.

Afterwards we went back to the small hotel we were staying in. I listened to the radio. In the north the situation was deteriorating. Electricity supplies were being cut; young men were being shot on street corners. Hothead politicians cajoled and threatened; roadblocks, sometimes made of trees felled across the highway, claimed their victims.

And then, as we travelled back, the government – the power-sharing executive – fell. The rebellion that had been mounted by the Loyalists had defeated the British Government. It had shown that if enough people refuse to be governed, they can bring down a government imposed on them. An optimistic attempt at compromise had failed.

We listened to all this on the radio as we made our way back. Our journey was over. For a brief few days we had experienced the benign side of Ireland, the romantic countryside, the lovely rural pubs where you could buy Guinness at one end of a counter and everything from tinned peas to soda bread at the other. We had talked to people we met who had time to chat to strangers about anything and everything. We had asked nuns for a restaurant recommendation and received good advice. We had stayed at a farmhouse where the farmer's wife said that unfortunately no eggs were available because 'my hens have had an accident'. We never found out what the accident was. Ireland is like that. There are things below the surface that you never really get to know completely.

It was a time of great sadness. Years of conflict lay ahead until at last the Troubles would come to an end. I went back a few years ago, to a Belfast restored to normality. I walked the streets, now safe again, although on some walls you could still see the folk art of conflict – the slogans, the paintings of King Billy or the masked gunmen. I thought about that journey as I walked. I had been changed by the journey in ways that I was yet to discover. I had glimpsed hope and the dashing of hope, I had learned a bit more about the history of a country and how even the distant past can have a very long reach and can mould, and often disrupt, our lives. I had been made to leave a comfort zone of assumptions. Only love and forgiveness are capable of healing us; distrust, revenge, and confrontation are no solution. The learning of these things, I suppose, is a lifelong process – or at least the reminding oneself of them is. That in itself is a journey.

A SCOTTISH LESSON

BY KEIJA PARSSINEN

If you are going to have your heart broken somewhere other than your home country, there is probably no better place than Scotland in February: the sky and sea a matching gunmetal gray; the rain and wind to buffet your body, as your heart feels buffeted; those endless seaside trails on which John Keats once ambled on a walking tour above the rough waters. Scotland is moody and beautiful, perfect for unpublished, twenty-one-year-old poets newly inducted into the halls of heartache.

I had chosen to spend the spring semester of my junior year at St Andrews University mostly because I was too scared of the French to brave Paris with my choppy language skills and big American body. But from my vantage point years later, I see that perhaps the gods were looking out for me – how terrible it would have been to be heartbroken in the City of Light! I would have eaten my weight in profiteroles, sneered at the entwined lovers in the Jardin du Luxembourg, perhaps thrown myself off the bridge with all those lovers' padlocks on it.

But Scotland had the feel of commiseration. Scotland, I knew from having watched *Braveheart*, did suffering well. There, I could openly weep on my two-mile walk to campus without fear of embarrassment, thanks to the slanting rain. I could stand on a cliff overlooking the North Sea and feel like the wronged heroine of a Charlotte Bronte novel. And when I got lonely, I could steal into Ma Bells, get pissed on Strongbow, and gaze longingly at my classmate Prince William, imagining my future as the first fat Queen of England. I knew if I sat there long enough, stared hard enough, he would start to wonder about the girl in the electric blue leather jacket that, conveniently, zipped off into three different lengths.

When I got drunk enough, I would actually start to believe in my betrothal to William of Wales, fretting over images of my coarse American relatives at the wedding: my father giving a crude toast alluding to my non-virginity, my brother doing the worm on the dance floor, sis doing karaoke to the Clarence Carter classic 'Strokin''. Guzzling my third pint, I decided I would have to wear a distractingly huge fascinator, perhaps with a life-sized peacock atop it, to keep all eyes on me.

The heartbreak came early in the semester. Far from close friends and family, I wanted to curl up in my twin bed in David Russell Hall and never leave. And I did indulge this desire, to a degree: I took long, boozy baths, forcing my roommates to bang on the door and say things that sounded angry, though it was hard to tell; in a Scottish accent, everything sounds emphatic. I bought a burner phone and plowed through phone cards; for twenty quid, I could usually get five minutes with mom, just enough time for me to stop crying before being cut off.

In Scotland I learned that pain, when suffered in the right place, could be beautiful. The day after I received the email from the boy I loved, telling me that he in fact loved my best friend, I took a walk with a few acquaintances along the Fife Coastal Path. I had cried much of the previous day and not slept well that night; my body felt leaden and my head, gauzy from exhaustion. As I clambered over stone walls and squelched through mud, I could do little more than exist in the moment, breathing the coconut scent of the gorse, feeling the mist off the sea, listening to my companions chatter in the easy way of people who have not just had their hearts squashed. I put one foot in front of the other and felt glad to be alive, on this path, with these near-strangers.

If I had been at home, I would have forced my close girlfriends to go to endless coffees to help me work through things; I would have wallowed. But being overseas meant I had to internalize, rather than externalize, my pain, a grain of sand I would turn over and over in my gut until I could make it into a pearl, something bearable. While I waited for that to happen, my mouth was forced to speak quotidian words to strangers, and my body was forced to move over unfamiliar terrain.

In this way, through familiar, meaningless speech, and unfamiliar, meaningful action, I began to heal. I learned how to dance a ceilidgh, did a homestay with a coal miner's wife who taught me to hate Margaret Thatcher, and developed a crush on a beautiful boy who talked fiction and poetry with me after our Scottish literature class. I stood in the ruins of the Cathedral of St Andrew and, gazing at the dome of sky that formed the cathedral's roof, felt a Wordsworthian sense of the sublime; it was difficult to imagine Wordsworth having patience for my small tragedy. Life was too full of mystery, of joy, of days spent trying to 'see into the life of things'.

At semester's end I rode a bus to the Highlands, and in that dreamscape, purple with heather, I shook off 'the heavy and the weary weight of all this unintelligible world' to run headlong and naked into frigid Loch Ness at midnight. That swim wasn't pleasant, but I recall it fondly because, like the sadness I'd previously endured, it jolted me from comfort to prove I was gloriously alive.

A SINGLE STEP
BY MRIDU KHULLAR RELPH

Family legend has it that when my parents decided to move back to India after a three-year posting in the United Kingdom I, all of nine years old, put my foot down and declared that I was not going to leave my beloved London. The London where all my friends lived. The London where I had already become a writer. London, my home.

When it became clear that I was not to have my way, I cried for weeks. Then, in a stubbornness that has marked my character through most of my life, I vowed to return one day, on my own.

For the next several years, I wrote long letters to my best friend in England and my class teacher, the one who had given me a golden sticker with her address printed on it. For years, I looked at the sky, watching planes passing by. 'One day,' I said to my mother every time, 'I will be up in the sky on that plane. It will be my turn to go abroad.'

By my twenties, London had become a distant dream, what with visa regulations making it all but impossible for a writer like me to settle anywhere but in my own country. I wanted to travel, however, and so after months of applying for writing residencies, fellowships, and grants, I had finally heard from a non-government organisation that was willing to sponsor my visa. To Ghana.

So now, here I was. Up in the sky, on a plane. Going abroad.

A Single Step

It was common enough for Indians, especially middle-class men and women, to head to better opportunities in the West. What was relatively uncommon was a twenty-something Indian woman packing her bags and heading off to Africa on her own. It never occurred to me, however, that I wasn't going to the developed world in search of the so-called better options. I was on a plane in the sky. As far as I was concerned, I was finally living my dream.

This wasn't to say that I wasn't absolutely terrified. I had wanted to leave India, by any means necessary, because my culture and its treatment of women stifled me and repeatedly threatened to crush my dreams. I wanted to, needed to, get away so that I could create a life for myself, find my own way in the world.

'I travel not to go anywhere, but to go,' Robert Louis Stevenson once said. I wanted to go. But I was woefully underprepared.

Women in my culture, heck, in my country, have traditionally not been permitted to travel alone. Not only are we thoroughly unequipped for it, what with basic lessons in survival denied to us (Wait, so you're not supposed to drink seawater? Why won't that quench your thirst?), but we're actively discouraged from the idea, with sordid tales of women broken and brought down to their knees when chasing after independence and a free spirit.

Were we supposed to feel sorry for the woman who set off to cycle across the Middle East and was raped three months into her journey? Or the foreigner who should have known better than to venture out into the dark Delhi night? Or the twenty-something who wanted to live alone but then complained when strange men broke into her apartment?

If you were going to chase this dream of independence and autonomy, I had been warned repeatedly, you were responsible for all the evils that would befall you. Don't come crying to us if those are the choices you are making.

I had squashed these voices in my head – some of them loud representations of my own fears – and had frequently travelled through the country alone. But so far, I'd always travelled around India, where I knew the people and the culture. Even when I arrived in a place where the language was unknown to me, I knew I could confidently read the situation, blend in, find help, and create fallback options for myself.

The biggest gift my education had given me was not the language that formed the bedrock of my writing career or the ease with numbers that allowed me to put a business head on my artistic shoulders, but the knowledge that there was an entire universe out there, a whole world full of people who did not live by my culture's rules. When my parents had bought a computer and got an Internet connection for the first time in my late teens, I spent hours looking at photos of large American cities, small English towns, the cafes of Paris, and the small windy lanes of Brazil. I pretended to study at night when everyone else was asleep and instead, stayed up until three in the morning watching repeats of travel and food shows on TV that drilled in me just how limited and small my world was.

Now, suddenly, my world had expanded. But my courage had not expanded with it.

I arrived in Accra and on finding that my sponsoring organisation had no clue what they were doing, got myself a hotel, and fretted about what I was to do next. The heartbreak of knowing that I would need to return to India soon, where I would be trapped again with no way out, squeezed my chest and left me breathless.

Depression hung over me like a heavy, persistent fog. I was not seeing the world; I was locked away in my hotel room for days hiding from it.

I was in Africa, in Ghana, a country where I knew no one, had no cultural references, no sense of reading a situation, no people to call in an emergency. What if I was raped, or worse? What if I got so depressed that I wanted to kill myself?

But I had been raped once before, in my own country, and I had survived that. I had done that. I had gotten so depressed that I had wanted to kill myself once before, and I had survived that. I had done that, too. I had picked up the broken pieces of myself, glued them back together, and become whole for another day. I had taken the long and torturous journey of the single step and that single step was all that I needed. It was enough. I had taken that one step, then another, then another, until I was walking again.

I had done that.

What then was so difficult about a goddamned trip to the beach?

I picked up my pieces. I glued them back together. I embarked, yet again, on the journey of a single step.

I considered it a success when I left my hotel room that next day, the entire hotel the second, and the neighborhood in which the hotel was situated on the third.

On the fourth day, I left the city altogether and found myself in the coastal town of Teshi, a suburb of Accra known for its exquisitely handcrafted coffins. I was curious to see these coffins, which I had been told were designed to reflect the deceased person's trade. Fishermen were buried in coffins made to look like fish, pilots in jets, and cellphone salesmen in large Nokia phones.

I walked down a long dusty road, with wooden huts scattered randomly across either side, expecting to see dozens of shops competing for business. Instead, I found just the one. I climbed the wooden steps into a wide open space that made me feel I was walking along a pier. There were no walls, just long, framed windows, and I was pleased to find that my effort had not been in vain. The coffins were not what I would describe as high art, but they were strangely stirring.

The story goes that a popular craftsman was building a chair in the shape of a cocoa pod for a village chief when the chief died suddenly. Instead of finishing the chair, the artisan turned it into a coffin instead. A few years later, a beloved grandmother of one of the craftsman's apprentices died. They built her coffin in the shape of an airplane. She had always wanted to go on one, and in life, never could. In death, they wanted to give her that final voyage.

'The Ga tribe find beauty in death,' I had written a few days ago, to an editor who'd been interested in a story about these coffins. I was keenly aware, even as I wrote the sentence, that this was one of those bumper sticker messages that didn't stand up to the scrutiny of stark reality. But the coffins also reminded me of the Buddhist monks I had met in India, who believed that the art they made was impermanent like them, to be created, enjoyed, and then washed away. These coffins, too, beautiful and precious as they were, were ultimately headed for the ground. The final destination was dust. Life was going to fuck us all in the ways that life always does. But maybe we could see the beauty, be beautiful in the spaces in between.

Could I? Could I learn to see the joy in my freedom of today instead of worrying about the entrapments of my future?

Over the next month, depressed or not, I forced myself to leave my hotel room every single day. I watched Bollywood movies with Mary, the receptionist at my hotel. I went on a day trip with a Ghanaian woman I met in a restaurant and her five-year-old son. I visited the home of the college student who was worried about his math exam and tutored him as his roommate watched television in a part of the room separated with a curtain. I sat on the side of the road with the woman who had asked me for money and heard her life story. I told her mine.

I went to the beach.

Every day felt like a challenge. It was as if the world was testing me. You want to travel alone, you Indian woman who dares to think she can survive independently in this rough and tumble world? Let's see if you can handle being stuck in a taxi with a man you don't trust. Will you be able to find your way back to your hotel with no money and no directions? How well will you deal with being called a 'fucking Paki'?

I forced every day to be a success. I met one person, who introduced me to another, who introduced me to another, and soon I had a chain of people, a network of friends supporting me, holding me up, refusing to let me fall.

Eventually, I ran out of money and days on my visa and it was time to go home.

I arrived at the airport four hours early. I sat on a chair opposite the boarding gate and read a book I had bought from a roadside stall in the city. I waited patiently until the gates opened and then I queued up behind the two people ahead of me until I reached the counter. I placed my passport and my ticket in front of me and was told, abruptly and rudely, that I wouldn't be able to board the plane because they had overbooked it and I hadn't reconfirmed my flight.

I argued with the man at the counter, but when nothing worked, I stepped away, and then stood there rooted to the ground. I started to cry, big, panicky sobs that made people turn around to look at me. I shook my fist at the man on the other side of the counter, who was gleefully handing out boarding passes to people who slid cash into his palm. I felt angry and betrayed at the outrageousness of it all.

When I calmed down, finally, and looked up, I understood that it was in all that I had lost and would lose that lay the seed to what I was just beginning to find.

I had put myself out in the world, I had made myself available to failure, but also to exploration, to the moments of beauty. I had eaten alone in restaurants, spent days in my own company, made unlikely friends, found myself in precarious situations and learned to trust my own instincts about them.

In Ghana I had learned, for the very first time, to completely trust in myself.

This was what it was to travel alone. You had to learn to live with you. You had to learn to like you. You had to learn to trust you.

I went back to my chair opposite the boarding counter. I calmly watched my flight take off without me. I grasped, perhaps for the first time, that nothing could trap me any longer. I may not have fully grown into my courage in Ghana, but I had experienced a small sliver of it.

I had taken the long and torturous journey of the single step and that single step was all that I needed.

It was enough to set me on my way to becoming the person I wanted to be. The writer who would go on many solo voyages, have many exciting adventures, and meet many incredible people. The writer who would keep her promise to her nine-year-old self and eventually find her way back to her beloved London.

THE NIGHT IS YOUNG

BY YULIA DENISYUK

My guide Mohammed dismounts his camel, takes off his worn leather sandals, and steps on the hot desert sand. The onset of dusk is adding a hint of sorcery to the dunes that loom all around us and I can no longer see the homes of Merzouga village behind the rare Saharan palms. I cling to my camel, Bob Marley, and follow Mohammed into the desert for an overnight stay.

Bob Marley's flesh is hot against my skin. The sun is still strong and I appreciate the elaborate red cloth turban Mohammed tied on my head a minute ago. Through the narrow slit in the turban, I track Mohammed's indigo blue tunic, aglow in the ochre dunes, as he guides us deeper into this land. I lose sight of him when we cross a large dune, a sleeping giant, and realize that a camel thread in Mohammed's hand is the only tie connecting me to another human. I have to believe that the thread is strong enough.

Bob Marley takes careful steps, sinking to his knees but coming back out each time. After a while, the camel and I get into an ancient rhythm, advancing as one through the desert. The quiet dunes surround our small caravan and at times seem to cover us whole. Still we keep going. Mohammed gazes far beyond the shifting horizon and charges ahead as if following an invisible path etched into the dunes.

The Night is Young

I catch the last glimpse of the sun before the next slanted dune hides it from view. The air cools down and my camel perks up. The night is quickly falling on the Sahara, and Mohammed's slim silhouette is dissolving into the darkness. I pull on the camel thread to ensure we are still connected. As if he is sensing my fear, Mohammed turns and sends me a bright wide grin. He must be only a kid, eighteen or twenty at most. I realize I don't know much about him, except that his family lives in a nearby village. By the time I go back to New York, he'll take ten other people on this nightly trek.

I too will have business to attend to upon my return. I have left an unfinished conversation in New York that began years ago when I started working as a marketer and soon recognized this path was not right for me. Not satisfied with my status quo but afraid to change it, I continued working and tormenting myself and my loved ones for years. At last, one mild spring night in New York, a close friend of mine asked, 'Why are you wasting your best years on something you do not care for?' The question hung unanswered that night but kept simmering in my mind all the way to the African continent.

Mohammed suddenly breaks the silence with his first words to me. 'Algerian border.' He points somewhere far, smiles, and says it again, 'Algerian border, there. We are close.'

Ten minutes later our caravan stops at a low valley formed by a circle of barely visible dunes. I say goodnight to Bob Marley as Mohammed helps me dismount. The camel, unmoved by my good manners, lies down for the night and we step into the dark.

The sand is now cool to the touch, a welcome change from the earlier furnace. I drop my bags and provisions and run up the nearest dune. There, on top of the mound, the first star of the night emerges into view. In vain, I try to decipher its elusive flickering message and finally go back down.

Below, Mohammed unhurriedly tends to a fire. His long lean limbs look fragile and graceful at once. I half expect him to turn around and tell me, 'You become responsible, forever, for what you have tamed.'

Instead, he pours me a hot cup of tea, 'berber whiskey', a mixture of fresh mint leaves and odd mountain herbs that grow in the nearby mid-Atlas mountains.

The tea soothes my limbs, sore from the two-hour trek across the impermanent dunes. Mohammed takes out a large cylinder drum from Allah knows where and starts humming a simple tune, gently at first, but louder and louder with each beat.

Zamaza, zamaza
A-zibi-bauwi-zibiba
Asalam-aleykum a mama
Asalam-aleykum a baba
Zamaza, zamaza
A-zibi-bauwi-zibiba.

I pick up another drum, smaller in size, and join in.
Zamaza, zamaza
A-zibi-bauwi-zibiba
Asalam-aleykum a mama
Asalam-aleykum a baba
Zamaza, zamaza
A-zibi-bauwi-zibiba.

Mohammed pours me more tea and I look up at the skies. The earlier single star of the night has bloomed into a plentiful garden of light, with myriads of tiny and large constellations woven into one bright carpet. This richness of space, lost on city dwellers, is re-igniting a fire I thought to be almost dead. I run back up to the dune and throw up my hands. 'Fearless,' I whisper. 'Be fearless.'

Oceans away from home, I finally say out loud what I could not bear to speak of before. I am afraid to be average. I am afraid to fail. I fear vulnerability, forgetting that in it lies greatness otherwise hindered by safety. Driven by fear, I continue to make life choices that steer me away from all that is risky and grand – creativity, freedom and passion. I have become a passenger in my life, watching the years unfold to someone else's scenario.

The stars keep shining as I cry and fall into the sand. My fear, acknowledged, quietly walks off the dune.

Some minutes later, I find Mohammed sitting atop the same dune, his face barely visible under his heavy turban. Only his eyes are alight, twinkling with kindness reflected from the flames of the fire below. We sit together in silence for a while, surrounded by stars, and then start our descent. As we slide down, Mohammed offers his second and last words of the night to me. 'The night is young,' he says.

The night is young.

DECELERATION

BY EMILY KOCH

In: one, two, three, four. Pause: one, two. Out: one, two, three, four.

I collect beaches. From South Africa's south coast surf to closer-to-home Cornwall and Devon, from the hot stylish beauty of the French Riviera to California's rugged Big Sur stretch, from the beach where I took my first baby girl steps in North Carolina to the Greek bay where I worked alongside the man who would later become my husband. What E E Cummings wrote is true for me: 'it's always ourselves we find in the sea'. So when a cheque arrived in the post from the insurance company of a motorist who had run me over at a pedestrian crossing, I knew I would use some of the money to add another stretch of sand and sea to my collection.

In: one, two, three, four. Pause: one, two. Out: one, two, three, four.

Needless to say, that moment, when I was swept off my feet by a Renault Laguna, was life-changing. I broke both my legs, damaged ligaments in both my knees, and smashed the car's windscreen with my head – landing on the cold, wet tarmac next to the strewn contents of my handbag. It took me three months to re-learn how to walk, and three years to overcome my injuries enough to achieve my goal of running a half-marathon. The recovery wasn't pretty, but the survivor's adrenalin that followed my accident put me into turbo mode. I started living too fast. Not drugs, wild parties and late nights: my vices were rushing, trying to do too much, pressurising myself. I had learned that life was short, and that I couldn't assume I would have enough time to achieve everything I wanted to. I'd been given a second chance and I needed to use it. I had to do this, this, this – now, now, now. There's nothing wrong with getting as much as you can out of life – but it took me a while to realise that doing it at breakneck speed was not necessarily the best way to go about it.

In: one, two, three, four. Pause: one, two. Out: one, two, three, four.

After five years of this frantic, post-accident life, I travelled across the world to the blue lagoons, extensive reefs and white beaches of the Maldives. I expected I would have time to reflect, relax, recharge and soak myself in salt water – but I could never have anticipated the full effect the trip would have on me.

In: one, two, three, four. Pause: one, two. Out: one, two, three, four.

While I was in this little paradise in the middle of the Indian Ocean – think hammocks slung between palm trees, fresh seafood, outrageously colourful sunsets and cocktails to match - I learned to scuba-dive. It wasn't something I had ever had a strong desire to do, but from my first few days snorkelling on the house reef, I knew I needed to see more of the spectacular sea life – and to do that, I needed to go deeper. I enrolled on a beginner's course and went diving off our island, as well as further afield via trips on the floral garland-strewn local boats, known as dhonis, jumping in flippers-first and exploring everything the South Ari Atoll had to offer. I wasn't disappointed. We saw turtles, manta rays, multicoloured shoals of parrot fish, countless varieties of cheeky trigger fish, starfish, grey reef sharks, and my favourite – the black, white and yellow-striped (and flirtatiously named) oriental sweetlips.

I learned a new skill, saw amazing creatures and underwater scenery, and got to share it all with new friends. But that wasn't all. It was diving around the island of Vilamendhoo that taught me, after these years of fast living, that there is a particular beauty in going slow.

It's all in the breathing.

In: one, two, three, four. Pause: one, two. Out: one, two, three, four.

My ever-patient instructor Hussein instilled in me the need to breathe almost as if I were asleep – slowly and deeply. You need to save the air in your tank when you are diving. A tank will last longer when you take deeper breaths, because you will need fewer of them. The slower you breathe, the longer each breath stays in your lungs and your uptake of oxygen increases. I learned to inhale for four seconds, slowly, then pause for a couple of seconds, then exhale for another four.

In: one, two, three, four. Pause: one, two. Out: one, two, three, four.

And the benefits of slowness come elsewhere in diving, too. Water is much harder to move through than air – think how hard it is to wade across a swimming pool. So you need to conserve energy – swim slowly, turn slowly, do everything as if you are in a slow-motion video clip.

In: one, two, three, four. Pause: one, two. Out: one, two, three, four.

The thing was, once I got all of that into my head, I couldn't get it out of there. I moved slowly on land; I breathed slowly on land. It felt good: I was noticeably more relaxed. And while I was moving in slow-mo, I started to notice more.

The wildlife on this tiny island – nine hundred meters long by two hundred and fifty meters wide – was not restricted to the sea. I started to see more and more of it, appreciate it, and enjoy watching it. In the morning the sand felt cool under my bare feet, and was covered with trails left by hermit crabs, as if long gold-link chains had been laid across the beach overnight and left their imprints. I could sit with my feet dipped in at the water's edge and set my watch by the appearance of a school of baby blacktip reef sharks, who would swim laps of the island in the shallows. At midday I would wash my sandy feet with a ladleful of cool water from an urn on the decking outside my hut, leave wet footprints across the wood and watch them evaporate dry in the heat. If I was lucky, a thirsty heron would stop by as I sat there, and take a drink from the same urn. At dusk, the fruit bats would wake up and fly excitedly from tree to tree – the best place to see them was floating on your back in the swimming pool in the middle of the island. After dark geckos would scamper up the white-rendered walls of the hut, playing in the warmth and glow of the security light.

In: one, two, three, four. Pause: one, two. Out: one, two, three, four.

Move slow, breathe slow, watch slow – then you will see more, live more, and learn more. I'm still working on it.

FLIGHT PATH

BY CARISSA KASPER

I peer out from the back seat of a 4WD traveling through the Andes of southwestern Bolivia. Columned cactuses flank the sides of the road, some reaching thirty feet in the air, with fuzzy white toques on the ends of their green branches as if to protect them from the chill of altitude. In the sky above, a horizontal rainbow shines parallel to the ground, a half-halo prism that mingles with feathered cirrus clouds. Below lies Valle de la Luna, where fragments of mountains rise like red stalagmites. We wind around the corner and a new mountain appears: it is smooth and wide, banded with pink, green and red, like a flag has been laid over its expanse, silk settling in its folds.

A village of adobe houses is tucked below the mountain. An Aymara woman walks from her home in chola dress: braids beneath a bowler hat perched on her head, a pleated navy skirt and white blouse. Her shoulders are wrapped in a woven shawl that holds a large load on her back.

I imagine the weight she carries on my shoulders, my body walking in the thin air. My asthmatic lungs tighten and my breath quickens.

Elena, a Quechua woman in almost identical dress, turns from the front seat to offer me a bag of coca leaves. '*Usted piccha*,' she says, as she grabs a handful, tears them, and places the wad between her cheek and molars. She passes the bag. I rip the tapered leaves, a tea-like odor releasing, and place their bitterness in my mouth. My lips begin to numb.

I pass the bag to Corrina, a British woman in her twenties with blonde hair and pink cheeks, who sits to my right. She takes a handful. Andean people use coca medicinally, primarily as a suppressant. They use it to stave off hunger, thirst, pain and fatigue. It is also very effective against altitude sickness. As we climb to 3600 meters, this has become one real possibility

Corrina passes the bag to Oliver and Rob, her best friends since childhood, who sit next to each other in the back seat. They are at the start of a three-week trip through South America, intending to cover as much ground as I have in the last three months. I met them last night at a hostel in Tupiza. We hired a driver and a cook, Manuel and Elena, to take us through the high Andean plateau to the Salar de Uyuni, the largest salt flats in the world.

Groups of three backpackers can be difficult to join as a solo traveler. Next to couples, they can be the most exclusive. Pairs of friends are often sick of each other. Larger groups tend to be partying, and welcome whoever wants to join. Solo travelers are the easiest to meet, as they look for respite from their own thoughts, conversation and connection.

We crest a mountain and descend into the high plateau of the Andes. The sky opens. The winding mountains we've traveled all day are pushed to the horizon, their tips white-capped and cascading like waves along the austere blue. The land is stark and barren, covered only by sparse bunch grass in tufts like an alpaca's tail.

We no longer pass any other vehicles. We no longer see Quechua women walking. There are no villages on the horizon. No animals cross the land. There is no water, and the wind is still. Everything is silent.

I shuffle in my leather seat. 'So what does the rest of your trip look like?' I ask the group.

'Lake Titicaca, Inca Trail, Machu Picchu, Cuzco, Colca Canyon,

Galápagos,' Corrina replies, then turns to Oliver. 'Where are we staying in Lake Titicaca?' They both grab copies of the Lonely Planet guide.

Manuel and Elena sit in front, talking in Spanish. I've only picked up enough to order food, find accommodation, and ask the who, what, wheres. In Spanish, I have no past and no future; I can speak only in the present. I tell myself relationships are in the experiences we share more than the words we speak. But I know the way we see is shaped by the words we are given.

We continue driving along the flat expanse of the Altiplano, the sameness of the landscape blurring into itself, as if we haven't moved at all. The never-ending horizon is wide open, just like the Canadian prairies that I'd traveled as a child, Dad off work from church, Mom on school vacation, my sister and I in the back. We would drive to the imposing edge of the Rockies, grateful for the break in scenery. Dad would begin to stop on the side of the road to collect pieces to take home: river rocks, mineral water, cedar saplings, and we would protest. For him, it was never enough to know a place; he had to possess.

Soon, the 4WD approaches a one-street village scattered beside a brown creek. A chapel peaks in stark white against the mountains. Black boulders lie scattered out front, as if they'd tumbled loose from the shadows of the cliffs and rolled like soccer balls onto the lush field. Outside the brick school is a basketball court, its smoothness foreign in the rubble of the Altiplano. We pull up outside a three-bedroom mud home, exit and stretch, inhaling the thin air.

Manuel begins to unload our bags and boxes from the roof rack. The four of us struggle to keep up. Elena leads us into the home, where a short Aymara woman stands and nods hello. They speak in the hard consonants and rolling vowels of Quechua, a language spoken even before the rise of the Incan empire in the 13th century, and its fall to the Spanish in the 15th. A language which anchors its worldview with such adverbs as *qhipa*, which means both behind and future, and *ñawpa*, which means both ahead and past. For speakers of Quechua, you face your past, and you turn your back to the unpredictable future.

Flight Path

A soccer game has sprung up in the field beside the creek. Oliver and Rob walk over. The players motion for them to join in and they accept. I sit on the grass beside the field to watch. An older man, maybe forty, heads down the field dribbling the ball. Oliver falters against the fine technique of his opponent, and he passes and shoots. A miss. At six feet tall, Oliver quickly overtakes the competition when the goalie lobs the ball back his way. On a breakaway down the right, he arcs toward the opponent's net, shooting toward the far corner. The goalie dives, falls short, and it's in. Oliver runs back across the field, his teammates high-fiving him on the way.

Nobody welcomes you like a small town. People root for you. On the prairies when you leave, you get cards from the little old lady who attended the church your father used to preach at, in waving scrawl: 'I see by the paper that you have passed your exams with flying colors. We women from Battleford think of you as a little girl and are always interested in how your life progresses. You do well.'

But in Saskatchewan, everyone already has an idea of you. There are expectations and ingrained patterns of routine. You fall into the role you were raised in, the person you were told you could be.

The next morning, we wake before sun breaks, loading the 4WD by moonlight, and drive to San Antonio, a 16th-century silver mining town, abandoned after Indigenous and African slaves rebelled against the Spanish. Layers of black peel from the sky slowly, moving from opaque to blue-grey as we approach Uturuncu, a volcano looming at 6000 meters. At its base – just beyond a hill green from rich mineral deposits of ash – is a pile of rubble. The ruins appear as an extension of the mountains, spilling from the cliff behind the village. A few peaks remain intact, scattered at odd angles.

Manuel stops the vehicle, motioning for us to get out. The British friends are sleeping in the back. I look outside, then nod my head, and step outside. I walk slowly through the ghost town beneath the shadow of Uturuncu. I keep my eyes on the ground, moving around the large rocks. The remaining walls are larger than I thought, and I peer around each corner before turning. I walk into the sole enclosed building in the village and look up at the faint twinkle of dimming stars as the sky warms.

At first, I love being alone. It's silent, and it's only mine, this moment. But as the sun rises, the volcano is bathed in pink and the white ash around its peak glows while the land remains shadowed. I turn my back to the volcano and walk out of the enclosure to the car. What would it have felt like waking each morning and seeing your impending death rise first?

The sun climbs higher as we cruise along the Altiplano, as flat and barren as yesterday. Slowly, everyone rises. I am wide awake after exploring the ruins under a looming volcano. I feel jittery, like I'm on my third espresso, but I haven't drunk anything. I reach into my backpack, and grab my journal.

Inside, I come upon cards that I think my mother has written, one for each month that I had planned to travel. But instead, I open the envelope to find my father's handwriting. I grip the card hard as I read, bending his words: 'Look around. What do you see today? What is the sky like? What about the lay of the land – flat, hilly, or…? Do you hear any birds singing? Is there water around – rain or a stream, or a pond or lake? Take it all in. It is so precious. It is the core of what sustains us. Dad.'

I draw in his sentences in one big breath, afraid to exhale and lose this kindness, afraid to become bare in my need. I don't understand my reaction – his gentle words sit heavy in my throat like particles of sand. He was there through my childhood, not a drinker like his father, never raised a hand. The mud of my memory holds only small drops of him, more feelings than occasions: listening from my basement room for the tone of his footsteps, at the dinner table learning to predict what he wanted before he asked, walking home from school through the snow knowing he'd forgotten to pick me up again. But then there are moments like this; I hold the father I want in my hands.

I allow his words to move through me until I feel the father who wants to know what I know. The sky is the same as it might be at home. Bright white sun. He would see the same shade of blue if he looked up.

Flight Path

The lushness has given way to bare earth; even the bunch grass is sparse and flattened. The land has begun to roll, and I can see a silver lake in the distance.

We turn right and approach a sunken marsh, surrounded by a rock pit of rounded red cliffs and covered in grass, wet with sitting water. Brown and white llamas feed in the oasis, bubblegum pink and true blue ribbons tied around their ears like a schoolgirl's pigtails. I get out slowly and walk among them, shoes soaking up the moisture. A white alpaca approaches with a woven necklace. She is elegant with her long neck, pursed lips, almond eyes and luxurious fur. I wonder who loves her so.

We pile back in the 4WD and drive until we arrive at a building standing alone. It is made out of bricks of salt; we are near the Salar.

We unload the 4WD as the sun dies, and begin to walk inside. An older woman stops us. She speaks rapidly to Elena, gesturing to the room behind. They are talking in Quechua, and I do not understand. Eventually, she gestures for us to follow. We enter the home and inhale the smell of blood in the salty air.

Inside a long dark room, an Andean condor lies dead, his body upturned on the dank earth floor, resting on broad shoulders with a torso the size of mine, black-and-white wings spread ten feet, blood and twisted beak lost under feathers. His white ruff, a fur stole around his neck, is stained red. Two long claws reach towards the roof, middle talons extended as if to curse the world in which he was killed. His bald head is crushed under his own weight, his neck twisted in an impossible angle, his curved beak pointing up.

My body slackens at the sight. Elena gestures hard to continue. We follow, set our bags down in the far room. She turns to us, '*El condor es muerto.*' The condor is dead. 'Porque?' I ask. But I cannot understand anything in her response. I want the language to understand. She tells us to go, and we walk past the condor once again, the smell of death clinging to me. Back and forth we travel, unloading baggage in his large presence.

Elena cooks dinner as we work: rice, beans, chicken, and for me, a vegetarian, an egg. We eat slowly on a blanket outside as dusk settles. I push the egg around on my plate, yolk seeping onto rice, onto beans. No one wants to go inside, but night crawls toward us, and finally we concede. We rustle to find comfort, and eventually flashlights turn off. I am the last one up.

I lie awake in darkness. My stomach rumbles. I try to quiet it, turning on one side, then the other. It begins to flip, and I grab my flashlight and stand up. I brace myself for the walk to the pit-toilet down the hall from the bird. I am sick in a bad way. My body overtakes fear and I run. One minute I'm on the toilet, the next I'm standing above it puking. Eventually, empty and weak, I walk back to bed, my beam of light resting on the black mass on the floor.

Before I have the chance to fall asleep, my stomach begins to churn again. I grab my flashlight and stand. Back and forth I travel all night, passing the condor, his eyes reflecting light from a limp neck. I want to know how he arrived here, to desolation and death. In Andean mythology, the condor rules the upper world. What is wrong with this god? He has no predators, living up to 80 years.

I begin to weaken as I walk: the stench of the bird, the salty air, my own body. I need to breathe. I rush outside past the condor, look up, inhaling the frigid and thin air. The stars are brighter than I could have ever imagined, brighter even than from the prairie fields of home.

———————

Under the wide starry sky, a memory rises: a winter night when I was a child. I was doing my homework at the kitchen table, white sheets of French spread over the surface. Dad entered. He was mad, slamming things around. I knew before he even looked at me. He started to pick up my papers, telling me, 'Clean up your fucking mess.' He was high on his own anger, in denial of his mental illness.

I sat still, quiet. My sister was in the living room, watching, silent. He continued to yell, moving through the kitchen, down the hallway, to the back door, with my homework. I yelled, 'What are you doing?' following him to the landing at the back door as he threw my sheets of French into the air. They drifted down and settled, white against snow. 'I told you to clean up your fucking mess,' he said, as he held the door open. I put on my boots, my jacket, my mittens. Outside under the stars, I picked up the crisp sheets, crackling like footsteps on snow.

I look up from the Salar, and imagine the condor flapping his wings as he rises through the salt-brick doorway, gliding on thermals over the entire salt flats. I imagine him soaring in sparkled fabric, so close to the stars, high above the Altiplano. I see him searching for his partner, his mate for life, soaring for a nest built in the cranny of a cliff. I see him dying of loneliness, crushed under his own weight.

The group wakes at five in the morning. I am dehydrated and shivering in my bed. They tell me to get in the car. I rise and walk past the condor one last time. Inside, I fall asleep as they load baggage.

I wake to sun rising in crimson, blood-orange, and flamingo-pink over salt flats. The Salar is brittle and sparkles, cracked into hexagons outlined with raised lines of salt, like a beehive opened and flattened. The crunchy flat protects a pool of brine that hides deep beneath. All around me, sky touches salt, reflecting off white incandescent desert like a field of prairie snow.

There are no points of reference. I am only here, and this is all there is. It is stark, pure and open. I own only what is on my back. Think only of what is happening right now. There is a shadow soaring. The cracks of the Salar gleam white, seams knit tight in the openness. I can hear my own voice. I will carry it back home.

INTO THE CONGO
BY JESSICA SILBER

Forty feet beneath me, one hundred feet above me, and for a hundred-mile radius around me, the forest was bellowing. Standing on the raised camp deck, I was eye-level with the canopy of the Congo Basin. The chirps, howls, hoots and screams that surrounded me suggested a place rich with life, but the sounds were disembodied. My eyes probed the landscape. I saw clusters of vines seize and shake; I saw leaves release from branches and float downward. But I never saw the twitch of tail, or the flutter of wings, or the grip of the horny foot that shook them loose.

This was frustrating, because I was here to see. Gorillas, specifically. Six hours earlier, I had arrived in Odzala-Kokoua National Park with seven other gorilla pilgrims – all Americans who'd endured the paperwork, cost, and 24-plus hours of flying to come to the Republic of the Congo, just to experience a moment in the presence of the world's last western lowland gorillas. In the gray haze of morning, our aircraft rolled onto a lawn that had been scooped out of the jungle specifically to welcome pilgrims like us.

I stepped out of the fuselage and took my first look at the second-largest rainforest on earth. I saw an obscure thicket of vegetation under a heavy sky.

Three waiting men in khaki stepped forward from a fleet of 4WDs.

Karl, in his early twenties but with a sure-footed confidence, introduced himself as the head guide. We regarded him already with gratitude: here was the leader who would guide us to the experience of our lifetimes.

But there was business to take care of first. Karl confirmed politely with a smile that there were no toilets at the airstrip, only rainforest, and that this would be the reality for miles.

Thus prodded, I and two others walked to the edge of the airstrip to take care of business. We folded ourselves, origami-like, to fit into the vegetation. Inside the breathing, heaving forest, we found ourselves completely invisible to each other but observed by hundreds of millions of spoon-billed, heavy leaves that quivered atop slender stems. I felt miles away from the women just a few feet from me.

'That is marantaceae!' Karl shouted over the engine as the 4WDs muscled into the jungle, and spoon-billed leaves slapped against the vehicles. I'd heard the word before in reference to the family of tropical plants that dominated this forest, but the term had been unwieldy and unmeaningful to me. Now, confronted with uncountable billions of marantaceae, I understood the challenge that the researchers in Odzala faced when they first attempted to study the gorillas. Even a family of 400-pound individuals could glide away in this landscape.

At camp that night, sipping on fizzy gin and tonics with shreds of lime, we gathered for a briefing on what we were about to experience.

Gorillas are dying and their conservation has been mismanaged, Karl explained. They are unlike almost all other species on earth. They have emotions and solve problems; they comprehend some of our language; they are self-aware. Yet as the human population nears seven billion, the western lowland gorilla population plummets toward 100,000.

Those dire statistics had brought us here. Some of us had previously trekked in Rwanda or Uganda to view the mountain gorilla, a species that was – you winced to think of it – even more critically endangered than the gorillas we were about to see. They described those gorillas' gestures and displays of comfort and affection. They described seeing wonder in the eyes of the babies. They described it as life-changing, mind-bending, activism-inspiring.

I was ready for that life-changing moment. I hoped I'd be struck with the same inspirational thunderbolt when a gorilla looked at me.

Dr Magda Bermejo, the project's leader and chief researcher, joined us after dinner to talk about her work as we reclined on cushions that generously absorbed back the moisture of the rainforest. Straightforward and serious, she had dedicated years of research to the preservation of the western lowland gorilla. Over the course of 10 years, she and her team had worked to earn the tolerance of the area's gorilla families. They had endured the resistance of the marantaceae and a devastating Ebola outbreak. They earned the gorillas' trust and the community's support, and laid the foundation of a tourism venture with a set of protocols, accommodations, an infrastructure, and a purpose: bring people here, show them the gorillas, and then send them home to evangelize their plight.

Then she said something that surprised me. 'In the beginning,' she said, 'when guests came, we saved the gorilla tracking for last. Not anymore. You have to go out to see them first, to calm your obsession with gorillas.'

She explained that in our lust to encounter these animals, we'd fail to appreciate each part of life that sustains a gorilla: the fruit that they eat, the time of year when the trees drop the fruit, the birds that disperse the seeds of the fruit, the trees that yield twigs for the nests of the birds. 'You miss the forest for the gorillas,' she scolded gently.

My eyes opened to darkness at 4.30am the next morning. Outside, a creature cried and cried, its lungs ramping up until it was all-out screaming. As the sky bruised into dawn, we gorilla pilgrims ate breakfast in silent meditation. Our minds were already with the gorillas, imagining what sharing their space would be like, wondering if the dials on our cameras were poised to the right settings.

Before we hit the trail, Karl introduced our trackers, men critical to the success of our expedition. David and Calvin had grown up just miles away. They were among the few people on earth who had mastered the language of broken twigs and decaying fruit, who could isolate the single important notes in the vast jungle orchestra. While we sipped coffee in the dark, they'd tracked the gorillas to their previous night's nests. With this head start, they would trace the gorilla's steps – and their swings, and swaggers – through the marantaceae to wherever they were now.

Backpacks swung onto shoulders, we departed camp. Raindrops hung indecisively from the tips of marantaceae. Insects tuned their instruments.

I wasn't sure how far or long we'd walked when we heard the first, heart-stopping bellow; I would realize later that the Congo obliterated the concepts of time and mileage, scrambling these units of measurement. David brought out a pair of garden-type shears and clipped the foliage for what seemed like years. Finally, in the dim growth, I saw a face – a gorilla, concealed by marantaceae and, by the sound we'd heard, annoyed by our approach.

It saw me, too, and moved its head to better perceive me through the forest. He or she stood still, focused and surprised. Then, in a tree, we saw a female gorilla appraise us, touching her finger to her lips as if unsure what to do. She turned and climbed higher, her ropy limbs hooking on vines and trunks, her motions circular and fluid, regarding us over her shoulder from time to time.

Time hung like a weight as we watched a whole family emerge. For the first time since we'd arrived, the forest felt silent. Our camera shutters boomed like slamming doors. All too soon, at a signal from David, we snapped our final pictures and returned to camp.

Back in camp, I sat on my deck and replayed scenes of an hour that had been planned for months but that was already in the past. I scrolled through the images on my camera. Elation was replaced by something that resembled disappointment: there was nothing there that *National Geographic* hadn't already done better. No image was adequate to communicate what I'd seen. There was no new information here that would persuade the world against extinction.

I set my camera aside and tried to discern if I'd found new clarity about the state of the world. I fumbled for something inspiring to say when people asked what I'd learned. Yes, I had pictures of the gorillas. But I was increasingly sure that I hadn't absorbed their primate wisdom.

Hours passed as I sat on the deck. Slowly, the forest seemed to habituate to me. Spiders the size of my thumb flickered up the edge of my pants. Butterflies settled on my discarded hiking boots and froze there in a sort of trance state. I accumulated ants and fallen twigs. When I stood to shake them loose, the butterflies convulsed into life, saturating the air so completely that I had to shut my mouth to avoid breathing them in whole.

'Back to reality now,' one of my fellow pilgrims had sighed as we trudged back to camp, though in fact we still had a week to spend in the rainforest. In the days following our gorilla sighting, we plunged again and again into the vibrating rainforest.

On an excursion out of camp one afternoon, Karl pointed out a brilliant jewel-pile of butterflies feasting on a heap of dung. I squatted to zoom my lens in on them. I thought of the butterflies that had exploded into the air at my tent, and commented on how many there seemed to be here.

'That's a good thing to see,' Karl said. 'Butterflies are a sign of a healthy rainforest. A healthy any ecosystem, actually.'

How? A butterfly's biological needs are so precise, their metrics for survival so small, that if you see them recurring year after year, it means the region has a stable enough climate to sustain their annual life cycle. I suddenly marveled at this cluster, a glittering still-life on a steaming pile of poop that was unaware of their role as a spokespecies for the health of the planet.

My anxiety began to ripen into awe. As the days passed, I recognized the shapes of plants beyond the dominant marantaceae. Suddenly, no two leaves appeared the same – as though each plant had been confronted with the same question of survival but had come up with a different answer. I came across a species that curls its leaves when touched, and we took turns stroking our fingers down its stem, causing it to shiver and retract. Each time we passed this plant, I paused to tickle it, engaging in a fresh dialogue with the forest that started when the obsession with gorillas ended.

One afternoon, as I trailed behind the group, a flicker of movement on the ground beckoned to me. I stepped closer. It was a scene of carnage: an army of ants overtaking a grasshopper. The grasshopper thrashed pitifully. The ants were improbably huge, as if each segment of their bodies were magnified 100 times, and they were relentless.

I felt a screaming pressure on my calf. My eyes dropped and zoomed to see renegade ants seizing my boots, my socks, the hem of my pants. Sweat formed immediately as ants used their jaws to pickaxe up my legs. A member of our group noticed my panic and shielded me as I tore at my clothes, dislodged the last of the ants and composed myself, but I spent the afternoon slapping intruding hairs away from my face, or startling at the unseemly lunge of a marantaceae leaf.

The Congo was a full-body experience, I thought the next day, as I stepped carefully over a hissing rope of ants that bisected our trail. It was impossible to appreciate with sight alone. We had come to see gorillas, but for the rest of the trip, we could not rely on our eyes to give us the returns we expected. Rarely did an animal reveal itself. Rather, a noise or track would make us twist and contort just in time to see the whip of a disappearing tail or the flash of an iridescent feather.

But instead of disappointment, I felt breathless elation as again and again, we experienced meaningful encounters from suggestions of a presence. Karl saw the knuckle-drag of a chimpanzee and his eyes widened as he appealed to us to consider the possibility of our sharing the same space with wild chimps that might never have come into contact with humanity before. As I considered this, I felt a thrill that I had never experienced from staring at something and clicking a shutter.

Here was the V-shaped footprint of a Congo clawless otter. A tree that evolved without bark so it wouldn't be engulfed by strangler figs. A skyscraper of spider webs, built communally, where all spider residents split the spoils that fluttered in. Humans could also eat a spider's web in an emergency situation, we learned, if they were inclined to boil it into a foul-tasting stew.

One morning, we waded across a shimmering *bai*, a salt marsh rich with minerals, into the jungle. As we neared the edge of the forest, hundreds of green pigeons rose from the trees in a tremendous exhalation. As we stepped into the jungle, smells crawled up my nostrils: rotten and sweet, vegetative and fresh, sticking to my face and clothes.

Suddenly, the bush near us spasmed. At the front of our cortège, Karl's whisper had all the urgency of a scream: 'Bongos!'

We moved clumsily toward the source, hearts pounding, then caught our breaths and squatted to glare through the lower stories of vegetation for a sign of the elusive antelope. But it was our ears that had to re-awaken, to step out of their supporting role to the eyes, and provide information. How many footsteps were those? How large was the animal? What direction was it going? What the hell was it?

There was the flash of a red rump, less impressive than the thunder of its sound. In the quiet of the bongos' retreat, a hornbill flew overhead with such gusto that its wings sounded like propellers.

Perhaps to distract us from the disappearing bongos, Karl began to explain how hornbills effectively disperse seeds in the rainforest. The birds' guts go easy on seeds, and their flight range is impressive, spreading the seeds a generous distance from the parent tree.

No one had probably ever visited the Congo just to see a hornbill, I thought, a scruffy bird that looked as though someone had welded two beaks onto its face. Yet the Congo existed partially because of the work of these birds.

As we emerged from swampy forest into dry savannah, nearly at the end of our walk, the forest emitted a loud wail to my left. I kept walking, assuming this was another yowl of a bird.

But Karl gasped. 'That is a chimpanzee!'

Our heads whipped to the side, and yes, could it be? – there was a black form moving in the branches of the distant trees. Our hands flew to binoculars and cameras. Karl herded us into a semicircle, chattering with unconcealed excitement. 'This is unbelievable! I cannot believe this! They have not even moved at the sight of us! This is incredible. Incredible! I have to say this could very well be the first time they have seen humans. Yes, this is very possible, even probable.'

Wild chimpanzees, unaccustomed to any human presence – how many creatures left on earth could share that distinction? Chimps were even more skittish than gorillas, and it had taken years for Dr Bermejo to get the gorillas to tolerate her. Travelers wouldn't come to the Congo with a hope of seeing a chimpanzee. A gorilla was a more reliable draw.

A deep mechanical rumble jerked my eyes away from the chimps to see the supply plane ascending from the nearby airstrip. When I turned back, the chimps had melted away. No one had managed to take a decent photo; no long lens would ever be long enough. I would have to be content with the memory of that first long wail, the wobbly mental image of their long dark bodies.

Still, we were exhilarated. We replayed the scene as we returned to camp in a 4WD, revisited by the same enthusiasm we'd had for the gorillas. Night fluttered down on us, and ahead of the vehicle, two pennant-winged nightjars fireworked into the air, long feathers like a trail of smoke.

I thought back to what Dr Bermejo had said about our obsession with gorillas. Was it because we saw gorillas as extensions of ourselves? Was it because we believed that if every person came face to face with a gorilla and recognized him or herself, we would elevate their status to something that requires our urgent and personal care? But then again, I thought, people came face to face with gorillas all the time in zoos. There was something about the forest that activated their magic.

As humans, we don't see the forest as an extension of ourselves. But it began to dawn on me then that we, like the gorillas, were extensions of it. Being in its midst, I had the impression that if you leaned on a tree for just one cosmic moment, your hand might sprout into the trunk and you would coil up it for energetic miles until you burst into the canopy, gasping for light. That if you let a bare toe linger too long into the mud, your humanity would dissolve and you'd sweep up into the circulation of the rainforest. All of your cells would shoot up into the tree trunks and convert from matter into sugar and drop down to the ground as big fruit that burst open with rot, to be dismantled and carried off by ants as morsels and molecules that were once your hair and eyelashes and fingernails.

As I approached my final moments in the Congo, it was the entire ecosystem that had kneaded me into awe and delight.

On one of our last nights in camp, we embarked on a night walk. Equipped with headlamps and torches, we stepped into the screeching bush, shining lamps onto millipedes, watching for flashing eyes, listening to bats lunge at the bloated fruit of strangler figs.

Karl asked us to turn out all of the lamps, to absorb the sounds of this new environment. The lights blinked out and the hoots and howls seemed to crescendo in my ears.

I thought of that first day as I stood on my deck, straining to see, frustrated by the invisible source of the sounds. I thought about the work of the hornbills and the shyness of the chimps and the sense of hope that a group of butterflies can bestow. I thought about Dr. Bermejo's appeal to see the gorillas, to feel moved by them, but to strain to appreciate everything else, even if it required more effort.

In the darkness, I closed my eyes and listened.

THE WHISPERING LIGHTS OF LOFOTEN

BY CANDACE ROSE RARDON

If it weren't for the Northern Lights, I would never have found myself in Svolvær – the largest town on the Lofoten Islands archipelago in Norway, located just north of the Arctic Circle.

My journey began with a three-hour ferry ride across an unruly arm of the Norwegian Sea called the Vestfjord, every flex of its currents causing a list in the boat and a lurch in my stomach. I spent my first night in a tiny fishing hamlet with an even tinier name – a singular Å crowned with a ring and pronounced 'oh' – and it was here I had planned to spend the duration of my five days on Lofoten, not least because of a hostel in the village. For a writer and artist, finding affordably priced accommodation in Scandinavia seemed nothing short of a miracle.

I had arrived in the heart of winter, to haiku days and darkness that drew itself around me like a shroud. Everything was new – the roiling sea, the gusts of snow, a pair of white hares darting in and out of headlights. There were mountains everywhere, sharp and formidable, and even at night, even in the dark, I could feel their presence giving shape to the world. But what impressed me most deeply was the presence of life in such a glacial landscape – many of the neat timber homes had been painted a rich red, a shade I would hereafter think of as Lofoten red, and every window glowed with the soft orange gleam of a lamp. It was like nowhere else I had ever been.

The only thing open on my first morning in Å was the kind of one-stop shop that anchor small towns the world over – a white wooden building housing a general store, gift shop, museum reception, and even the office of a Polish historian specializing in north Norwegian fishing traditions. While I waited for my groceries to be rung up – an eclectic mix of dried apricots, dark chocolate, and other provisions to last me the week – I noticed a printout of activities posted by the door. Despite its remote location and the time of year, Lofoten was brimming with options: from snowshoeing and sea kayaking to winter nature safaris and walking tours. What caught my attention, however, was a guided Northern Lights tour – for if anything had drawn me to Lofoten, it was the chance see the Aurora Borealis for the first time in my life.

The only issue was that the tour departed from Svolvær – two islands and several bus rides away. With some reluctance, I let go of my plan to hole up in quiet Å for five nights and began working my way up Lofoten's rugged, windblown coastline, reaching Svolvær two days later. There was no hostel in town, so I settled on the cheapest room I could find at such late notice – a guesthouse about which all I knew was its name: Kunstnerhuset.

My decision to join the tour paid off. We had only just set up our cameras about an hour's drive outside Svolvær when the first faint glimmer of fluorescent green appeared above us. Not a minute later, the auroras arrived in full force, an iridescent arrow shot from one edge of the sky to the other. I had never thought of the lights as moving before – that they actually dance, leaving luminescence in their wake, their shimmering edges as soft as the sand in an hourglass. I had never known they have a path to follow, a set trajectory, a sacred circle of light encompassing the magnetic pole at its center.

I fell asleep that night with a quiet sense of completion, believing I had seen everything I had come to Lofoten to see. I slept in the next day – not a difficult thing to do when the sun doesn't rise until 10am –

then made a breakfast of apricots and coffee, and spent the rest of the morning working on an illustration commission in my room. At two minutes to noon, I decided to take advantage of being in a guesthouse and asked the owner if I might have a late checkout.

Her name was Bente – 'a very traditional name in Scandinavia,' she had told me the night before – and I found her vacuuming another room across the hall.

'Of course,' she said upon hearing my request. 'There is no reservation for your room tonight, so please take all the time you need. The room is yours. I won't be cleaning it until tomorrow.'

I was so moved by her kindness that I felt compelled to continue our conversation. I asked Bente how long she had owned the guesthouse.

'Oh, no,' she said. 'I just work here and live in the manager's apartment. The house is owned by the North Norwegian Art Center. They also own one of the galleries you might've passed in town. In fact, the name of the house, Kunstnerhuset, means 'artist house' in Norwegian.'

This would have been serendipitous enough for me, but Bente continued. 'We actually have two studios upstairs. I can show them to you, if you like?'

I told her that I would like this very much. The studios were located at either end of the house, with several bedrooms for artists set in between. In the first studio we visited, several easels stood around the space, as though in conversation with each other, and the air was thick with turpentine. The room had white walls, high peaked ceilings, and windows that stretched to the roofline, not unlike those of a cathedral – and I could not have imagined a better focal point for such an altar: the magnificent snowy peaks surrounding Svolvær.

We returned to the first floor, and almost as an afterthought, Bente said, 'You should see the guestbook.' She led me into the living room, where among a pile of magazines and coffee table ephemera lay three very substantial books. The one that Bente handed me had a thick leather-bound cover, with a decorative seal and accompanying border

that seemed almost Polynesian or tribal in design. Its name –
Gjestebok, Kunstnernes Hus, Svolvær – had been embossed below the
seal in gold. In the afternoon sunlight, both the leather and gilded
letters seemed to glow.

Sipping a cup of Earl Grey tea, I soon realized this was no ordinary
guestbook. Knowing it was a house for artists, I perhaps should have
been more prepared for what I encountered – that on every timeworn
page, next to each name and note of thanks, there would be art.

The book spanned nearly forty years – from the house's founding in
1954 all the way to 1992 – and held art of every medium: pen and ink,
pastels, watercolors, acrylics, crayons and collage. There were portraits
and pop-up glaciers, seagulls and seascapes, and those same red cabins
I myself had grown so fond of. Some of the drawings were humorous –
cartoons of bad weather reports, two cats pawing at a pot of fish stew
– but others moved me with their beauty, washes of delicate color
depicting Lofoten's unique blend of sea, sky, and soaring peaks.

I could feel the weight of history in my hands – the dozens of
languages and nationalities represented, and the myriad visions of
Lofoten they'd left behind. As John Kendrick from Lake Placid, New
York, wrote in February of 1976, it was 'beyond beauty, beyond
description.'

But it was another note – one of the few others in English – that left
me in tears. On 17 May, 1954, an artist named Frank Schaeffer had
written: 'Coming from the far south, I have been the first painter who
had the privilege to live in this home. Back in my homeland, Brazil, I
will never, never forget the time I spent here, maybe the most fruitful
for my work I ever lived. To express my gratitude and admiration I find
no words.'

Realizing how far I'd been hunched over the guestbook, I leaned
back in my chair and took a final sip of tea. It was then that I
remembered something my two Northern Lights guides had shared
with me the night before, on our initial drive out of Svolvær.

'If you are on the plains up in Finnmark,' they said, referring to the northernmost corner of the country, 'then you can actually hear the sound of the lights. It's like a humming – the humming lights, the whispering lights. One of the indigenous tribes of Scandinavia, the Sami, have known this for as long as they have been around, but two years ago, it was proven [by scientists] without reason for doubt. The reason it makes sound is the discharge of electrons into the atmosphere, but the Sami people also have their stories: that the Aurora is their ancestors, their past going over the sky, watching over them.'

I thought about the seemingly random sequence of steps that had led me to this place – stumbling across the printout of activities in Å, scrambling for a last-minute hotel in Svolvær – and wondered if there hadn't been a subtle magnetism at work; that just as the auroras rely on science as much as they do on serendipity, so too does our own trajectory through the world orbit a sacred, invisible center. We move, we dance, we take risks and leaps of faith, and yet still we stay our course.

I'd journeyed to Lofoten to see the Northern Lights, but it was the light of these souls of artists past I now know I was meant to find – my own whispering guides watching over through time.

IN THE COUNTRYSIDE

BY MARILYN ABILDSKOV

What I remember now is the house. Large by Japanese standards, it had five bedrooms, three bathrooms, a large combination kitchen–dining room-living room with a fireplace in its center, windows everywhere, perfect light.

A view of snow country from every angle.

And two sisters. One had long hair, the other short. One was lush, the other angular, thin. They both dressed in natural fibers, Indian print shirts, long colorful skirts, sandals. They did not look like most other Japanese women. On trains, in the markets, women were often strikingly chic but rarely dressed so casually or looked so effortlessly bohemian.

Years later I've forgotten their names. But I remember how they looked and how one night that winter, they walked arm in arm down the hallway. They were barefoot, wearing thin robes. Their faces were freshly scrubbed, radiant as they whispered and laughed lightly.

The older sister's hair fell like a curtain in front of her face.

The younger sister worked in a shop downtown that sold clothing imported from India. Hand-beaded sarongs, long embroidered wraps, pure chiffon stoles, hand-woven cotton weave shawls. She spoke perfect English.

In The Countryside

'Where are you from?' she asked when we first met. 'What are you doing here?'

Her questions themselves were not unusual. Others often asked foreigners like me the same things all the time. But their questions – 'Your job, what is? You work where, by the way shall I ask?' – sounded as if they had been cut and pasted out of order from an out-of-date textbook.

Her questions, by contrast, sounded natural, unflustered.

When I told her I was American, from Salt Lake City, Utah, she said, 'Oh, yes, I know Salt Lake City. It's Matsumoto's sister city.'

There were no exclamations at the ends of her sentences as there were on others' I'd heard. She smiled but did not giggle or reach to cover her mouth.

I lingered, hoping to continue the conversation, then bought a blue and white cotton square scarf that I would later use as a tablecloth.

I introduced her to my American neighbor. I felt envy and relief when the two began seeing each other regularly – envy because now they had someone and I did not, relief because now someone else would have to listen to my American neighbor's monologues.

The American and I were both assistant English teachers in junior high schools, working in Japan on the same sister-city program. I spent a good deal of time at his apartment during my first months, relying on him. He was fluent in the language, he understood the customs. He'd lived in Japan before. And he was generous, loaning me books and CDs. But with that generosity was a price: I had to listen to him hold forth. On the brilliance of Bruce Springsteen. On the medicinal qualities of pot. On the virtues of meditation.

We lived next door to one another in drafty old apartments made colder by their proximity to the river. Identical in layout and size, our apartments felt dramatically different. He filled his right away with dishes, CDs, small Buddhas, blankets, books. Mine, by contrast, had only the bare furnishings provided by the government to foreigners like us – a rice maker, a kitchen table, a *kotatsu* (low wooden table), futons, a pillow filled with beans.

I put a calendar on the wall, its impressionistic watercolor calligraphy a mystery to me, and tried to convince myself to like the spare look. But the apartment didn't seem spare so much as empty and cold.

For New Year's, the American invited me to join him and his girlfriend to celebrate. She lived with her family in a house in the Japanese countryside. We would spend a week there with her parents, her grandmother, her brother, and her older sister, who, the American told me, I would like very much.

We arrived in late afternoon, the sun casting shadows. The younger sister showed me to my room, which I would have to myself. I set my black overnight bag down on the tatami mats and thought how small that bag looked in this large empty room.

That night I listened as the family talked while preparing dinner. The grandmother said she'd heard from a neighbor at the *sento* (communal bathhouse) that the youngest boy in the Sato family was ill. The younger sister cut up vegetables to go into udon. The oldest sister ran her fingers through her little brother's hair, saying it was so long, he was starting to look like a girl.

I was grateful to dry dishes after dinner, to feel momentarily useful, to observe the lovely symmetry of teacups lined up on the open shelf as I listened from the outskirts to the family talking effortlessly.

On the second day the sisters' mother put me to work, asking me to fix stamps to the family's red and gold New Year's postcards, containing messages in *kanji* I could not read.

In the afternoon, the younger sister drove us to a coffee shop where my American neighbor and I and the two sisters drank cafes au lait and the older sister doodled on napkins but wouldn't show us what she'd drawn. She'd been to art school in Tokyo, I learned, and doodled the way others daydreamed.

On the third day, I asked the older sister what her favorite music was. She smiled and said, 'Reggae, of course.'

At night we watched American movies with Japanese subtitles.

'Oh, to have such elegance,' the older sister said, watching Audrey Hepburn in Roman Holiday, lamenting what she described as her own never-quite-put-together style. I was stunned. She looked plenty put together to me.

Her younger sister told her she was beautiful and asked, how could she fail to recognize that?

'No one ever appreciates what they have,' I said. The older sister laughed and said, 'It's true, it's true, a far-reaching, sad, international truth.'

That night I lingered in the empty hallway on my way to the bathroom, taking in the small archways that cut into the walls, alcoves that, as if this were a museum, showcased ikebana under single spotlights.

Each night the women in the family prepared elaborate dishes. Broiled fish cakes in the shape of rising suns. *Konbu*, a kind of seaweed, which the sisters' father said symbolized joy. Skewered prawns cooked in sake. Mochi rice cakes. 'Traditional New Year's foods', the sisters' mother said.

The American translated the grandmother's story of a neighbor who had recently grown fat as a pig. Everyone laughed. I wasn't sure what was funny but I laughed and tried to look as if I did.

By the fourth day, I was restless and hoped we would put on our tall boots and go for a long walk in the countryside, but we didn't. Instead, we slept in late, then lounged again between meals and the sister's brother taught me how to play *karuta* with face cards, which he quickly won.

The weekend was so languorous and the family so lovely that it felt like a movie, one where the slow plotting would lead to something. Maybe someone's dark secret would soon be revealed.

At night, after everyone had gone to bed, I wandered back into the living room to sit on the couch in the family room and stare into the last embers of the fire, then out the window at the shimmering snow, homesick for my cold apartment in Matsumoto.

On New Year's Eve, we drank warm sake and ate cold soba, which 'would cancel our bad lucks', the oldest sister said. She drew her knees up to her chin at the long kitchen table as her brother wrapped his arms around their grandmother and kissed her on her gray head.

The grandmother said she hoped I would come back, that if I came back in the spring they could take me to Tsumago, a town nearby that was restored after the war. The town looked as if it were straight out of the Edo period. 'You'll walk down cobblestone streets,' she said.

At 11pm the younger sister brought out snacks, *oyaki* dumplings and bamboo leaf-wrapped *sasa-zushi*, and the older sister opened two bottles of champagne. Everyone laughed and cheered when the cork popped. We drank more and broke open edamame, piling up the bright skins of soybeans into small green hills.

Midnight came and went without fanfare. I was grateful to avoid the awkwardness. Who would have kissed me at midnight? Who would I have hugged?

By 1am, nearly everyone had gone to bed.

The older sister and I lingered as the candles at the center of the table burned. She poured the last of the champagne into small teacups. It seems impossible to imagine now but we spoke easily into the night. She spoke a bit of English and I understood a bit of Japanese and both of us were loose-tongued, tipsy from all the champagne.

What did I think of Japan? she wanted to know. Did I know what I wanted to do afterward? Did I have someone waiting at home for me? I told her I loved Japan but felt lonely much of the time. That I didn't have any idea what I would do once I finished the year. And though I'd been seeing a man back in the States, it was over now. We still exchanged letters but they were more friendly than romantic and I knew even these exchanges would not last.

'What about her?' I asked.

In The Countryside

She did not know what she wanted to do. She loved to paint, she loved to draw, she knew she did not want to live in a big city like Tokyo, but beyond that? Her future was unclear. As for love, she shrugged and sighed and stared into her empty teacup. 'I have no one,' she said, laughing lightly, then something that I wasn't sure of but imagined translated into a version of but what's a girl to do?

She was beautiful in the candlelight in her loose gray cashmere sweater, her long hair shiny like a lacquer box. She seemed like someone who'd stepped out of a foreign movie and because I was with her, now I had stepped into one too.

Then she asked matter of factly, did I? Want to?

I understood perfectly, immediately. And I understood that this was my chance. I was in a quiet house in the country. I could do whatever I wanted.

I burned with pleasure as the champagne took hold.

In the spring, the city moved both my American neighbor and me into apartments in a new building on the other side of town. Here the flats were bigger and newer and nicer all around. He continued seeing the younger Japanese sister, going to her house in the country on weekends, taking her to concerts in Tokyo, making her dinner in his apartment at night. I continued living alone.

I'd see the two of them sometimes from a distance, standing outside her shop downtown or carrying groceries into his apartment, a picture of good luck, good looks and, what seemed to me, unreachable happiness.

A year later, when I was running errands downtown, the younger sister stepped outside of her Indian shop and waved to me in the sunlight, asking me if I could talk. We hadn't seen each other in months. She seemed agitated. A tiny bead of perspiration had settled on her upper lip. Did I know? she asked, stammering in a way she never had before.

Did I know what? I asked.

'If he was. . .' She hesitated. 'You know,' she said.

But I didn't.

The American and I rarely talked now. I'd started spending time at an expat bar where I'd made friends and fallen for an engineer from Brazil who'd recently returned home. He'd told me he wanted to come back to Japan to pick up where we'd left off but I hadn't received a single letter from him.

Was he trustworthy? she said.

Now I hesitated.

'Did something happen?' I asked.

He had, she said, something wrong with him. Something on his penis. A rash. Did I know anything?

I wanted to tell her she should move on, that she could do better, that I didn't trust him, that I never had. But on the basis of what? That I'd found him arrogant? Irritating sometimes?

I said I didn't know anything.

The Brazilian engineer moved fluently between three languages, Portuguese and English and Japanese, as if each one were his native tongue. One night at Scotty's, our town's expat bar, we'd cordoned ourselves off and for the rest of the night, it had been just the two of us talking for six hours straight, closing the bar down before dawn.

'I have to go now,' he had said, one hand on my shoulder, whispering in my ear. What I heard was something else entirely: I need you and how. But then he made it clear with a quick flick of the wrist that he wanted us to leave together and so we did, unlocking our bikes outside the bar and beginning the rituals of our courtship: talking and then following up that talk with the dignity of a simple walk.

He walked me home that night by way of the Matsumoto castle and asked me, once the castle's garden came within sight, what I thought of bonsai, the Japanese tradition of pruning trees. I said I didn't like the idea of stunting a tree's growth for the sake of aesthetics and besides, I liked my gardens wild and lush and ridiculously overgrown.

In The Countryside

But when we reached the castle gardens and were standing right in the middle of the bonsai garden itself, I changed my mind. Maybe it was the wash of the early morning light or maybe it was Ricardo's presence or maybe it had something to do with the air, which was, I see now, the air of youth: still full of possibilities then. Once we were in the garden itself, standing there with only our bikes between us, the stark, monastic beauty of this finely manicured garden with its Japanese maples and pines struck me as gorgeously ordered and, at the same time, wild in some inexplicably contained and subtle way.

Maybe I was wrong, I told Ricardo that night. Because this is beautiful, isn't it? A paradox.

Yes, he said. A paradise.

The American told me about a teacher he worked with, a small slip of a man. Takahashi-sensei was in his sixties and drew a Buddha every day. He said his sketch in charcoal was penance for some earlier sin.

What could it be? I asked my American neighbor at the time. What had Takahashi-sensei done?

The American didn't know.

When the older sister asked me on New Year's Eve if I wanted to, I remember thinking how strange it was to understand. But I did. I understood her question. I understood my own reticence too.

I smiled and thanked her and said I was flattered, but no.

She took my hand and we laughed like schoolgirls, staring at the last of the candle's wax, agreeing that love was hard to find no matter where you lived, and then she brought out a large carafe of water and two glasses and we drank until the candles died and small squiggles of smoke filled the air like messages only we could read.

I slept deeply that night in the elegant borrowed room, the sun on the snow in the morning waking me from a strange, untranslatable, un-filmable dream.

Now Takahashi-sensei would be in his late eighties, if he's still alive. His back would be bent, his hands arthritic. If he still sketches each day, his mark now would be a single gesture, not a full rendition of Buddha. Just a brushstroke.

Maybe it's not penance that drives him or some single dark secret but a desire to pay homage to the complicated memory of the past, to all the loveliness and loneliness of how we circled one another then, to the constancy of Eros that coursed through our blood, to the way we loved and hurt and refused each other then, believing the paradox was a paradise of sorts, that we could live in the dream house of youth forever, that our longings would never end.

Maybe his was the sin of commission. Maybe his was the sin of omission. It doesn't matter now.

Like those snow-covered fields in the Japanese countryside that looked one way from a distance but surely up close must have been something else.

FOCUS
BY SHANNON LEONE FOWLER

In the spring of 2002, my boyfriend accepted a teaching job for the Communist Party in China. Shortly after his arrival, he phoned me in exasperation saying he didn't know what he'd been thinking. He hated crowds, was impatient in lines, and couldn't use chopsticks. But he loved his students and was fascinated by the country – a place torn between communism and capitalism, still faithful to doctrine but seduced by the Western world. Sean had been hired to teach marketing.

Near the end of Sean's contract, I took a short break from my PhD research studying Australian sea lions and went to visit him. As young Westerners – I was twenty-eight and he was twenty-five – I found that we had a kind of celebrity. Everywhere we went, people wanted to pose with us for photos. They'd wrap one arm around our shoulders as if we were old friends, make a peace sign with the other hand, and smile into the summer sun for the camera. Then they'd thank us and walk away, without ever having asked our names.

In the few photos of the two of us taken with our own camera, Sean had been concerned about cultural sensitivities. As a consequence, there's an awkward distance in these images – a blank space between our bodies, my head only coming up to his armpit, his hands hanging out at his sides. Our relationship is blurred. Over thirteen years later, our photos from China are still stuck in a cardboard box. I prefer my memories. They're in better focus.

———————

We're walking down a busy street in Chángshā and a small child, being pulled by his mother's hand, twists out of her grip to turn and yell at us.

'*Yáng guǐzi!*'

'*Zhongguoren!*' Sean shouts back.

The child stares at us, wide-eyed and open-mouthed, then doubles over giggling. I am impressed. 'What did the kid say?'

'He called us foreign monsters.'

'What did you yell back?'

'Chinese person.'

———————

At a bustling city market in Běijīng, Sean and I are rummaging through piles of cheap, mass-produced Mao trinkets. My favorite is a wristwatch where Mao's arms circle like the clock hands on an old Mickey Mouse watch. Sean's particularly amused that most of the watches don't work.

We spend the hazy heat of the July afternoon collecting presents for his family and friends back in Melbourne: a knock-off Gucci bag for his sister-in-law, bright silk pajamas for his nieces, pirate DVDs for his mates, a wooden Buddhist mask for his mother. Sean's never satisfied with the first thing he sees. He wants to check every booth to make sure he can't do better. We weave back and forth through the market, surrounded by smells of cooking oil, chilies, cigarettes and car exhaust. When we've finally explored hundreds of stalls, he leads me by the sweaty hand back down twisted aisles and cramped corridors – back to the best bag, the perfect PJs, the cheapest DVDs, and his favorite mask.

It's a muggy night and we're visiting a group of Sean's students back in their dorm. Posters of boy bands and David Beckham are plastered over the walls. Someone has cooked a large pot of noodles to share and it's almost unbearably hot inside, but the students don't seem to notice.

As we slurp noodles and listen to the roar of traffic, it's clear something is up. Finally, Leon says there is something they'd like to talk to us about. Chris leans forward, glancing suspiciously over his own shoulder and whispering. 'No one outside China knows what we are about to tell you and even in China, no one speaks of it.' They begin to describe a demonstration that ended violently in Běijīng.

Sean replies. 'Yes, Tiān'ānmén Square. We know about that.'

The students stop, chopsticks in mid-air, to gape at each other. They say over and over again, 'You are not supposed to know of this.' It takes some time to convince them the outside world has heard about Tiān'ānmén. They themselves have only heard rumors and aren't exactly sure what happened or how many died.

The students are troubled, but increasingly defensive. Leon and Chris dismiss accounts we give them with waves of their hands, certain outside China we didn't get the correct story either. Once the students realize the massacre made headlines around the world, they seem even less comfortable talking.

Later, another foreign teacher tells us he'd been visiting Taiwan when it happened and there were candlelight vigils and protests. When he returned, photos of these vigils were published in Chinese newspapers, with captions claiming the Taiwanese were celebrating Taiwan's return to Mother China.

We're leaving Chángshā for Zhāngjiājiè and Sean thinks it'll be easier if Chris and Leon buy the train tickets for us. It's a complicated system, with different windows for foreigners, and it all requires hours of waiting and standing in lines. We go to the train station and Chris and Leon take their place at the end of a line. Sean and I wander around, holding hands, trying to decode signs, and figure things out.

The floor's sticky with used tissues lying next to overflowing ashtrays, and the air conditioning seems to be on its last legs. People stand around, listlessly smoking or punching keys on their flip cellphones. After about two hours, Chris and Leon come to find us.

'No available tickets on Thursday.' The boys shake their heads and shrug.

Sean asks, 'What about Friday? Or Wednesday?'

The boys look at each other, blink, and then back at us with blank faces. 'You said you wanted to go on Thursday. Why would you want tickets for Friday?'

Another two hours later, and we're finally leaving the train station with tickets-in-hand for Tuesday. It's only then I notice that the metal detectors at the entrance are apparently optional. People can choose to go through, or they can opt to go around.

———————

In a cheap restaurant filled with warm and vinegary-pungent steam near Huá Shān, Sean and I are surprised to find the menu in English as well as Mandarin. But the translations are more entertaining than informative. I suggest Chick with Sky, or Head from Small Animal in Special Breath.

Although Sean can now speak a bit of Mandarin, he hasn't learned how to read the characters. When we try our luck and point, there are usually disastrous consequences involving some kind of animal's feet. Sean does know how to order a handful of dishes and I resign myself to our usual plates, *qiézi* (braised eggplant) and *yú xiāng ròu sī* (shredded pork with chili). But he's also able to order one of our favorites, *páigǔ* (row of bones, or spare ribs).

While we wait for our food, we wash our chopsticks in hot tea, as Sean's students had instructed. Our tepid beers arrive first. I start to reach for the green Yanjing bottle, but Sean's already started to pour my beer into a glass.

When the food gets to our table, it's rich and complicated, with far more complex flavors than the Chinese food back home. Sean orders another round of beers while I'm in the restroom, and fills both our glasses as I return to the table. He winks a blue eye, and his dimple pops as he grins and raises a toast. The beer goes particularly well with the *páigǔ*, which is decadent and delicious with its sticky, juicy, salty-sweet heat. At the end of the meal, Sean and I peel ourselves off the plastic seats.

Thousands of pale grey figures stand at attention below us, their ranks stretching into the pit's farthest dim corners. Each life-sized soldier is unique – details of topknots and armored coats, some with mustaches or beards, others now missing their hands or heads. It's hard to imagine how the Terracotta Army must have looked in full color.

'What do you reckon about us coming back? Living in China for a year, Miss?'

'Not Běijīng. Maybe Shànghǎi….' We're young and in love, and anything seems possible with Sean. I know he's interested in the emerging markets, thinks there will be opportunities for someone who can speak Mandarin and English, who has a background in marketing.

'It's all about right place, right time. Don't you think, Miss?' We look out over the ancient sea of warriors, the air so thick with dust and history it sticks in my throat. 'And here we are.'

Focus

Sean and I are ready to leave the heat and humidity of inland China behind, and are looking forward to the coastal breezes of Shànghai. But first, we're stuck in our hard sweaty seats for the twenty-hour train journey.

We've been lucky to get seats at all. Every single hard and soft sleeper, even the last soft seat from Xī'ān was sold out for weeks. The aisle is crowded with people standing and smoking and eating instant hot noodles, holding onto plastic bags, cardboard boxes and bicycles. The man seated across from us balances a straw basket with two live chickens.

For the first few hours, we watch the scenery through the train window. The city traffic, smog and concrete give way to flat yellow fields of cereals and grains. Steep mountains shimmer in the hazy distance, and muddy-colored rivers practically steam in the summer evening heat.

Sean's been taking me hiking in China: through dripping green forests surrounded by thousands of towering quartz pillars in Zhāngjiājiè, up and down the steep steps of Huixin (Mind Changing Rock), Tian Ti (Heaven's Ladder), and Yao Zi Fan Shen (Somersault Cliff) on the sacred mountain of Huá Shān, and winding along stony ridges wrapped in fog on the Great Wall. But the landscape here continues to stagger me – the enormity and the uncontained wildness.

As night closes in, the train windows go black and we lean into each other. Sean flicks on a light and turns to the folded down page in our guidebook, reading again the description for the mid-range Ren Min hotel we've decided to splurge on in Shànghai.

'Air conditioning, clean pressed sheets, Western toilets, and a decent shower. Ours to be had soon, Miss. Very soon.'

I have no idea he'll propose to me, wrapped in those clean pressed sheets in that cool room the very next day. For now, he flicks the light back off, tilts up my chin in the dark, and kisses me.

Only ten days after we got engaged in Shànghai, Sean was stung by a box jellyfish off a beach in Thailand. We'd gone to Thailand for a quick break, an easy holiday after the difficulties of traveling in China. We were kissing in shallow water, my legs wrapped around his waist, when the jellyfish wrapped around Sean's legs below me.

More than thirteen years have passed. I think of China, and our trip there together often, even if our photos remain stuck in a cardboard box. And I imagine the snapshots of us posing with the locals who never knew our names now sitting in photo albums all over the country. Locals who will also never know that these photos captured some of the last moments of Sean's life.

A TICKET TO VIENNA

BY ANN PATCHETT

When I was 29 and living in Montana with my boyfriend, I took a year-long fellowship at Radcliffe College and moved by myself to Cambridge, Massachusetts. At the time I had thought it was too great an opportunity to pass up, but only weeks later I could see what the decision was going to cost me. When I called our apartment in Missoula late at night, no one answered the phone, and when I did manage to reach my boyfriend, he was distracted, evasive.

Broken-heartedness was not upon me yet, but I could see it clearly up ahead – the bright lights of a car coming towards me in the night. I considered going back to Montana to stake my claim, but if the damage to our relationship was already done – as I suspected it was – then leaving Radcliffe just meant I would be out of both a boyfriend and a fellowship.

In Cambridge the days grew shorter and colder. I trudged back to my tiny apartment from the library, past the Brattle Theater, past Sage's grocery, past the American Express Travel Agency. Something about the travel agency stopped me. I looked at the posters hanging in the window: the Eiffel Tower, the white sand beaches of Tahiti. Maybe my assessment of the situation had been too limited. Maybe I didn't need to be in Montana or Cambridge. I put my hand on the door and went inside.

A Ticket to Vienna

I'm sorry travel agencies don't exist anymore, at least not as the plentiful dream shops they used to be, those wide windows advertising the beauty of the world, the men and women behind the counter always there to help you go.

When I was 20 I'd won a writing competition, and the prize came with the explicit instruction that the cash award was to be spent on the winner's development as a writer. That summer I bought a Eurail pass and knocked around Europe with a girlfriend until the money ran out. It was Vienna that stuck with me, the cafes that lined the Ringstrausse, the catacombs beneath Stephansdom, the glorious Hofburg Palace.

I had always believed that someday I'd go back. And so I left the travel agency that night with a plane ticket in my coat pocket and a week's confirmed stay in a pension. I would go in December for my thirtieth birthday. The travel agent was impressed by my spontaneity, as was I. I didn't have a lot of money in those days but there was enough for a single impetuous decision. Walking back to my apartment I found I had a different view of myself entirely: I was independent, adventuresome. I wasn't sitting around waiting to see what someone else decided about my future. I was the master of my fate. I was the captain of my soul.

'Vienna?' my boyfriend said to me over the phone. 'By yourself?'

I pictured a distant future in which people sat around a table at a dinner party, each guest reminiscing about what he or she had done on their thirtieth birthdays. I would tell them I went to Vienna. By myself.

I got a booklet of travelers' checks and $200 in Austrian schillings. I got a new passport. At the end of November I told my friends in Cambridge goodbye and they wished me an early happy birthday. I packed my bag and put it by the door. My plan was to call for the taxi to take me to the airport at 5am. I sat down on the edge of my bed and waited. It was 4am, and then it was 4.30am and then it was 5am. I kept telling myself to pick up the phone and call the taxi. I told myself that I could walk into Harvard Square and find one. It was 5.15am. I had planned to get to the airport early. There was still plenty of time to make the flight. I sat there and looked at the clock. It was a quarter to six.

Was I not brave enough to go by myself? Was I afraid of missing my boyfriend? Was I sick? Scared? Was I having a premonition about a plane crash that I didn't understand? I had no idea. All I knew was that I wasn't standing up. I wasn't picking up my bag. I wasn't picking up the phone. It was as if there was something very heavy sitting on my head, holding me in place. It was six o'clock. I lay back on my bed, still in my coat, and cried. I was ashamed of myself. Four hours later I woke up with a fever and started vomiting. It went on like that for five days.

I can't remember ever being that sick or that happy. Whatever it was that struck me down in my apartment would have struck me on the plane. And then what? I would be this sick in the airport in Vienna. I would have made it to the pension somehow, boiling with fever, not speaking German.

I called a friend who left ginger ale and soda crackers outside my door. I slept through my thirtieth birthday and the day after that. My boyfriend called to check on me. I got better. After Christmas he confessed that he'd fallen in love with one of his students.

We had lived in a furnished apartment in Missoula and didn't own much. He mailed me what was mine in a few large boxes. Everything hurt and nothing killed me. I took my paper ticket back to American Express. The prepaid room in the pension was a complete loss but the travel agent told me I had one year in which to use the ticket to Vienna.

The autumn before I turned thirty-one I was living in Nashville. All year long I had heard the plane ticket ticking away in my desk drawer like a biological clock. I still planned to go and go alone but, having failed at my departure once, I was having a harder time making a commitment. In the meantime, I had been on three dates with a nice man named Karl who had recently been divorced. His wife had left him and he was very much adrift, having to rethink everything he knew about his life. On our fourth date, I looked at him across the table in the restaurant. He wasn't a stranger, he worked with my mother, and yet he wasn't someone I actually knew. But what did life ever come to without a few risks? I asked him if he wanted to go to Vienna.

Yes. He said yes, and then he said it again without giving it another thought: Yes. It reminded me of the night I had walked into the travel agency. I told him that, because of my ticket, we would have to go soon. He told me that soon was not a problem.

I hadn't meant this as a dating strategy but it functioned as one just the same, so I pass this along as advice: If you meet someone you like, ask that person to go with you to Vienna.

As it turned out, we were in Vienna for Karl's birthday, which was a couple of weeks before mine. We ate pastries filled with marzipan and walked along the Danube holding hands. In the catacombs we struck up a conversation with a young woman wearing a backpack. She was traveling alone. She was, I think, from Alabama. When we walked away, Karl said she looked tired and broke and that we should invite her to dinner, and so we went back and found her and brought her with us to a wonderful restaurant called Drei Hussars. We drank little glasses of freezing, syrupy vodka with peach pulp in it. I wondered if someone might have invited me to dinner had I made it to Vienna a year before, and then I remembered no, I would never have been able to leave my room.

Karl and I had made plans to spend half of our trip in Prague, but on our way to the train station he saw a very old set of silverware in a shop window. Since his divorce, Karl no longer owned silverware. In fact, he didn't really own anything. After some discussion with the store owner, he bought the forks and spoons and knives and had them shipped to Tennessee. The transaction took longer than we expected and because of this we missed our train. There were no other trains to Prague until the next day. We stood in the vast station with our suitcases, looking up at the board.

'Budapest,' he said, scanning over our options. 'I've never been to Budapest.'

I allowed that I had never been to Budapest either, and so we took that train instead, because at that particular moment it mattered more who we were with and less where we were going. In fact, that continues to be the case. Karl bought me a thin gold ring in Budapest to commemorate the day, and eleven years later I married him. We had been in such a rush and then were in no rush at all, proving that we were both impetuous and careful in the extreme. Proving that we were in love, and that Vienna was a city worth waiting for.

THE ROAD TO OAXACA

BY FRANCINE PROSE

On our living room wall is a wooden box about the size of a medicine chest, painted entirely black, and missing a door. Inside are shelves, and on the shelves are eight figurines: the skeleton figures commonly associated with the Mexican Day of the Dead. Held at the end of November, the festival is an occasion for Mexican families to remember and honor their dead – with flowers, with altars commemorating their lost loved ones, with picnics at the cemetery, and with comic-grotesque figurines, like the ones we have. Though not exactly like the ones we have: ours are female, skeleton-women with thatches of wild white hair, each bent over a desk on which there is ... a typewriter. We call our mini-installation 'The Dead Prose-Writers Society'. We call it 'The Secretarial Pool of the Dead'. When I found the figurines in Oaxaca, in 1986, it seemed to me that they might have been been made especially for me: a writer, a woman with long hair, who then worked at a typewriter, and who – for as long as I could remember – had been fascinated by the Day of the Dead, its art and rituals.

That trip to Oaxaca was the first real travel we undertook as a family: me, my husband Howie, our son Bruno (then eight) and our son Leon (then four). We were young, we were brave, we were energetic: it never occurred to us that a journey from the Hudson

The Road to Oaxaca

Valley to the Mexican Highlands was in any way adventurous. Mostly, what I thought was: this was someplace I'd always wanted to go, a festival I'd always wanted to witness, an excuse to take the kids out of school. And it truly never occurred to me (nor could I possibly have known) how profoundly the trip would change our lives.

We flew from JFK to Mexico City and from there to Oaxaca. We stayed in a beautiful hotel that had once been a 16th-century convent. There was a swimming pool in the central courtyard; one could dine beneath the arches of the cloisters; lush purple bougainvillea climbed up the pale stone walls. Our room was dim, cool, large, with enormous high ceilings; at night haunting music filtered softly in from the street outside.

It's always tedious to hear people describe how wonderful a tourist spot used to be before it became 'overrun' with other tourists, but that was the case with Oaxaca, then. The city was quiet. We were often the only outsiders around when we visited Oaxaca's remarkable art treasures: the gorgeous cathedral, the Basilica of Our Lady of Solitude, the exuberant Baroque churches, the leafy, restful zocalo, the pedestrian streets decorated for the festival with paintings made from colored sand and with flower petals arranged to form the pictures of the saints and the Virgin of Guadalupe; with makeshift altars featuring images of the dead and offerings – cigars, bottles of tequila, favorite foods – of objects that the dear departed had enjoyed in life; and with the orange marigolds and velvety deep-red celosia blooms that are traditional for the holiday.

Our hotel found us a competent, patient and exceptionally knowledgeable taxi driver named David – the kind of cool guy whom our young sons instantly looked up to – who drove us to provincial towns where local craftsman wove rugs, carved brightly colored animal figures, and distilled mezcal, and to the nearby archeological sites: the huge, ruined pre-Columbian city of Monte Albán, where a pyramid, a ball-game court, and a series of walled plazas provide among the best preserved examples of Zapotec architecture, and to Mitla, the jewel of

Zapotec civilization, much of it built between the 7th and 12th centuries, its standing walls still decorated with complex and extremely beautiful ornamental friezes.

I'd been to Mexico before. I'd traveled in Europe, Asia and North Africa; Howie and I had spent time in India. But it was totally different, traveling with the kids, seeing these gorgeous historical sites, this brave bright new world, so unlike their bucolic upstate New York home – through the eyes of the children. It was on that trip that we, as a family, fell in love with travel, as a family. Over the next decade, we took trips, as often as we could, as many as we could – to Rome, Venice, Sicily, Paris, the Loire Valley, and – thanks to the generosity of the Fulbright Foundation – we were able to spend five months in the former Yugoslavia.

That first trip to Mexico was not without its hitches. One Saturday afternoon, strolling through Oaxaca's fascinating, sprawling 20 November market, I felt a slight tug on my purse and moments later discovered that some clever thief – with the deft touch of a master surgeon – had slit my bag with a razor, and removed a packet containing all our passports and our plane tickets home. In a panic, we returned to the hotel, where we were told that nothing could be done until Monday morning, when the American consulate would open again. Not knowing what else to do, we told the kids to put on their swim trunks, went out to the pool and – as the boys splashed happily in the water, our crisis already forgotten (by them!) – Howie and I ordered a round of margaritas, made strong and served in styrofoam cups. By the time we'd finished our second round of drinks, we thought: whatever. We were not going to let this spoil our vacation. If nothing could be done until Monday, we'd try to have fun and keep cool until Monday, when the consulate would solve our problem – which it did. Temporary passports in hand, plane tickets reissued, we finished our trip and said our regretful (actually tearful on the part of our younger son, Leon) goodbye to Oaxaca.

Perhaps one reason that Leon was so grief-stricken by the prospect of leaving Oaxaca was that he'd developed an intense, little-boy crush on the beautiful waitress in the cafe alongside the zocalo where we went, every morning, to drink fresh squeezed orange juice and people-watch. Leon was very small, very cute, and had a very bad case of laryngitis, which didn't stop him for trying out the few words of Spanish he'd learned. It became a kind of ritual: when it came time to ask for the check, we'd send Leon, who'd croak out the words '*El conto, por favor*' in his throaty, husky voice: such a deep, large, unexpected sound to emerge from the mouth of such a small, delicate boy. And the beautiful waitresses would unfailingly dissolve into gales of warm, appreciative, fabulous laughter.

Now, more than thirty years later, Leon is married to a Mexican woman, our daughter-in-law Jenny, who is also beautiful and who has a warm, fabulous laugh. Often, we return to Mexico, this time to visit the in-laws. This past Christmas, Leon and Jenny and their two daughters spent the holidays in Oaxaca. Every year, in advance of the Day of the Dead, Jenny and our granddaughters build an altar on their dining room table in Brooklyn with flowers, candles, offerings and photos of relatives who have died. Last year, my eight-year-old granddaughter put a copy of my latest novel on the altar, in case my mother came back from the dead overnight – and wanted something to read.

Was all this – the similarities between what happened on that trip and our current lives – a coincidence? An accident? I think not. Only the most unromantic and the most cynically rational could suggest that there is no connection, no magical correspondence, between that long ago-trip to Oaxaca for the Day of the Dead – and the way our family lives now.

THE LAND OF THE GREEN SHEEN

BY TC BOYLE

My mother's mother was a McDonald, married to a Fitzgerald (though a shadowy Dutchman by the name of Post was ostensibly my mother's father), and my father's father was a Boyle. Though I've never traced my lineage for fear of what I might find there, I account myself at least half Irish, which is good enough to claim some sort of ethnic identity, and so, in the spring of my fortieth year, in the company of my wife and three small children, I moved to Ireland for a period of three and a half months, just to discover what it would be like to live in the land of my forebears. Unlike most Irish-Americans descending on the Shamrock Isle (Murphys! Are there any Murphys in this pub?), I had no familial connections and no particular destination. I wound up, with the aid of the Irish Tourist Board, renting a grand eighteenth-century house just outside of Skibbereen, on Lough Hyne, where for a brief period I adopted the role of (ersatz) lord of the manor.

Arriving at Shannon Airport in the dim mist of early morning, accompanied by baggage enough for an exploratory expedition to the interior of Africa (baby seats, baby carriers, baby diapers and other infantile accoutrements forming the bulk of it), I found that my initial meeting with the Irish was unpropitious, to say the least. The men at Immigration were of a mind to send us back as refugees who looked to be gaining entry on false pretenses and who would clearly become wards of the state and no doubt beggars to boot, and I let my wife – willowy, sweet-faced, sweet-tempered and above all, reasonable, which I most emphatically in that place and at that hour was not – handle the negotiations. Babies shrieked. The luggage accumulated. The Customs men looked dubious. Finally, exasperated, I explained my business: 'I'm a writer,' I said. Their faces jumped with recognition, if not outright joy. 'Ah,' said they, 'a writer,' as if that explained everything, and vigorously stamped my passport and that of my wife and children, including the smallest baby, whose passport photo featured the image of a very large hand (mine) propping him up.

What followed, after the exhaustion of the all-day, all-night journey from Los Angeles, was the pre-Google searching out of the path to the rented house down a succession of miniaturized Irish roadways, and all of it while driving on the opposite (wrong, that is) side of the road. When we finally arrived, the local farmers, Mary and Paddy Burke, who were in charge of maintaining the house and farm for the absentee landlords, showed us around. The house was six times the size of the one in which we dwelled in sere, sun-blasted Los Angeles, with a grand entrance hall and various parlors and a library lurking about, as well as a succession of mysterious wings. I'm sure Mary Burke was sizing me up as she showed me around, coaxing out the details of the utilities and the linen closets and such, while already, above us in one of the bedrooms, babies howled themselves to sleep. Outside the windows, on the vast rolling lawns that gave on to Lough Hyne itself, were perhaps a dozen cows. I said to Mary, suckering her in: 'You know, I'm not really all that familiar with livestock – tell me, when it rains, I'm supposed to bring the cows into the house so they won't get wet, right?' She let out a laugh and we were instant friends. She was Irish and so was I.

The next matter of importance, if not survival, was my daughter's schooling. Kerrie was then in second grade and she had a full seven weeks left to go in the semester when we unpried her from the grasp of the LAUSD and rudely dragged her off to the land of the green sheen.

Accordingly, on the day after our arrival, I telephoned the Master of the Rath School in Baltimore (Baal-tee-már), Michael Collins, and explained our situation to him. We were not taxpayers, we were not citizens, but our daughter required schooling and could he help us? 'Bring her over,' he said, and the next day, following his directions, I drove the rented car over an unpaved road with a stripe of shin-high grass sprouting down the middle of it for fifteen minutes or so, doubtful, very doubtful, nothing but sheep and green hills and the occasional farmhouse to guide us, but then, mirabile dictu, the Rath School appeared at the bottom of a long deep-green hill, set there like a beacon against the pound and slash of the ocean. Michael himself greeted us. 'Give her half a day,' he said, 'and see how she adjusts.' When I returned to pick her up, the entire schoolyard rushed to the car to wave her farewell, the chorus of children's voices crying, 'Goodbye, Keddie, goodbye!'

What am I trying to say here? That the Ireland of my experience was a relaxed and welcoming place, the diametrical opposite of smog-choked, freeway-clogged LA, that the Burkes were a delight and that Michael became – and still is – one of my closest friends. And that because we were living in a village and had a child in school alongside the children of the local residents, we fell into a way of life that was very different, I expect, from what the average tourist (Murphys? Any Murphys here?) might come to experience. It was my first taste of living abroad and I was deeply gratified, enchanted even, LA instantaneously relegated to another sphere altogether.

There were the cows. There was a bower of rhododendrons leading to the lough, there was a rowboat, there were fields, a long winding gravel drive, a series of ancient iron gates to keep the cattle out of one field/garden or another. And there was the mailman, whose presence and practice were vital to me then, as I was plowing through proofs of an enormous novel at the time as well as sending out stories to various magazines. After pulling open the cattle gate at the base of the long drive each morning, he would placidly drive through, stop to close the

The Land of the Green Sheen

gate behind him, re-enter his car and wend his way up the hill to the house, where he came silently into the grand entrance hall to lay the letters on the table there. Best of all, it rained, rained constantly, and this was no small consolation to a writer having to contend, day after interminable day, with the riot of sunshine that was LA during the scorch of summer.

If this was writing weather (and I was productive during my time on Lough Hyne, composing most of the stories that would comprise my third collection, *If the River Was Whiskey*), it was also drinking weather. In that era, Skibbereen was a town of some 3000 souls and featured, give or take, seventy-odd pubs. I can't say I visited them all or even half of them (all right: a third maybe), and of course, there were pubs in Baltimore and Skull that merited a timely stop or two, but I quickly found the ones that truly sustained me. At first, being a foreigner and not knowing quite what to expect by way of reception, I was chary of entering them, but soon got over that. I'd been there a few days when I worked up the courage to try the most rustic-looking pub, set down a stone alley decorated with fifty or so shining and neatly stacked aluminum kegs. My wife was with me, and since I wasn't sure whether or not the sexes were segregated in the bars then (in one, men unaccompanied by females were confined to a separate room, owing, I imagine, to bloody historical encounters), I tentatively pulled open the door and peered inside. This was a long narrow place, featuring perhaps ten or twelve bar stools in a rigid line. Each was occupied by a farmer in a tweed jacket, a tweed cap and the black gumboots they all wore as a matter of practicality (rain, mud, ordure). And each of them was a twin of rapier-eyed, savage-beaked Samuel Beckett. They all turned their heads as one, and I, thinking of Vladimir and Estragon, backed quietly out the door and eased it shut behind me.

A week later, when I was more acclimated and knew the girl at the bank, the greengrocers and all three butchers, I went back to that very pub, clapped on my beret and had a good raucous time, looking, in the dim mirror over the bar, faintly Beckettian myself. I remember the wait for a pint of Guinness while it settled into its perfect blackness with its half inch of creamy foam on top, and the little glasses of John Powers whiskey that by necessity accompanied it. And the music. The music was a constant, and on the very rainy day that washed out the school parade and community fest on Clear Island, we all crowded into the three pubs there and everyone spontaneously broke into song, accompanied by the odd mouth harp, banjo and set of clacking spoons. Most of all I remember the silence that fell over the wet fields and the misted lough and the grand old house too, the five us sitting around the peat fire for story time, all well, all right, in a time longer than time.

Was the trip life-changing? No, not in the sense that my discovery of Flannery O'Connor or John Coltrane was – it was just life-living. I re-read Joyce that summer – *Dubliners*, *Portrait* and *Ulysses* – and I attended a performance of Synge's 'The Playboy of the Western World' at a tiny stone community building on Sherkin Island and for the first time really, actually got what it was all about. Was that life-changing? I suppose so. But then so is every experience, every moment, including this one, as I sit here all these years later, seeing Ireland in the synapses even as I stare out at a stormy sea on the Central Coast of California. The point is that while I've been back to the Isle many times since, it's always been on business – book business – whereas for those glorious three and a half months, I was able to live and write and truly inhabit a place that was at once foreign and familiar too. And that made all the difference.

BRAVE IN MALAYSIA

BY KAREN JOY FOWLER

My daughter, Shannon, is good at many things, but traveling is one of her special skills. When she proposed a trip to Malaysia, I said yes instantly. And I didn't do much in the way of preparation. I figured Shannon would have a plan.

So I didn't actually crack open the guidebook until we were on the plane and on our way. We flew China Air, which didn't seem to board so much by seat number as by rugby scrum. We'd both asked for the vegetarian option, which turned out to be a sinister black, foul-smelling, gelatinous mass. I feared it would eat me before I could eat it. Which I was never going to do. I couldn't even have it sitting on the tray in front of me.

All around us, other passengers were tucking into instant soups they'd brought in their carry-ons. The smell of ramen noodles drifted through economy class. I have never wanted anything so much. It was in this fragile state that I read that Western women were being physically attacked by Muslim fundamentalists in Malaysia.

The year was 2001. I showed Shannon the relevant paragraphs in the Lonely Planet guide. It was clearly not news to her. 'I was hoping you wouldn't see that,' she said. 'Anyway, that's not the part of the country we'll be in.' Asked and answered.

Brave in Malaysia

We landed in Kuala Lumpur, and went immediately to a Thai place called the Ginger Restaurant. For years my Australian friend Justine has been complaining to me about American Thai. 'Too sweet,' she said. 'Thai food is all about the balance of flavors.' In the Ginger Restaurant, I finally understood what she'd been talking about. American Thai food is too sweet. We would return to the Ginger again and again, every time our journey looped us back through Kuala Lumpur.

But it was viciously hot in Kuala Lumpur, and after just one day there, we went in search of cooler weather. We toured tea plantations and hiked in the Cameron Highlands. We spent a few days on Tioman Island, where we swam in an ocean so warm as to be unsettling, and strolled among Komodo dragons. We slept at night with mosquito netting around our beds, our sarongs our only blankets, and the soothing white noise of the overhead fans. I tried to put those attacks on Western women out of my mind. I never felt unsafe. But I did often feel that, even in our long-sleeved shirts and skirts, with our hair carefully covered, we were unwelcome.

Then we flew across the South China Sea to Malaysian Borneo. I had read Robert Payne's *The White Rajahs of Sarawak* back when I was in college, and I felt virtuously prepped even though I didn't remember a word. Kuching was friendly and simply beautiful. We walked along the waterfront, which was strung with lights. We took pictures of each other with the Great Cat of Kuching, Yong Kee Yet's relatively recent cat statue, its paw out, waving to us. We ate some delicious peppered shrimp. What was not to love?

We went to the English language bookstore to top up our reading possibilities. The people at the register ahead of us had extended earlobes, full-body tattoos, and extreme piercings. They paid for their books and exited the store. Immediately, the people behind the counter fell about themselves, laughing. 'Americans,' the clerk explained to me. 'From Santa Cruz!' There seemed no reason, at that particular moment, to admit to being from Santa Cruz ourselves.

We caught a bus to Bako National Park. Signs on the way in and all around the park warned us – Beware Naughty Monkeys. This made me think that the monkeys would be mischievous, possibly in delightful and photogenic ways. Like Curious George. We had come, at least in part, to see the proboscis monkeys, and we did see several of these, though far away, nearly hidden in the trees.

The naughty monkeys, in contrast, we saw from much closer up. We had no sooner debarked, on our way to the dormitories, than a troop approached. At first we were very pleased. Look how close to us they are coming! Why, they don't seem a bit frightened of us! And then they came closer. And closer. And we began to see that they didn't seem a bit frightened of us because they weren't. They spat at us and bared their teeth. They surrounded us, howling and hooting. The largest male singled me out. He came at me with some speed, screaming furiously. Even as he was charging, I expected, I hoped, that he would turn aside at the last minute. I saw that he was furiously erect, in both meanings of that word. I had just one moment of realization that it was entirely possible something very bad was about to happen.

Fortunately, the only crime on his mind was theft. He snatched my toilet kit from my hand and took it up into a tree. Above my head, he opened it, took out each item one by one, bit it, and threw it angrily to the ground. I'm guessing he'd expected something more delicious than my shampoo. He continued to scream and display. The rest of the troop kept a ring around us, menacing.

When my kit was empty, the male came down and charged me again. What was planned this time, I don't know; I had nothing left to steal. But a large British man stepped between us and shouted at him. I was pretty awed by this display behavior, awed and grateful. It worked. The monkeys moved on and I was able to retrieve my personal items, all now with serious tooth marks.

My daughter and I took a long hike to calm down. We found the shy proboscis monkeys, and appreciated the way they stayed so far away from us. We had dinner, and laid our sleeping bags out on the bunk beds in the tourist dorms. We'd imagined we'd be sharing – there were maybe twenty bunks to a dorm – but tourism was light that day and we had a whole room to ourselves. Or so we thought.

We turned out the lights. Shannon seemed to be having trouble getting comfortable. I heard a lot of restless rustling. This went on for a while. Then Shannon said, 'Mom, I think there's something in the room with us.' The light switch was at the foot of my bunk. I sat up and reached for it. The room was empty.

I turned the light off and the rustling began. I turned the light on. The room was empty. But a tube of Pringles that I'd had in my backpack was on the floor with the side chewed off. I retrieved it, disposed of it in the lidded trashcans. Got back in bed. Light off. Rustling. Light on. Nothing. This time when I turned the light off, I didn't lie back down. I kept my hand on the switch and the moment I heard a noise, I flipped it again. Nothing.

In the end, we slept all night with the lights on. The next morning at breakfast, another American woman approached us. 'Can you believe the size of the rats here?' she asked. Apparently the rats in her room had not been as speedy as the ones in ours. 'Rodents of Unusual Size,' she said.

Back in Kuching, my daughter turned 27. When I asked what she wanted to do for her birthday, she said karaoke. We had never karaoked before. It was about time.

We chose a bar on the waterfront; there were not too many people there, though everyone else seemed to be male and Japanese. We arrived during a lull, got our drinks and began thumbing through the musical selections. We decided on 'California Dreaming.'

It was not available, the proprietor told us sadly, so we picked 'Hotel California' instead.

Not available, the proprietor said.

We struck gold with 'Leaving on a Jet Plane.' There were several singers ahead of us in the queue so we settled in to wait our turn.

The first man took the mike. He did an Elvis song. He was incredible. He was better than Elvis. We began to feel a bit uncomfortable.

Four more performances followed, each one better than the last. These men sang their hearts out. Our uncomfortableness grew. The next three songs were then announced. 'California Dreaming' would be followed by 'Hotel California,' which would be followed by 'Leaving on a Jet Plane.' The stage was empty, the men in the bar looking at us expectantly. Somehow we ended up committed to three songs.

We saw no path but the one forward. The songs were all pitched too high and we'd had a bit too much to drink. I found 'Hotel California' particularly difficult; we stumbled our way through it. But anyone can sing 'Leaving on a Jet Plane,' and that was our most solid performance. Still, not Elvis, not by a long shot.

When we finally left the stage, it was to warm and generous applause. The other singers came by the table to say encouraging things. Sometimes it was hard for them to find the words. 'Such a brave performance,' one of the virtuosos told us. 'Very, very brave.'

I am not the traveler my daughter is. This is something I know about myself – I think I love to travel, but what I really like is knowing that I'm going on a trip, and then remembering it afterwards. I am so good at remembering that I had a good time, I'm never sure if I actually did.

Did I have a good time in Malaysia? I was often uncomfortable under the gaze of disapproving men. It was extremely hot and yet we were wearing our modest long sleeves and often hiking somewhere steeply uphill. Shannon hikes very fast, so I spent many hours gasping for air and soaking in sweat. For three days a dead fish floated in the small waves of the beach at Tioman Island, and I remember thinking that the water was so hot, the fish were cooking. There was that moment in the National Park, facing the monkeys, when I was genuinely terrified.

But I do believe I had a wonderful time. I remember how blissfully I slept under the overhead fans, how good the Thai food was. I remember the Komodo dragons.

I remember Borneo in particular, the beauty and friendliness of Kuching, the lights reflecting in the water, the Great Cat Statue with its enigmatic face. Borneo, I think to myself. I love Borneo. Borneo was that place where I was very, very brave.

MOLDOVAN ODYSSEY
BY ROBIN CHERRY

'Do you have mold cell?'

I'd just gotten off the plane in Chișinău, the capital of Moldova, when a woman accosted me. It was my first visit to my father's ancestral homeland and this wasn't how I'd imagined it would start. But then how could I have known that Moldova's leading cell phone provider would be in the middle of a marketing promotion?

My father's ancestors fled Moldova at the end of the 19th century and research suggests that I should be grateful. And not just because we missed the early 20th-century pogroms that decimated the country's Jewish population. Ruut Veenhoven, who runs the World Database of Happiness, pronounced Moldova the unhappiest country in the world. Eric Weiner, in his happiness expose *The Geography of Bliss*, couldn't wait to leave and wrote 'there is nothing I will miss about Moldova.' But is it really that bad? I came to Moldova to see where I came from and to see if it really is as unhappy as all that. In the spirit of full disclosure, I rigged my happiness research trip a bit by timing it to coincide with Moldova's two-day National Day of Wine.

After I recovered from my cell phone assault, I realized that the taxi my hotel had promised was nowhere to be found, so I hired a cab and headed to the Hotel Gloria. As a violent rain fell, the driver put his hand out the window and manually guided the wiper across the cracked windshield so he could see where we were going. Unfortunately, he had no idea where we were going. The gas light came on as the gauge neared empty. We snaked up and down muddy roads lined alternately with faux art deco villas and hulking Stalinist office blocks. Finally, we pulled up to the metal gates of my hotel. I climbed the curved cement staircase past a regal lion statue and a kitsch porcelain pug. It was as if the New York Public Library had merged with Hunan Wok.

I checked into my room, where the faux deco decor was accented with highly flammable accoutrements. The sheen of the bedspread was outdone only by that of the gold-flecked curtains.

I headed to the restaurant and slipped into a red velvet banquette. The mirrored ceiling was festooned with turquoise chandeliers that lit up the ancient Rome-inspired mosaic floor below. I pondered the relationship between an earnest American and his smoldering Moldovan date until he said, 'We need to find an ATM.' Then, an elderly man in slippers shuffled in and turned on a karaoke machine which played three songs in constant rotation: the theme from *Love Story*, 'Speak Softly Love' from *The Godfather*, and Barbra Streisand's 'Woman in Love' played on a recorder. I wrote 'creepiest place ever' in my journal and wondered if coming to Moldova was a good idea after all.

The first morning of the festival, the skies let loose a deluge of freezing rain so the National Day of Wine celebration was moved from the center of Chișinău to the city's exposition center called, you guessed it, Moldexpo. If you assumed, as I did, that the festival had been moved inside, you would be mistaken.

I hailed a cab to take me to the festival, assured by the receptionist that it wouldn't cost more than 15 lei (roughly US$3). When we stopped, the driver demanded 20 euros. 'Nyet, 15 lei,' I responded triumphantly in my remedial Russian. 'Private cab. No rules,' he grunted back in English. I offered him 50 lei, but he scoffed at his country's currency. Then I offered him US$5 and he said he would take both the lei and the US$5 bill. I gave him US$5 and got out of the cab, daring him to follow me, certain I was safe as my Russian wasn't good enough for him to possibly make out my threat.

The opening ceremony of the two-day Day of Wine was in mid-Soviet-style swing, with dark-suited men standing around a microphone issuing proclamations to muted applause. Suddenly, a thundering sound erupted. Cricova, Moldova's state-run winery, had started its Eurovision-worthy extravaganza. Strapping young men in lederhosen emerged from a tent, parading flaming tiki torches as a stentorian narrator intoned a panegyric to the wines of Cricova. Like a Ricola ad come to life, complete with long Alpine horn, the refrain Cri-Co-Va rang out as the dancing young men were joined by lithesome female singers. Despite the miserable weather, the youth of Moldova smiled, laughed, and performed with gusto, joy and, dare I say it, happiness.

As I walked the grounds, I entered a historically-themed tent presided over by Bacchus (played by a craggy actor with a sour face who lamented that he had to violate historical accuracy by wearing socks under his sandals because of the cold). Dancing female servants and stoic Roman attendants swirled and milled around the tent. Suddenly I saw a young centurion who was the spitting image of my father as a young man. My father died two years ago, and it was his family that had both left and brought me here. I suddenly felt connected to this strange little country that almost no one has heard of. And despite the freezing rain, the shockingly bad design, and the corrupt and incompetent cab drivers, I was loving every minute here. I strolled among the tents, tasting lovely wine from proper bottles as well as some less-refined vintages from repurposed plastic water bottles.

It rained almost the whole time I was in Chişinău. I came in from the rain at Las Taifas, an elegant take on a rustic country farmhouse where I enjoyed a delicious dinner of grilled pike perch washed down with a bright, Moldovan chardonnay. When I went outside, someone had stolen my cab and I had to wait an hour for a new one. Another time, the driver took me to the wrong hotel on the opposite side of town. Finally, three hours later, I returned, exhausted, to the New York Public Wok.

I'd dreamt of coming here for years. I knew it wasn't going to be Shangri-La. The former Soviet Union never is. But little things clicked into place. I visited the house where Russia's greatest poet, Alexander Pushkin, ironically exiled for his poem 'Ode to Liberty', lived from 1820 to 1823. While Pushkin complained about boredom and backwardness in the city, by all accounts he had a lively time, bedding the wives of local nobles, fighting duels, and falling in love with the beautiful gypsy Zemfira (who, alas, ran off with a fellow gypsy, who murdered her). He started his masterpiece, *Eugene Onegin*, in this small house that today houses the Pushkin Museum. Today, it is filled with period antiques and photocopies of his manuscripts (the Russians kept the good stuff; the originals are in St Petersburg). The Moldovans take great pride in Pushkin's visit. There is a statue of Pushkin that's identical to one in Moscow except that the Muscovites could afford the entire body, while the Moldovans could afford only an enormous head. One of Chişinău's main streets is named for Pushkin, although with comic informality, it's listed as Al Pushkin Strasse. And I was mesmerized by the National Museum's WWII battle diorama complete with a filmed loop of planes flying across the backdrop, dropping bombs and crashing into the landscape covered with authentic ammunition.

My last night in town, I had dinner at the Symposium Wine Club, a stylish cafe tucked under a grotto-like ceiling. I tried mămăligă, the national food of Moldova, a soft mound of polenta filled with sour cream and topped with cheese, garlic sauce, and fabulous homemade pickles. My great aunt used to reminisce about mămăligă, but as she didn't cook, I'd never tasted it before. Although it sounds like an unfortunate female condition, mămăligă is delicious. This is not the food of an unhappy people. The menu offered affirmations that were both amusing and quaintly sweet, like 'The smoking food on a large plate is pretty much like the sunshine on a summer day' and 'May all the problems disappear and the life become more wonderful.' Moldovans even have a saying, Hai Narok, that's said at the beginning of a meal and conveys wishes of good eating, drinking, health, and happiness.

I'm not saying it's easy to live in Moldova and I'm not saying my four days were a true representation of life in an emerging democracy. I'm just saying that most of the people I met were far from the morose misanthropes I'd seen portrayed elsewhere. And that my trip to my father's homeland was everything I could have hoped for. I travel a lot and often feel at home, but this is the first time I've truly come home. The first time my feet touched roads that may well have been traveled by my great grandparents over a century ago.

I woke up on my last day in Moldova to find the sun out in full force. After I checked out, the receptionist gave me a bottle of wine to remember my visit. The driver arrived. The receptionist paid my fare and we sped off to the airport. The gas gauge was on empty the whole time, but like my entire trip, against all odds, everything worked out just fine.

TRACKS IN THE SAND
BY ROBERT TWIGGER

Steve was my buddy. He had been on an expedition across the
Canadian Rockies with me in a birch bark canoe when he had lost the
top part of his thumb, sawn off by a nylon rope when the canoe got
caught in a vicious current. His whole top thumb joint was gone but
some sort of vestigial nail was lurking and a thin crescent regrew so it
looked almost normal, until you took a second glance. The accident
had happened while towing the canoe through deep, ice-cold rapids.
Now I was asking Steve to do some more towing, this time through the
opposite terrain – dry not wet, hot not cold, in fact the hottest, driest
section of the Sahara, down in the righthand corner of Egypt that
borders Libya and Sudan. We would be taking turns towing a
homemade trolley – four motorcycle wheels and a baseboard that
carried water for ten days, over 100 litres of the stuff. Our mission: to
find a lost temple deep in the Sahara.

A strange German explorer called Carlo Bergmann – Google him and
you can see his amazing desert discoveries – had found evidence that
ancient Egyptians had penetrated far into the Egyptian desert. Cologne
University had spent 20 years looking for evidence of the Pharaohs in the
desert and found precisely zero… They drove 4WDs and lived high on
the hog. Carlo Bergmann had two camels and went alone, season after

season, searching for the old routes through the desert and meticulously following up clues in the manuscripts of the first explorers of the region a hundred years earlier. In one piece of research he'd found a local reference to a stone temple 18 hours southwest by camel from Dakhla oasis in southern Egypt, the place where Steve and I would start our journey. A camel caravan can average five kilometres an hour, so Bergmann reckoned on the stone temple being 90-plus kilometres into the desert – but what he found was far more intriguing. Because Bergmann was very concerned about his discovery, the exact location remained a secret. But retracing Bergmann's track, we might just get lucky....

We didn't have camels and we didn't have 4WDss. I had been in the desert only a few times and, frankly, the place scared me. Or rather camels plus desert, or cars plus desert unnerved me. I needed to keep it simple. Also, in keeping with my tightwad approach to adventure travel, I had decided manpower was the best way forward. And, to be honest, I'd also become a little bored with the clichéd image of the lone Westerner with camels or dusty jeep and existential freedom, etc. It was time to burst the bubble and what better way than a pretty ludicrous-looking trolley made in a few hours in the Cairo bazaar? The axles and wheels had been fitted to a piece of plywood I had bought for US$5 from a scrap wood shop out near the Cairo ring road. The metal work had been fabricated late at night in a workshop that specialised in making bicycle-powered delivery vehicles – heavy-duty stuff that was reflected in the 30kg weight of the trolley. But the one thing I'd learnt in my few trips into the desert was that most of it wasn't soft sand, and this beast would roll very easily over the hard, dried-up lakebeds and gravel plains that constitute most of the Sahara. Just so long as we could get across the dune barrier....

This had been remarked upon by every desert explorer leaving Dakhla in the last hundred years. Between 10 and 20km south of the oasis was a barrier of dunes which varied in width from five to 30km, depending on where you tried to cross. The maps were not much use –

they were still mostly white blanks and Google Earth just seemed like cheating. To me there is always a fine line in travel between ignorance and over-preparation. I often like to visit places with no map or guidebook; of course sometimes I crash and burn and miss all the great sights. But sometimes, just sometimes I stumble on something brilliant and overlooked and joyous to behold and I am the first to remark upon it. One thing is certain: when you travel without decent maps, you spend a lot more time looking at the place you're travelling through. Which is the main idea.

We drove to Dakhla along the desert road with the trolley on the roof in bits. We assembled it and left the car in the garage of a government hotel in the oasis. By mid-morning it was getting hot. Though this was early November and the cooler season should have arrived, it was still 30°C in the daytime. We now had to negotiate about 5km of sandy fields and irrigated gardens that marked the outer rim of the oasis. Every time we thought we'd finally be in the real desert, there would be another dank and reedy irrigation ditch to cross.

The dark, still slightly earthy sand was soft and dirty and the trolley sank into the surface. Our sweat was soon caked in dirt. Even though we let the tyres down until they were squidgy, we still had a hard time pulling the trolley. There was a simple rope attached to the front and, like a tethered beast, the man in front just heaved and struggled forward. We passed the last palm trees, the last bits of spiky grass and small tamarisk bushes. The stagnant smell of the irrigation ditches gave way to the dusty, almost smoky smell of the desert – very faint, almost no smell at all. The sun was going down. By the end of the first day I calculated I'd drunk ten litres of water – we had budgeted on drinking five.

Ten litres washing through your system takes out all the minerals and electrolytes. Small wonder that I was throwing up at sunset when we finally made camp behind a small conical hill, mercifully out of sight of the last dwelling and the fields.

We could look back at our own narrow-tyred tracks now cutting through clean, rather than churned-up, sand. There is a subtle shift

146

from car tracks and messed-up sand being the norm to pristine sand and no tracks of any kind. When, after hours of nothing, you find a single car track unspooling like two ribbons over a line of dunes it somehow looks mystical and strange, like the yellow brick road, a path somewhere important….

There are few better feelings than sipping a cup of tea in the desert while watching the sun set, the immense quiet when the wind finally dies down, the sharp and welcome chill of nightfall.

Sleeping under the stars, without a tent, I watched the slow turn of the Great Bear and Cassiopeia rotating around the pole star. It was like a clock; from their relative positions I began to be able to guess the hour. The dawn came cold and stealthy; we almost missed the moment when the sun broke the long, flat horizon in a sudden rupturing dazzle, filling all around us with instant warmth.

There was no breakfast for me but just tea with sugar. We had already evolved a system for the trolley: one at the front and one leaning/pushing on the back with the rucksack frame as a kind of handle, as if the whole trolley was some kind of giant old person's walker designed for the limping idiot at the back. The one benefit of being at the back was you could alter the angle at which your feet hit the ground. This was supremely important if you wanted to avoid the hot-stinging nightmare of a full-sole blister, popped but quickly refilling…. Steve meanwhile was fine. He told me he never got blisters, which, annoyingly, seemed to be true.

All too soon, we were at the dune barrier.

Our luck was in as the north-facing side was hard-packed and only the flip side was loose sand – which we descended by lowering the trolley by the rope, one guiding it to make sure it didn't flip over. The trolley ran well on the hard sand – I say hard though perhaps a 4WD drive would have cracked through the crust and sunk, but for our comparatively light trolley with under-inflated tyres it was not a problem. The great German desert explorer Gerhard Rohlfs made much of the difficulties of this set of dunes – which he crossed with twenty camels in 1873 – but then he did have some sponsors at home he needed to impress with his hardships. Amazingly – to us – we crossed in about three hours, onto a completely flat plain of hard sand that seemed to stretch forever. 'I think I can see another line of dunes in the distance,' said Steve. Well, maybe.

The hard sand gave way to a surface of flattened rock that was sharp in places. It was hard to tell, as it was all white in colour and the sun was burning down all white. I was drinking far less than yesterday – mostly as hot sweet tea, which worked much better than simply swigging from the bottle. But somehow we managed to puncture a tyre.

We had a spare and a spare inner tube and I quickly changed the punctured one. But when I tried to use the foot pump, it creaked twice and exploded – sand had blown inside its innermost workings, and pumping down hard on it broke it away from its frame. It was useless and unfixable. By some strange happenstance I had thrown an old bicycle pump into my bag but with no connector. So we still couldn't inflate the tyre.

Soft tyres in the desert are good. They keep you afloat on softer sand. But flat tyres are useless, terrible in fact. The hard wheel pushes through them into the surface. The tyre skids round the wheel and gets destroyed. If we couldn't re-inflate the tyre we'd be in trouble.

Of course the connector from the foot pump was a different size – but I saw that the end piece – if I cut it off – could be jammed with tape into the bicycle pump. We had duct tape and surgical tape and using both in liberal quantities, I fashioned a new and barbaric pump connector. The tyre re-inflated and we were on our way. This simple mechanical fix was almost the most dramatic point in the whole journey – when you're all alone and far from home, that's often the case.

But where was the lost temple? And all the Stone Age artefacts I had promised Steve? In my previous sojourns into the desert I had always found perfectly chipped stone tools. In the hotel where we stayed there was a pile of such tools found by other tourists. I scanned the ground in front of me, hardly looking ahead. Nothing. Not that there was a huge amount to see in the distance either – a few black bumps far away, which we steered for, using the GPS as a compass heading southwest as Bergmann had.

As I hinted earlier, it wasn't a temple he found. The cathedral-sized lump of rock, roughly worked around its base with a sort of dry stone wall, actually turned out to be a 'water mountain'. This was a water reservoir and storage point in the last days before the desert completely dried out around 3500 years ago. On the walls of the water mountain were fifth-dynasty hieroglyphic carvings alongside a good number of earlier nomadic rock art; this was a unique site in Egypt, showing the demise of one culture and the rise of another. It also demonstrated that the extent of pharaonic rule was much greater than previously imagined.

Things were going easier now. We had a routine: one man at the front for 45 minutes and then at the back for 45 minutes. Unlike an hour, which sounds quite long if the going is hot and blistery, 45 minutes sounds almost bearable. Slowly we made progress. Going around 4km an hour, we made 30km on the second day.

The landscape began to change. We entered a white space on the map that was actually riven with dry, sandy canyons. We kept a lookout for rock art but the rock was all rotten and shattered by heat and cold. Rock art, as I'd later discover, was usually on unexposed or north-facing flanks of harder limestone where it could not be eroded; around here it was all reddish crumbly sandstone. And still no tools. Steve was cheerful, though, and towing well. We had reduced our water intake to about four litres a day – at least half in tea and cooking. It seemed that the body was fooled into absorbing water better if it was part of food or a hot drink than if you just glugged it cold (or tepid). Maybe plain water sent a signal that water was not scarce and it got diverted into cooling via sweat. Or maybe it was adding sugar and salt that helped. Either way we were inadvertently copying the Bedouin way of dealing with thirst as they rarely drink unadorned water.

Another day, another camp. We used the boxes of water (we had boxes full of water bottles) as protection from the wind for cooking. In the afternoon the wind could suddenly get up, only to die out around

9pm. Sitting round a tiny crackling fire of sticks picked up while walking, with the wind howling and stars visible with incredible nearness and clarity above, is my memory of the desert night. When author and desert pilot Antoine de Saint-Exupéry called his memoir *Wind, Sand and Stars*, he got it absolutely right.

Walking on sand has a certain nightmarish quality about it. Every footfall is the same. The only variation is whether it is hard or soft sand. Soft sand becomes something feared and loathed as you lose power with every step sinking in. And every footstep being the same, the sand moulding in the same way, means the very same part of the foot gets rubbed time and again. No matter how slowly you walk in shoes or boots, your feet get sweaty and the skin becomes soft, as soft as having sat in a warm bath for an hour. The damage is terrible! Next time I will definitely wear open-toed sandals.

Steve said he was OK. I noticed he took off his boots and socks at every rest stop, though, wiggling his toes in the dry sand. Maybe that was his secret.

The air first thing in the morning was always cool and 100 percent clear. We were now almost 100km from any kind of road or human habitation and must have been inhaling the cleanest and most refreshing air on earth. Champagne air….

We entered a region of hundreds of small, 100-metre-high conical hills. It was like a place of giant termite mounds. They were made of shale, sometimes still with a limestone cap that had prevented their complete erosion. The shadows cast by the hills provided welcome relief. Steve, with his excellent eyesight, spotted *alam* – stone markers hundreds of years old that marked the old camel routes through the desert. Those routes are gone now but the markers remain. One of Bergmann's techniques was to follow such *alam* tracks and see what lay on either side. It seems that the ancient caravan routes lay on top of even more ancient Egyptian trade routes through the desert. Now we were getting somewhere.

But after another day of toil, the alams seemed to have vaporised in the clear desert air. There was nothing now, no tracks of any kind. Just sand. Small two-metre dunes. More flat sand. A vast bed of compacted gravel. Then we saw something rather chilling: our own tracks, our own wheel marks – two narrow lines suddenly crossing our path. It was straight out of Robinson Crusoe. We must be totally lost, we thought. The GPS (admittedly an old model) must be completely wrong…. We're going to die out here.

But a closer look at these tracks showed that though they were cut through the gravel surface, they were filled with white sand, fine white sand that had blown into them over ages. I measured the width – though the tyres were as narrow as ours, the gauge was marginally wider, only an inch or two, but enough for me to know these were not our tracks. They had been made much, much earlier. I had read about tracks in gravel lasting in the desert for a hundred years or more and these looked like those made by a very light small car – similar to an Austin Seven or a Baby Ford. Sure enough, I later discovered that in 1934 the Ford Motor Company had sponsored several adventurous explorers to take their 'baby' Fords deep into the Sahara.

The ancient car tracks extended into nothingness on either side. Ahead there was a shimmering mirage, a kind we had become quite used to where castle-like shapes moved each time we tried to fix their position. We had come far enough. Made our own track. Maybe that was enough.

A year later I went back into the same desert with some Bedouin driving a 4WD. We were there to drop water for a camel trip a friend was making. The experienced Bedouin driver tried but couldn't get through the dune barrier. We made a big swinging detour around the end of the dunes some 50km west of the oasis. Quite by chance we found a fresh track. This was, of course, unusual. No one came into this part of the desert, not even the smugglers from Libya who preferred a more northerly route. The track was maybe a week old, the Bedouin said. We followed it because that is what you do in the desert: tracks are always less unpredictable than open country. Hours later I saw something I knew – an outline of rock I had seen on Bergmann's photographs. It was

AN IRANIAN-AMERICAN IN INDONESIA

BY POROCHISTA KHAKPOUR

In December 2015, I was slated to go back to the country of my birth: Iran. Nearly a year before, an editor at *Conde Nast Traveler* had contacted me wondering if I might be interested in being sent to Iran. She did not of course realize that this would be my first trip back to the country since I was three, nor that there would be substantial complications given that I was a dual citizen (I became an American citizen in 2001, but Iran refuses to recognize US citizenship since I was born there), and that after a new batch of imprisonment of Iranian dual citizens, the trip would be cancelled (Jason Rezaian, the Iranian-American journalist who had been imprisoned for 18 months in Evin Prison, was released just weeks after my planned trip). I remember feeling more gutted about this loss than anything else in my life – a trip where I'd explore Tehran, Shiraz, and Isfahan. It felt so important for me to go back to a place I did not know but still called home.

The closest I'd been to Iran since I left was flying to Australia for various book festivals in the spring of 2015. My Emirates flight stopover was in Dubai and I calculated that I was only 750 miles from my birthplace. As we approached the night skyline of Dubai, I looked down at the same sky-view glitter of my refugee home Los Angeles, but with the notable Burj gleaming shamelessly like a sword. My many hours there on both legs of the flight were relatively fruitless – I searched into the faces of nearly everyone, as I knew Dubai had a substantial Iranian population, but that did not yield much. More than that, I was in awe of the fact that I was in a region where the majority of people were somewhat like me – Middle Eastern, of a Muslim culture. But you are hard-pressed to see that in a hub like Dubai International. As I bought cartons of Gauloises at the Duty Free, I marveled at all the East Asians, Europeans, and even Americans around me. I was not going to get much of a cultural experience here.

But what I did not realize was that during the flight from Dubai to Perth, I'd fly over Iranian airspace. I wouldn't have known this if not for the flight-tracker monitor in front of me – but there it was, as if Iran was no big deal, as if revolution or not, it was a country that existed, that you could go to, that you could just casually fly over. I watched those very cities that I was planning to visit in December announce themselves underneath me in a flash: Tehran, Shiraz, Isfahan, plus Qom and Masshad. Outside the window it was just before dusk and all you could see was a hazy brown of mountain upon mountain. For a second I felt like my longing could fill the whole plane and everyone had to know. And after a couple weeks of touring through Australia, the thing I looked forward to most was the ride back: Iranian airspace yet again. This time I was not so lucky to have a window seat and I nearly flattened the old South Asian grandmother next to me as I leaned into the window. Sorry, it's Iran, I was born there and I haven't been back, I said to her. She didn't seem to understand, as my body weight still was up against her. I pulled back. I muttered to her, but really to myself, I'm going to go back one day soon.

I haven't yet. But half a year later, I found myself on another long international flight, this time on Cathay Pacific via Hong Kong to Jakarta, for more book festivals. It was on the final leg after Hong Kong – a city I'd been excited to visit my whole life, after growing up with so many Hong Kong kids and their action movies – when a realization hit me: my trip to Jakarta would be the first time I would be in a Muslim country since Iran. I started to imagine what this could mean: veils, prayers, Korans, beads, all the paraphernalia of a childhood I had mostly missed, but that was to be mine. On this book festival circuit, Ubud, Bali, was the focus, but I'd agreed to do satellite programs in Jakarta and Semarang and my affiliates there had arranged for me to speak at several colleges. I had no idea what to expect, but I somehow seemed to know this experience was going to be significant.

Semarang was my first proper city and I had little idea of it, other than we'd be there for a couple days, that I'd speak to two colleges, and then we'd be off to Bali, where I was staying at a very upscale resort and there would be so many parties and great food and good writer friends – in other words, none of my trip organizers had really wanted to speak much about what Semarang had to offer. When we landed on the Garuda flight from Jakarta, I immediately was taken with the colorful prints on the clothes of nearly everyone, matched even more brilliantly with headscarves. I realized I was probably the only person who could call Islam her culture who was bareheaded, not to mention tattooed, in a tank top, wearing garish lipstick as if dressed for an American spring break. I wondered if they could tell; if they could, they were too polite, or perhaps too disapproving, to look. Maybe I was invisible, maybe in a good way.

At the hotel, as tired as I was with nearly no sleep in days, I could not pry myself from the window. Semarang is the largest city in the province of Central Java and looked not unlike the Los Angeles of my '80s youth – the sky a murky yellow-gray, smog and haze competing for complete saturation. But if you could spot a handful of bikers on highways there, here nearly everyone was on a motorcycle. And it wasn't those Vespas of Rome. They were simple cheap old motorbikes and on top of them you had far more than just the driver, but his companion and often a child or two or even three. You were in a land where there were bigger issues than safety and you got the feeling these cyclists were not on joyrides, but commuting urgently to work or home. I asked my handler why this was so popular, and she blinked at me as if I was kidding, snapping, Of course they are cheaper than cars. I watched with admiration as they zigzagged with little attention to lanes, ran red lights, made spontaneous U-turns, and honked mercilessly. The chaos had a logic to it, the way that once you actually drive in New York City, you come to understand. Your attention is the substitute for rules. Hypervigilance gets built into you as survival, and you ease into it. If I had more days there, I would have likely been converted as a rider myself.

But I had work to do. I was to deliver those two talks, and I was dreading them. It took arriving at the first destination to understand just how challenging that experience was to be. The representative from the US Embassy seemed very relaxed about my duties and assured me it would be the sort of talk I was used to, no preparation necessary. Had they read my books? I wondered. Probably not, she said, but not to worry, it would be easy. On my crumbled schedule, the program publicist had written that the talk was to be 'a discussion with acclaimed author and *NY Times* contributor Porochista Khakpour, exploring her life, background and work as a woman of Iranian-descent with Muslim lineage. How has her identity contributed to her personal journey and literary career? And what place does the concept of America, and the 9/11 WTC bombings have in her work?'

Easy enough, everyone seemed to say. But when I arrived at Walisongo State Islamic University, a public Muslim college, I saw a giant orange banner across a stage: 'American Corner Talkshow: Being a Minority with Porochista Khakpour.' I immediately felt a bit lightheaded – those wild words and their promise, plus the overpowering heat (it was 90˚F in Semarang; New York had been half that when I left) in a large room full of electrical fans, and buzzing with what seemed like hundreds of young people, seemed unendurable for me. I tried to focus on something, anything, but everything was a wave of color and heat and sound. The headscarves stood out – also the smiles. There was genuine excitement among them for ... me. They led me 'backstage,' which was a faculty lounge of sorts, where a lavish spread had been prepared for me – fruit, nuts, cookies, tea. Professors greeted me with huge smiles and handshakes. I started to hear 'Muslim author' a lot.

It is so good to hear a Muslim author from America, an administrator kept saying.

I finally had to say something. I'm not – well, I don't practice Islam. I am of a Muslim culture, but I don't... I had absently pointed to my head, but I also meant to point at my tattoos, my loud lipstick, my drinking, my history of drugging, my singleness, my lack of praying, all of it.

Everyone just smiled and nodded, and moments later, I was introduced by the US Embassy and handed a microphone. I began to ramble about my experience as an immigrant who had become an American finally in 2001 and then an Iranian-American author in 2007, hoping they would catch a word or two at most. But they were all watching and nodding, attentive. When the Q+A came around – an hour allotted for it – I imagined that since my book had not been taught, there would be no questions.

There were dozens and dozens.

How does it feel being Iranian in the US today?

How do Americans consider Muslims?

If I move to America, can I be respected as Muslim?

There was not a light question in the mix. I rambled my way through them and somehow the program concluded to much applause. Then I became aware of another Indonesian tradition – photos. Everyone wanted 'selfies' with me. A full half hour, I realized, had been allotted for the taking of photos. By the end of my day there, I had a few hundred more Instagram friends.

What followed was a polite and charming seafood dinner with journalists and academics at a local restaurant, and I found myself telling various people I knew I'd never see again that I would be back and that I would love to stay in touch. Then we were back at the hotel and I was informed by my handlers that tomorrow I'd be doing the same thing again. Different school, same drill.

An Iranian-American in Indonesia

They did not tell me that this time it was a Christian school, Soegijapranata Catholic University, in a far wealthier part of town. I was immediately greeted by hordes of faculty, who handed me elaborate snackboxes and lots of tea. The US Embassy rep had warned me that I'd have another banner, and so I blinked less when I saw the same giant banner, this time in purple with similar words: 'A General Lecture on Multicultural America: Being a Minority by Porochista Khakpour.' This time instead of a hot crowded assembly room, I was on a modern amphitheater stage. This was not a poor school. Of course there were no headscarves but you could easily see a difference in income level in the way the students were dressed.

There were the same questions, but this time about being Christian. It occurred to me that these students were the minority: Christians in a Muslim-majority country.

I tried my best, I felt inadequate, selfies upon selfies upon selfies, and that was that.

When we left Semarang for the airport the next day – bound for Bali, where the actual main event, the Ubud Writers and Readers Festival, would take place – I found myself thinking so much of that city. On the cab ride to the airport, the cab driver kept honking and honking.

'No one gets upset?' I asked my handler.

She looked confused. 'Why?'

'The honking,' I said. 'In America, it's rude or at least aggressive.'

She seemed surprised. 'It's courtesy and respect here. They don't want you to crash.'

Of course, I thought.

And of course, Bali was a dream, staying at a luxury hotel in the monkey jungle, having my first encounter with a proper Olympic-sized infinity pool, reveling in a festival that was as exhilarating as it was glamorous (we had multiple festivities at the royal palace), but it was not until my final days of satellite events, this time back in Jakarta, that I felt like I was in Indonesia again.

I would not have guessed that Jakarta, perhaps especially after the unexpected joys of Semarang, would become one of my favorite cities on earth. We had only a few days in this coastal city, at the mouth of the Ciliwung River on Jakarta Bay, on the world's most populous island. Everyone, including Indonesians, had warnings for me about Jakarta – that it was too dirty, too crowded, too loud, too ugly. There seemed to be little love for it. Just look at our sky, the taxi driver said as we boarded, and indeed there was Semarang's – and my '80s LA's – grey-yellow backdrop, though even more grey, in a way that made all the highway flora, amply planted, look almost surreal in their pinks and purples against the bleak newsprint tones of concrete and sky. Look at our traffic, he said later, much later, as it indeed took us some hours to get to my hotel; this was an expression many would echo, and a good reason to not explore much, everyone said.

But still I explored. Our base, the Artotel Thamrin, was clearly the hip boutique hotel of the city. Located in the city center, the hotel had collaborated with eight emerging visual artists whose work was on display in each hall and room. The effect was a sort of East Berlin hostel, a bit careless, a bit punk, but also very calculated in its young hipness. We walked all around the city center, poking in and out of stores, malls, and gem shops. The days were all about food: nonstop nasi goreng, that fried rice delicacy with skewered meats, satay, and all sorts of fried fish and fish dumplings. My favorite treat was a street food, *martabak*, which my team seemed especially excited to introduce me to. We sat at night with beers and these heavy cartons full of the sweet treat, a folded pancake filled with toblerone and butter, that seemed nearly impossible to consume as just a dessert, especially in the overbearing viscous heat of the tropical monsoon night. (I soon came to realize that everything I wore would be drenched. Jakartans explained to me that they all found it shocking Americans bathed only once a day – they not only bathed multiples times, they washed their clothes daily too.)

The city used to be known as Koningin van het Oosten (Queen of the Orient) in its colonial period, but today it was more 'The Big Durian' (after the horrifically-odored fruit that I had learned to avoid that trip), like The Big Apple. And it had that same New York quality: manic and urgent and all about work and the impossibility of work. It was a wonderful mess. All around, a diversity of architectural styles revealed themselves – from my modern base to Malay, Javanese, Arabic, Chinese and Dutch influences, the Old Town melting into the New with little hesitations. This place felt like an actual melting pot, my first since New York.

I found myself wondering if my hometown Tehran would feel like this, another question I could not answer.

Jakarta was of course a major Muslim capital too, with the population at over 85 percent Muslim, the rest Protestant, Catholic, Buddhist, and Hindu, mainly. This was my first city where I heard over loudspeakers all day, the azan, the Muslim call to prayer, and this turned out to be one of the most important experiences of my life.

My first memories of Iran are not happy ones – air raids, bomb sirens, panic and revolution and war, as I was born in the time of the Islamic Revolution and then the Iran–Iraq War. One of the memories I also have of that era is looking out the window facing my crib and seeing men wailing on rooftops in prayer. It's a memory that scared me, because it was tied to some change, something that my parents recognized as threatening, something tied to fleeing, something I would not understand as part of my culture for many years.

In Jakarta I woke to the sound, and my days were punctuated by the sound. At a dinner with journalists, some almost apologetically mentioned to me that the city for years had been trying to enforce getting mosques to lower the volume, but it was not always effective as it could be interpreted as disrespect to Muslims.

You don't want to offend Muslims, a journalist said to me, in total earnestness, a sentence I could never have imagined in America.

I found the sound so beautiful, and something that connected me to another world I belonged to. I found myself recording the prayers, over and over, and treasuring this folder on my laptop devoted to the calls of Muslim devotion in Jakarta. I even found myself trying to mouth the words one morning.

The other event there that tied me to this special city, was the satellite program's impromptu affiliation with a local poetry group, who had asked for us to make guest appearances at their local slam night on the rooftop of the Artotel. My traveling companion, an editor, and I, a bit reluctantly obliged – neither of us were poets – and imagined we'd just be in the audience, a bit clueless, as we were warned the event would not be in English.

But that night became such a significant night: again so overbearingly hot and humid that the air finally burst into monsoon downpour and the deck of the roof turned automatically into a covered vestibule for us, and a shelter of many special hours. The members of the group were young Jakartans who did not look so different from my liberal arts college students in New York. Many of them pointed out to us that they were part of LGBTQI organizations in town. They were all so excited that we lived in New York and wanted badly to speak about it with us. But of course they also wanted to show us their reading. They read all sorts of things, some in English even, perhaps to humor us – Sylvia Plath's 'Daddy' was rendered like horror theater by a young gay man, and then a Bukowski poem I'd never heard was uttered in a throaty whisper by a beautiful young woman in a tiny black dress and sky-high heels. They got it, these Jakartans, and I was reminded of my first slams in New York City in the '90s – so vulnerable, so powerful, so naked, so sheltering.

They kept asking for me to share something and I realized that just the summer before I had begun writing poems, but not with the intent of sharing them at all. Still somehow I was compelled to share with this group, and I dove into my laptop and found a draft of a rough poem. And they applauded me not like some famous author who was doing a reading for them, but like a peer. It was a beautiful feeling and I felt impossibly young and new and excited about words again in a way I hadn't for many years.

An Iranian-American in Indonesia

When I got back to America I thought of this group, Malam Puisi, so much, and we emailed and tried to arrange for me to Skype into their session as their night would be my day. All of Indonesia stayed with me so deeply – I stayed in touch with my handlers, I played the Muslim prayers over and over, I dreamed of even the dirty skies and the colorful prints and neon flora that fought its dismalness at every step. I felt downright haunted by its importance to me, how oddly I felt I belonged there, even when being pushed to speak about being a minority, in a country where for once I was culturally part of a majority.

The morning I left Jakarta, the sky was a burnt pink. The fires, my taxi driver said, 'Don't you know?' I didn't. I came to learn about it: palm oil and paper pulp companies illegally set fire to forests to clear land to plant more trees, thinking this was cheap and fast. This was an annual problem, and this time it had resulted in 8063 square miles of forests and other land burned, 21 deaths, more than half a million people sickened with respiratory problems and US$9 billion in economic losses, from damaged crops to hundreds of cancelled flights. He told me I was so lucky to be leaving then, and I remember feeling a worry for Indonesia that did not surface again for months.

Ten days after my last night there, the world fell into grief and panic over the Paris attacks, and every Muslim, anywhere you went, was suspect again. I became a news junkie again, on social media begging for tolerance for Muslims, often thinking of how I had answered the questions of those young Muslim students:

How does it feeling being Iranian in the US today?

It feels mostly okay. It has been a long road. Americans in the '80s were not so tolerant, but I have hope for our future...

How do Americans consider Muslims?

It took some time after 9/11 of course, but I would say the Americans I closely associate with are very tolerant and generally quite curious about Muslims, at least in the big cities. . .

If I move to America, can I be respected as Muslim?

I personally believe so, though it may take some patience and educating on your end. . .

But I worried about my answers, I worried about the world we were suddenly in, very much the post 9/11 one all over again and somehow worse. New York seemed to feel it was poised for another attack and I found myself in constant insomnia online late at night, inhaling news as much as I was battling bigots.

It was late one night, too late my time, that I saw the hashtag #PrayforJakarta pop up from my poetry group friends on Twitter. Right next to my Artotel, there had been an explosion outside a Starbucks and then another at a police station. At least eight people – four attackers and four civilians – were killed, and 23 others were injured. ISIS claimed responsibility within hours.

I stayed with my Malam Puisi friends on Twitter as they remained indoors, and I tried to gather news stories for them. Forgive me for sounding like an overbearing mother, but please stay inside and take precautions, I tweeted, Just in case. All I could think of were their performances of Plath and Bukowski, their open spirits, how they had brought us into their world so effortlessly, how they had not just offered but expected we'd stay in touch.

Back and forth we wrote, and their final words before I went to bed were, We're fine. We're not afraid. Thank you for your prayer. hugs

Hugs to you, back in my favorite city, I tweeted to them.

Funny, my favorite city is your city, their leader tweeted back to me.

I've been trying to write about that magical night of poetry on the rooftop of the hotel during the rains, I tweeted.

Please, write it. So I could read it aloud at Malam Puisi Jakarta's next event. We surely be happy to hear your story :) she wrote back. It was the last exchange we had, that terrifying January night.

This is my story for them, what I never got to tell them about. That for a week, I got to feel at home, in a country many thousands of miles away from all my homes. When I say I will be back, this time I know. I may not be able to go to Iran any time soon, but for now I might still be able to uncover pieces of it all around the globe.

CHANNELING EUDORA

BY NATALIE BASZILE

It's just after lunch and James and I are on the edge of Franklin, Louisiana's historic district, scouting for junk piles when we come upon a strange scene. Most of the houses in this tiny town look the same: prim, one-story raised Queen-Anne-style cottages and early 20th-century bungalows, painted powder white with forest green shutters. The lawns are all mowed, the hedges all neatly trimmed, and this time of year, the window boxes boast an abundance of cornflowers and phlox. But the house we're now approaching looks like none of these. Three times larger than any of its neighbors, its hulking wood frame rises above the street like Noah's ark run aground. Its architecture is vaguely Acadian – one wide, unbroken slab of shingled roof hangs low over plain wood posts, shrouding a long stretch of porch that folks down here call a 'gallery'. Two cockeyed windows flank a screenless front door in the middle of its blunt facade.

But for all of its mismatchedness and lack of proportion, it's the paint job that gets me. The house is painted four different shades of blue – cobalt, indigo, azure and royal – and even from the street I can track the jagged patchwork of overlapping roller marks where someone began painting in one shade then, because they ran out of paint or grew bored, switched to another.

And against this crazy quilt of color, the dozen or so black people gathered on the gallery stand out in bold relief. Adults and children alike, their complexions range from coffee to cinnamon. Some of the men smoke as they balance on rickety folding chairs, while the women hoist kids onto their laps to braid their hair. Two small girls squat in the sun-baked dirt yard while three older boys straddle the wooden arms of a tattered couch. Every few seconds someone pushes through the front door and claims an open seat, or stands, stretches, then disappears inside. It isn't the people as much as the sheer number of them, and the juxtaposition of activity and inertia, that amazes me.

It's not polite to gawk, but as we pass I press my face to the truck window, straining to take in the scene.

James sees me staring. 'That's the The Blue House,' he offers before I can formulate my question. His tone is casual, as though he's just told me we're out of milk.

'The Blue House?'

James nods. 'Mention to anyone in town that you saw The Blue House, they'll know exactly which house you're talking about.' He gives me a look.

We're almost past the The Blue House now, and James, who was born here and knows everything there is to know about Franklin, launches into a history lesson. Founded in 1808, Franklin, like all the other towns along the Bayou Teche, owed its early prosperity to the sugar-cane trade. But unlike other towns whose residents were French or Acadian, German, Spanish and African, Franklin's founders were mostly English.

'I tell you what,' James gestures toward The Blue House. 'Some crazy shit goes down with those people.' He explains that back in the 1970s, on the heels of segregation, a black woman bought the place for her immediate family. Over time, more relatives moved in, until now, as many as sixteen people – no one really knows for sure – call The Blue House home.

The fact that James is a white man, and I am a black woman, and we

are in the south, is not lost on me. But until this moment, I have wanted
to believe that race won't be a factor in our friendship. But as he talks,
though, I hear something beneath his words, something mocking and
dismissive, and as much as I try to ignore it, I can't. I've listened to James
brag about his English roots. I've not judged when he confessed that his
forefathers owned slaves. And in the past when I've asked, teasingly, if
he's sure he doesn't have any African blood in his veins ('Who doesn't?
This is Louisiana, after all!') – I've held my tongue when he's insisted on
his pure breeding, unwilling, against the odds, to entertain the idea that a
more complicated bloodline might be possible.

But I've heard this kind of language before. I know what people
mean when they say a neighborhood has gone downhill, or warn me to
stay away from folks who live 'back of town.' I know to whom they are
referring when they talk about people who don't want to work or are
always looking for a handout. I understand what people are suggesting
when they think they're complimenting me by saying I'm 'different'.

'This used to be a nice street,' James says. He casts a long, mournful
look down the street. 'Now look at it.'

'Back up,' I say.

Confused, James turns to me.

'Back up. Right now.'

James frowns, but obliges. He throws his truck into reverse and we
roll backward down the street. He eases alongside the curb and before
he can park, I'm sliding from the passenger seat and hurrying down
the sidewalk.

Now that I'm on foot I take everything in: the shredded window
screens, the chicken coop in the shaded side yard, the clothes hanging
from the line.

What am I looking for? What's my plan? The truth is, I don't know.
But my chest is burning and my heart feels squeezed.

On a research trip down here years ago, I passed a group of convicts
working along the road outside a town called Parks. Dressed in black-
and-white-striped uniforms, the kind you see in old movies, they

worked their shovels in unison while a white guard in a wide-brimmed hat cradled a shotgun nearby. Passing the group I felt a tightening in my gut, a sensation I always feel when I stumble upon some scene from the Old South. I had my camera with me and for a moment I considered stopping to ask if I could take a picture. But I was a woman traveling alone, and I drove on. I thought about that scene for the rest of my trip, and I think about it still.

As I approach The Blue House, Eudora Welty's book of photographs comes to mind. I've always loved her stories, but confess that I love her photographs more. Welty worked for the Works Progress Administration during the '30s, traveling around her native Mississippi photographing ordinary people – black and white, poor and poorer – as they went about their daily lives, struggling to survive. In her photographs, there's an ease with which people stand and look at the camera, an unfiltered honesty in their gaze. Welty's work is warm and intimate, unpretentious. You sense the compassion she felt for her subjects. Reynolds Price, in the book's introduction, writes that Welty's subjects felt a 'patent trust', and that she, in turn, worked to capture the 'stubborn valor with which [they] were meeting their lives in a chronically impoverished state . . . the lightly worn dignity . . . and vibrant strength' they summoned every day.

I have my camera with me again, and with Welty's work on my mind, I wave to the people sitting on the gallery. When they wave back, I walk up and introduce myself. I'm a writer, I say, writing a book set in Louisiana. I tell them I live in San Francisco, but that my father is a south Louisianan too, born in a town just like Franklin, only smaller, and we share a laugh, knowing how small his town would have to be. They tell me their names, we shake hands, and when the kids inch closer to ask me about my camera, I offer to take their pictures.

Before I know it, I'm surrounded by children wanting a turn in front of my lens. The older boys strike poses trying to outdo each other with their fierceness. They stand stiff and unsmiling, arms crossed in front of them like bouncers. The girls are shy at first, but with a little coaxing, throw their arms over each other's shoulders, smiling as much at the love they clearly have for each other, as at the idea of having their picture taken. There's a lot of laughter and a fair amount of pushing and shoving, all in good fun, and for the last shot, I urge them all to stand together. One big family.

I offer to photograph the adults, but they decline, so I thank them again. 'I'll be back,' I say. 'I promise.' The family waves and bids me a good afternoon. I walk back down the street toward James's truck.

'How'd it go?' James asks.

'Great.' The tightness in my chest is gone.

James glances at me, then slips his key in the ignition. 'I don't think anyone's done that before.'

'You should try it,' I say and turn to look out of the window. 'They're good people.'

That night, I spend an hour at the Walmart, printing 5" x 7" glossies of the photos I took. I buy wooden frames and a card and scrawl a quick note to the family saying how much I enjoyed meeting them. The next morning, I drive myself over to The Blue House. No one is on the gallery now, so I knock at the front door. And when a man in his early thirties I don't recognize answers, I explain who I am and what I've done and hand him the bag of framed photos. Later that afternoon, James picks me up in his truck and we resume our scouting. When he asks how I spent my morning, I don't mention The Blue House.

In the years to come, my friendship with James will be tested. When pressed, he will retreat into his white southerness. He will cower behind bigotry and small-mindedness, and take false comfort in the privilege he convinces himself his lineage holds. He will utter all the ugly words I prayed I would never hear, step aside while others do the same. Our friendship will not survive. But this is still years off. For now, we are good friends and I cling to the hope that the small space that has opened between us is just that – a small space – and that neither of us will be worse for it.

Meanwhile, the The Blue House is what I keep going back to. I imagine the framed photographs on a table somewhere inside, or maybe hanging from a nail above the children's' beds. All their faces bright with smiles, their eyes focused on my lens, while I admonish them to stand still. Just like family.

JASMINE AND OTHER
FLOWERS THAT MAKE ME CRY
BY SUZANNE JOINSON

It's the late '90s and seven of us are crammed into a minuscule film studio in downtown Damascus. We have just watched the first ever screening of an Arabic film called *Under the Ceiling* and the filmmaker is chain-smoking, anxious for discussion to begin. There is an extracted serving of tea and all eyes are on him. He leans back in his chair, taking his time, until finally he turns to me and says in English, 'So, as the voice of a Western superpower, do you think it is too long?'

I blush and panic. Then the room of five Arab men and one French woman laugh. It was a joke, and possibly I am the butt of it, but that's okay.

There is a cigarette break, and I go out on to the balcony to look out over the glittering nightscape. There are some cities I smoke in and some I don't. Damascus, of course, is a city for smoking. The minarets on the mosques are lit up by green neon strips and I can see them dotted around the city like jewels and up high on the slopes of Mount Qassioun.

My friend Nidal comes out of the hot, smoky studio. I met Nidal when he was an exchange student visiting my hometown in England. He invited me to visit, and now, three years later, here I am. If he is surprised at my impromptu arrival, he is polite enough not to show it. I am twenty-one, accepted into a room of film-makers who have studied cinema in Cairo, Paris and Moscow, and I tell myself: this is a taste of the life I want.

Some places feel like a haunting, but it is hard to tell if you are the ghost, or the person being haunted. On the balcony I am hit with the aroma of the roasted almonds, grilled corn, petrol and an elusive, fragrant scent I keep catching everywhere I go in this city.

'Nidal, what is that smell?'

He does a dramatic comedy sniff. 'Jasmine, silly.' I lean over the balcony and sure enough, down on the street below is a hedge clouded with an impressive amount of jasmine flowers doing their night-time thing.

'So, did you enjoy the film?' he asks.

The film, with Nidal translating quietly in my ear, was certainly long, a complicated story of friends, the city itself a character, but I loved it: the indulgent shots of the Damascene skyline; pink dusty walls and mysterious backstreets; and beautiful couples eating cherries and exchanging complex glances.

I nod. How can I explain to him that I want to stay in the atmosphere of the film, the city, this balcony, in the cloud of jasmine-scent, forever?

After the screening we sit in a bar, drinking Mexican beer, joined by gazillions of Nidal's friends and acquaintances. Damascus for me is ubiquitous with Arabic cardamom-laced coffee and cigarettes, I'm permanently wired here, and for an Islamic city there's a wide variety of beers available.

'I want to know about the cherry motif,' I say. All through the film glistening cherries sat in bowls, or were shared and eaten.

'We have a folk saying,' Nidal explains. 'When a woman is pregnant and craves a particular food – in this instance, cherries – the baby will have a birthmark in the shape of that food. Hence, the cherry. All about longing and loss.'

'I see,' I say, conscious of my youth, and of not really getting longing, or loss, or the profound symbolism of the cherry. His friends around the table proceed to exhibit their own particular birthmarks for me. I am shown a fish-ish shape on a calf, an almond-eye on upper-arm flesh. On the wall of the bar behind Nidal's head is a sign written in English.

Killing people is illegal. Unless it is in large numbers and to the sound of drums.

It freaks me out so much that I don't comment on it, but my eyes keep drifting back to it throughout our stay.

Nidal walks with me back to my hotel. We drift along the central corridor of the Souq al-Hamidiyya which comes alive in the evening. Lingerie shops offer a surprising display of glittering belly-dancer costumes, sequined miniskirts, lurid gold veils, silver vests, feathered pants, chains and diamanté-styled negligees; the eroticism of the underwear on show seems incongruous against the backdrop of old town Damascus, with its aching mosques and World Heritage site gravitas.

'What's with the all the racy underwear?'

'Ah,' says Nidal, skipping a little, 'did you know Rumi wrote 'who knows grace in dance, lives in God'?'

'Yeah,' I say, 'but does it have to be a dance wearing glittering gold feathers?'

'Well, in the Koran it says women must dance for their husbands.'

I realise he is laughing at my shocked face.

'Let's not go straight to the hotel,' I say and together, companionably, we walk around the old city, listening to the sound of our footsteps on the ancient cobblestones.

Damascus is not so much a city, more a memory, or an idea; a place from a dream, to fly through, or remember. As we pass tucked-in convenience stalls selling bottled water and phone chargers, something happens to me: I understand deep down, in the pericardial part of my heart, that I am a writer and a traveller and somehow these two things must be combined into destiny. Nidal is pointing out his favourite brand of fizzy drink as I think this.

'Shall we get some Orange Fanta? I think so, I think so.' He slips into the mouth of the hobbit-sized shop. I stand outside, weightless.

I want to share this conviction of my destiny – a writer! A traveller! But how? – with Nidal, but he is engaged in a momentous struggle with the lid of the Orange Fanta bottle, swearing, stomping his feet, and when the lid comes off, creating quite a mess.

'Nidal, I …'

'Shhh,' he says, and after a deep long swig of his nectar, buoyed on sugar and the pleasantness of the evening, he starts to sing, quoting, he tells me, the much-loved Syrian poet, Qabbani:

For I am the Damascene, whose profession is passion
Whose singing turns the herbs green;
A Damascene moon travels through my blood;
Nightingales … and grain … and domes.
From Damascus, jasmine begins its whiteness
And fragrances perfume themselves with her scent …

He spins around. 'By the way,' he says peering into dark, mysterious alleyways, 'now I am afraid I am a little lost.'

We float like seeds, not quite sure where we are, and I feel my ambition – or perhaps it should be called a dream – bed down inside of me, a crochet hook forever entwined with the scent of jasmine, the noise of a fizzy drink bottle being open, with being half-lost in a city that is as old as time, feeling the pulse of possibility.

———

The next day – my last day – hoarse from smoking and talking, I walk through modern Damascus rather than a city of my dreams: a car-jammed, polluted, chaotic metropolis that clings like smoke around the ancient centre.

173

I enter the Umayyad Mosque. At the gate I am given an abaya to put on, told to cover my head with my scarf. As I enter the courtyard I am quickly admonished by an elderly lady who whacks me with her walking stick to inform me that my robe is hanging a little too far to the left, thus showing an inappropriate glimpse of my shoulder.

The mosque seems to beat, like a heart. I take my shoes off and sit myself down on the well-worn carpets and close my eyes to listen to the chanting of the prayers, trying to be invisible.

My invisibility spell does not last long.

I am quickly surrounded by five children who have been flying around (there seems to me a marked difference between mosques and churches, in that children are relaxed in the mosque, allowed to skip about and play and run, whereas children in churches are scolded, told to sit still for hours on uncomfortable seats) and they clamber all over me, tugging my abaya, playfully pulling my hair. They have a paper bag and one of them holds it up to my face; I peep inside. Trapped at their mercy is a dusty-winged yellow butterfly clinging to the side of the bag and below it an unhappy terrapin.

One of the children thrusts his hand into the bag and puts the terrapin on my knee. I smile, looking down at the creature. Their laughter and giggles get louder, and one of them begins acting out a dance in front of me. At first I laugh along with them, faintly worrying that they will demand money at the end of the performance, knowing that I have no change on me, but then I realise that the little boy is pointing at me, and running his finger across his neck, in a gesture of death. The children all laugh hysterically at this motion; so encouraged, the boy does it again. I lean back in horror, inadvertently tipping the terrapin onto the carpet in front of me.

Just at this moment an official-looking man comes over and shoos the children away. In perfect English he tells me that the soles of my shoes, which are next to me, should be facing each other rather than flat on the floor. I quickly rearrange them. The smallest child starts screaming, and pointing. We all look down. The terrapin has disappeared under my abaya.

'Perhaps he is curious to see what is inside?' the man says to me, and I can't quite interpret the tone. I fish under the material to retrieve the creature, but then another child is shouting, pointing up: the butterfly has made a dash for it. It flutters haphazardly past the praying men, past the chaotic children, upwards.

'Where is he going?' I ask the man.

'Tahta al-Saqf,' he says. 'Under the ceiling. Sadly he doesn't realise there is nowhere safe in Damascus.'

I stand up quickly, thank him and leave.

I tell Nidal this story as I say goodbye to him at Damascus airport. 'Tahta al-Saqf,' he repeats. 'How strange.'

'Why?'

'Because that is the name of the film we watched, remember? *Under the Ceiling.*'

'Oh yes.'

'Will you come back,' he speaks to my shoes, 'if the naughty children in the mosque haven't put you off?'

'I will do everything in my power to do so,' I say.

'Well, I can't ask for more than that.' And he gives me, for the journey, a box of the brightest, sweetest looking red cherries.

It is 2011 and Nidal's email informs me that the 'revolution' in Tunisia is called the 'Jasmine Revolution', but for me, he says, playful, the jasmine belongs to you.

I have been back to Damascus four times since my first visit and through that time I have devised a theory about travelling alone as a woman. Without doubt, it has a certain frisson. It has challenges, it has advantages, but there are two survival rules I've devised over the years.

1. Don't close up and be suspicious of every man who speaks to

you; otherwise you give off a defensive air which actually accentuates vulnerability (in other words, relax).

2. And – this is very crucial – don't have more than one drink on social, out-and-about occasions because it's just not worth it.

I stick to these, but I have also developed a theory: cities in countries that have conservative notions of how females should behave are extremely safe for 'Western' females to travel alone. In these places you are likely to encounter politeness, friendliness, helpfulness, curiosity, respect and reserve, but also warmth. With this in mind, I am surprised that the Syrian Embassy has turned down my application for a visa. I email Nidal:

Me: So strange. I don't understand why I'm not allowed to visit.

Nidal: Things have changed, things are difficult, things are heavy. To be truthful, it's not a good time to come.

Me: I know, I know, but I still want to. To see you. To walk around. To drink Arabic coffee. To smell cardamom. Didn't you once tell me that 'a toothache in London is as painful as a toothache in Aleppo'? Aren't we all the same, whatever is happening? The writers and the teachers and the shopkeepers and the businessmen and hairdressers and the students of Damascus and London have exactly the same concerns: making money, finding love, getting pregnant, not losing glasses.

I am quoting him, from one of his long and whimsical, walking-around-the-city rants, so it is a surprise when Nidal, usually so gentle, funny and kind, replies in a harsh way.

Nidal: You don't know what you are talking about.

Five minutes later he sends another email with an apology and what he tells me this time – about being trapped in his apartment in central Damascus, powerless, unable to work, unable to leave the country because too many family members will be left behind, too frightened to have a bath in the evenings, jumping at every noise, bombs frequently going off in nearby neighbourhoods, good friends disappeared, under pressure to join certain factions – what he describes in this email gives me nightmares for three nights.

I dream of the ancient city: squares filled with dappled shade from the almond trees, crowded balconies, the low moaning of the call to prayers, cats creeping under cars, of being watched by a small girl with large brown eyes.

I dream I am in Damascus, trapped with my one-year-old baby daughter, a very strong sense of being hunted, trapped and terrified.

When I wake up, I email Nidal to see if he is okay, by which I mean alive, but I don't hear from him again for four years.

It is 2016 and the city I dream of so often doesn't exist anymore. It's been blown away by bombs, washed away with a thousand tears. Nidal, who is giving me a hug at Gatwick Airport on his way through England to Italy where he has a scholarship, tells me it will come back, a phoenix out of the dust.

I am not sure I believe him.

He is different and the same: older, thinner, and a new line runs through the centre of his eyebrows making him look permanently puzzled. He has been through things he doesn't want to talk about and his hand trembles, I notice, when he raises the coffee cup to his mouth. He still laughs easily though, wincing at the horrible airport coffee, making a face. I am grateful for that.

'I have something for you,' he says. It's a book, by a Greek author, Stratis Tsirkas, called *Drifting Cities*. Inside its hard cover is a dried sprig of jasmine, most of the fragile flowers lost.

'I know you like an overblown gesture,' he says. I lightly punch him in the arm.

We have a short time together, just an hour, before he takes his plane. The cafe is deserted and we are assaulted by piped music and a strong smell of grease. Under a nearby table a pigeon coos and bobs gracelessly.

'What the hell is a pigeon doing inside an airport?' I say.

Nidal looks at it, smiling. 'It's renegade. Walls and glass and borders and rules can't stop that bird. Way to go, Mr Pigeon.' The bird pecks, puffing its feathers, indifferent.

'I almost wish I had never been to Damascus,' I say, 'thinking of it being destroyed.'

But I know that's not true. As if reading my mind, Nidal says, 'That city will always be with you. It's the haunting that keeps you writing. One day you'll be back there, I know it.'

'Hmmm.'

The clock on the screen behind him is ticking off its seconds and soon he will be gone. Now is the time to say what I have always wanted to say to him. I watch him gather his laptop, his phone, bottle of water. There is a long white scar across the curve of his chin, I see. Another second clicks through, I say nothing.

'If you want to keep Damascus alive, then write about it,' he says.

I shake my head. 'It's too sad.' I have seen photographs. The destroyed souks, the ruined streets. Not to mention the people.

'Write about your longing for it then.'

'Yes.' I realise that all the words I have ever written have been an attempt to spirit me back to that balcony after the film, to the light tingling feeling of having the wherewithal to make a dream happen. By writing myself backwards through maps I can resurrect Damascus, as I knew it. I can fly through geography and history and time, for a short time at least.

Nidal is on the plane and I'm loitering in the airport concourse, not quite ready to go back to my life. I pick up the napkin he pressed into my hand. Meet me in Damascus when we are able to get back there? There is a badly drawn picture of a cherry next to it.

As I leave, the pigeon is being shoo-shooed by an airport cleaner shoving her brush at it with venom.

'How did you get in here, anyway?' she says to the bird, jabbing at it. I point up to the top of the glass casing of the airport.

'It must have flown in through there,' I say. There is a gap where the glass doesn't quite meet a metal window frame and beyond it, the bright blue sky.

'Well, I never noticed that before,' she says, staring up. I recognise the sensation of a story growing in me. It has an untidy pulse, a nostalgic flavour, and most of all, a strong smell of jasmine.

I WOULD GO

BY ANTHONY SATTIN

'Would you really go to Syria?'

I would.

'Well, you're braver than me.'

This brief exchange happened three years ago in southeastern Turkey in a place called Karkemish. I was standing with a man from the nearby city of Gaziantep, looking past the ruins where Lawrence of Arabia had worked four years as an archaeologist, past the iron bridge that once carried the Berlin to Baghdad railway, across razor wire and into Syria, over land that would soon be planted with the black flags of terror.

I would go, and in part because a very similar conversation had taken place some twenty years earlier. 'Syria? Really?' The reasons not to go then were many. Hafez al-Assad was in the presidential palace and, ten years after he had sent his army to crush an uprising in Homs, killing tens of thousands of his own people, his regime had a tight grip on dissent and just about everything else. Foreign travellers, when they were allowed in, were closely watched, none closer than foreign writers. A cloud of suspicion would hang over me as I travelled around the country. Perhaps the biggest reason not to go was also one of the most persuasive reasons to go: we knew so little about it how it felt to be there.

I Would Go

And so I went... I had a vague idea that I would find drab hotels, spectacular monuments, large welcomes, and conversations with people who would look over their shoulders while expressing anger about the way their country was being run. And I was going to write about it. Not a book (that idea came later), but I had persuaded a newspaper to publish the story I would write about my journey between Aleppo and Damascus, although first I had had to explain Aleppo to the editor, who had never heard of the place. 'It claims to be the oldest continually inhabited city in the world.'

Ancient history was a big part of the draw – I knew about the romance of Palmyra, the city of Queen Zenobia where great temples and colonnades shimmered far in the desert like a mirage. I knew about the Euphrates River giving life to some of the earliest of civilisations. I also knew there were the great castles from the time of Saladin and Richard the Lionheart, of which Crac des Chevaliers stood as the finest example. But when I arrived in Aleppo and walked up the worn marble steps of Baron's Hotel, I found myself intrigued by a more recent history that was hanging above the reception desk: a framed bill for a bottle of Corton Rouge champagne and a lemonade. It had been charged, in June 1914, to a 'Monsieur Laurence,' better known to us as Lawrence of Arabia. This more recent history was being discussed in the bar that evening, where an Englishman in tweeds was insisting they should make a museum out of the rooms that Lawrence, Freya Stark and Agatha Christie had used. It also hung around the private lounge of the owner, the wonderful Koko Mazloumian, who sat me down the following day with a shot of Armenian brandy and told stories from the hotel's glory days. When I mentioned the idea being discussed in the bar the previous evening, he complained with some satisfaction that 'if we turned every room where famous people have stayed into a museum, we'd have to close the bloody hotel.'

For a couple of days I revelled in the wonder of Aleppo's souks and its medieval citadel, which sat above them like a cake on a plinth. The place was lively, but this was before Russian and Turkish traders arrived in any numbers, and tourists of any sort were a rare sight. Aleppo, then, was a city for Syrians and for other Arabs and I found myself in a cafe with a large keffiyeh-wearing Palestinian and an even larger Iraqi with a finely trimmed moustache and bellow-like lungs that made his waterpipe bubble like a geyser. 'Why are you here?' they both asked.

Back in the alleyways, I was distracted by what I glimpsed of the beauty of a young Bedouin woman: veiled, loose-black-robed, showing only a graceful, tattooed hand and half an extraordinarily fine face, she walked a couple of brisk paces behind her husband. For some minutes, I walked several paces behind her. The variety of shops we hurried past was announced by the succession of smells – pungent, dusty spices, freshly slaughtered meat, baking bread, beaten metal and the flat smell of newly dyed fabrics – each lit, now that night was falling, by naked electric bulbs the size of ostrich eggs and fronted by fast-talking salesmen. None was faster than the Armenian silk merchant who wrapped a scarf around my neck and would have dragged me into his shop had the power not been cut. As he went to find a candle, I hurried on through miles of souk now lit only with candles and oil lamps, as they had been when medieval, Byzantine or Roman travellers had come here to buy and sell.

Outside the medieval gate of the souk, a crowd had gathered and was cheering the slaughter of a lamb: I arrived at the moment when the animal was already slumped on the worn stones, its life seeping away with its blood. While this happened, a band played the loose music of the region against a backdrop of extravagant floral arrangements. Then a dance troupe arrived, and when a video camera and its light were flipped on, I realised that we and the dying animal were celebrating the birth of a new shop.

Citadels, souks and slaughter. These were the images I carried out of Aleppo on the day I drove south. I was not planning to go directly to Damascus, but up into the mountains that separate the desert and Asia from the Mediterranean world. For even longer than Aleppo has existed, from before recorded history, people have fought over this land, not so much for what it contains as for the wealth and power it controls. Each one has left its mark: it is impossible to travel and not be reminded of their passing, from the Mesopotamian palace at Mari near the Iraqi border to the Greco-Roman-era desert city of Palmyra. But in the mountains, the most striking reminders come in the form of the citadels, castles, strongholds and watchtowers built during the two hundred tumultuous years between the 11th and 13th centuries, between the arrival and eventual defeat of the European crusaders.

Koko Mazloumian of Baron's Hotel had recommended that I look at Lawrence's book on Crusader castles and I took a copy with me as a guide. Lawrence was twenty years old and at the end of his second year reading History at Oxford when he walked out of Beirut, one midsummer morning in 1909, to see the castles between what is now Turkey and Jordan. Twenty years old and escaping a controlling mother and the awkward truth of his being illegitimate, he was gathering material that would guarantee his first class honours degree at university. He was also in the process of finding himself and his place in the world.

I followed his trail through the hills and between the castles, from Aleppo to Sahyun, hidden in the rolling green hills, from the colossal block of Markab, high on a bluff above a valley of extraordinary fertility, to the beauty of Safita, a lesser castle, but one with an upper chamber as beautiful as any Romanesque church I had seen in France. Then there was the glory of Crac des Chevaliers, which Lawrence rightly thought was 'quite marvellous' and which he judged to be the finest castle in the world. The Crac is both massive and beautiful. The road up to it wound through groves of almond trees that were then in blossom, and fields carpeted with wild flowers. I stayed the night at a simple hostel with a view across to the battlements and spent the evening staring at them while discussing the inevitable politics with the only other person there, the owner of the cafe. In the morning, I walked alone up the worn stones and into the keep. I wandered around the cathedral-like structure that was the refectory, the beautiful hall that turned out to be the church, with a Venetian-style loggia of unexpected curvaceously carved stone, and then climbed to the high point. I remember the chambers of the commander being bare but imposing and made beautiful by the window with its view over the countryside – I could see as far as the Mediterranean coast – and by the rosettes carved around the opening to frame the view.

But of the week I spent in the mountains, the most important moment, for me, happened in one of the most remote places. I was on the trail of the Assassins, the Shia group who ignored religious and cultural differences and were prepared to side with whoever best matched their interests. This flipping from side to side made them dangerous. Their knowledge of the mountains and their ability to hide made them more so: the reputation they had for fanaticism and for killing – from which we have derived our meaning of assassin – was well-deserved. Even the mighty Saladin had found himself vulnerable in those mountains. He had posted guards around his tent but an Assassin still managed to enter while the great warrior slept and left a note suggesting that he retreat before they killed him.

Yet I, like Lawrence, found nothing but hospitality. Lawrence had had to rely on it. There were no hotels in that part of Syria when he visited and he was travelling alone, on foot, in his bespoke suit, with a small bag and without a tent. So each evening he was obliged to enter a village and ask if he could sleep there. The response was always 'ahlan wa sahlan' (welcome), and he would be taken to the roof, engaged in conversation and fed, before being left to sleep.

I had been engaged in conversation in a small cafe on the road up to a place called Kalaat al-Kahf. I had been served some of the soft mountain cheese that was brought with bread and herbs and while I ate, some men came to talk. They couldn't remember the last time they had seen a western man in there and they wanted me to know I was very welcome. When I left, I found they had already paid for my food.

The *kalaa*, the citadel I was looking for, took some finding, but that was how it was designed. It had been one of the Assassin strongholds, high in the green, twisting mountains, and it was approached through a doorway cut through thick rock. I had to slide past fallen rocks and flourishing trees to reach the top, the keep. This had been the base of Rashid al-Din Sinan, the Assassin leader known to Crusaders as the Old Man of the Mountains who had terrorised the region. Six hundred years later it was still in use: a friend of the eccentric British traveller Lady Hester Stanhope was held captive there in 1816 and the place was only finally destroyed at her request. I sat at the top of the ruin as the sun passed towards the western sea, and I thought of Crusaders and Assassins, of Lady Hester, of young Lawrence who realised, up here in the mountains and because of the Assassins, that guerrilla warfare could be a potent weapon. I also thought about myself, and why I liked this country and its people so much. And then I thought no more, but sat on the rock for a long time, hearing the wind in the oaks and breathing the clean, crisp air.

At the first village beyond Kalaat al-Kahf, a man stopped me and, as people like him have been doing for longer than we can know, he invited a traveller into his house. Over a glass of tea, with his children staring from the safety of the doorway, he gently led me through a series of questions that established who I was, where I had come from, where I was going and why. I in turn asked about his land and what he grew on it, the size of the harvest and of his family, the state of the countryside and, eventually, the pinch of the government. Curiosity satisfied on both sides, I continued on my way, his younger sons herding me out as though I were some stray goat, until their father called them off and the breeze carried his blessings to me.

Eighty years earlier, Lawrence had written to his mother to explain why he wanted to stay in the region. 'I don't think anyone who has tasted the East as I have would give it up.' I don't think anyone who has had the sort of experiences I had would not want to return. I was attracted by the beauty of the place, by the history, but also by that sense of common humanity, by the sharing of the little that they had with someone they had never seen before nor ever would again. I found other reasons to go back to Syria: I wanted to look more closely at the castles and at Lawrence's travels, which I later wrote about in a book. By then I had made friends, whose company I enjoyed and found stimulating. Many of them have now left, or have died. But if you ask me that question now, I know what I would answer. I would.

THE GUIDE

BY LAURIE HOVELL MCMILLIN

On our third day in India, my 16-year-old son stops talking to me. This I can understand. India can be an assault to the senses – can turn your world upside down. I've been there myself. At age 20, I landed in Pune, and gradually, steadily, over the next six months, I became unhinged. So it's no surprise it's hard on him.

Not only that, when you are 16, you crave independence: That is your stage in life – your American samskara. And here he is, with his mom for Chrissake, whom he depends on for nearly everything. How to take a shower, where to put his feet, which hand to eat with. It's really too much. He can't even make himself understood in English to the English-speaking receptionist. They can't get his accent, or his idiom. He ordered 'a garlic naan and a Thums Up too' only to end up with two colas: 'Thums Up two.'

On the other hand, when I lose my wallet on the first day, stupidly leaving it in a rickshaw, Liam stands on the street for half an hour in my vain hope that the driver will return while I go to the police station: Liam, six-foot-one, muscularly built, dressed all in white cotton, stands there like a rock in a stream of probing eyes.

Certainly it must drive him a little crazy that his mother, whom he thought he knew, seems at home in this place. I love my little conversations in Marathi with vendors, rickshaw drivers, and waiters; I adore returning to the hand gestures and head movements that convey so much here.

No doubt it galls too that he recalls having been comfortable in Pune before, when he was eight, his brother six, and we traveled as a family. The boys had done famously back then; they had trodden broken sidewalks without complaint, adapted to the strangeness of eating by hand and sleeping under mosquito nets. They had learned how to play cricket and invented the game 'bottle soccer.' But there's a difference between being eight when you're really most concerned about playing with your brother and being 16 when you're differently attuned to the world.

The first two days in Pune are a rush of visits and errands – I want to see everything and everybody, buying Liam new cotton clothes on Laxmi Rd, making arrangements for tea and dosas with old friends. By the third day, though, we need to get out of the polluted, traffic-clogged city, and decide to visit an ancient Buddhist monument in the countryside.

A number of Buddhist caves were built throughout this area, and date back two millennia. In these caves, called *leni* in Marathi, workers created resting places and worship halls for monks and meditators by carving into the live rock of the mountain. Steadily, steadily they worked, chipping the rock until they had created prayer halls with stone columns and stupas to circumambulate, symbols of the Buddha's transcendence. Slowly, slowly they worked the rock, chiseling away to make tiny rooms for monks. Craftsmen constructed these rocky abodes not by building anything up, but, rather, by taking things away. So natural and beautiful did the carving seem, you could almost imagine that the carvers had discovered the columns within the stone – that they pulled rock out to reveal meditation rooms that were somehow already there, that they had happened upon rather than formed lotus flower decorations.

To get to the train station, the rickshaw jerks through a tangle of traffic and exhaust fumes. Outside the station itself, it's madness – humans waiting, squatting, spitting, pissing, staring at us gape-mouthed. We make our way to the ticket booth; the clerk wants to know, as they all do, What country are you? How long you are staying? Making our way to the assigned platform, we are constantly stared at; people swirl around to have a look at us, white and tall. Wary after losing my wallet, I have hidden my money in a pouch under my clothes, and I touch it periodically to see if it's still there. Finally the train comes and we push on with all the others.

We pass through Pune's outskirts, whose ugly names seem to say it all: Pimpri, Chinchwad. Slums back all the way up to the tracks – homes made of nothing at all, a sheet of tin, an old signboard, dusty old blankets. A boy stands holding his pants – he will drop them to shit after our train goes by. The world: it's all here for the viewing. I think of the Buddha when he was still a prince, and the forays he took out of the palace. Seeing the sick, the dying, the dead: it made him want to renounce the world.

On the train, peanut sellers, key chain vendors, and a stream of beggars work the crowd. A woman with her sari pulled tight over her head comes through, one empty hand to her mouth, the other held out: 'Please, brother, sister. Give.' We try not to meet her eye; no one gives her anything. Two blind singers enter the car, singing in Hindi: 'This life is nothing,' without you, I suppose, or maybe simply 'this life is nothing.' Hearing this sad song, passengers who had remained unmoved before pull out their rupees.

Then a lady comes, strong jaw, brash eyes, her fingers wound with ten rupee notes like a blooming flower. She taps each man and asks for money. She's a hijra, a kind of gender-bending figure of both good fortune and inauspiciousness. When she taps Liam, he shakes his head and looks away, but she won't stop, so I say, in Hindi, 'Stop that', and she turns to me, shrieking, as if I am a talking monkey. 'What is your name, monkey? Can I marry this boy?' She calls to her friends, sturdy in saris, their stubbly chins below mascara-ed eyes. They leer at us, and then they disappear at the next station. On comes a man with a two-sided drum and bells on his wrist. He sings beautifully and this time I am moved to pull out my money.

A mother and her son and daughter perch beside me. The girl greedily crunches the biscuits her mother gives her, standing in the aisle. Her younger brother calls out for water, then falls asleep, his head heavy on his mother's arm. 'That's my son,' I tell the woman. He doesn't look at us.

Finally we arrive in Kandala.

Once outside the station, I bargain with three entwined rickshaw drivers, who ask an exorbitant price. I walk away, then stupidly calculate their price into dollars, decide it's not so much really, and turn back to accept it. One man pulls himself free from the others, and we get in.

The rickshaw winds through packed streets. This village has none of the sophistication of Pune – no women in jeans, no shiny electronics stores. The road is lined with shops selling cheap glittery clothes and bottles of strange colored water, and people and vehicles jostle for space. I stare out while Liam keeps his head hidden, tired of being noticed, perhaps also simply tired of seeing.

Leaving the village, we pass a row of makeshift tents operated by tribal women with bare-assed kids squatting nearby. I try to engage Liam, but he will not talk other than to ask for a page from my journal to write a few notes. 'Is something wrong?' I ask. 'Do you want to talk?' He shakes his head. It's all so much – the language, the noise, the people, everything. India seems to force travelers like us to become philosophical: Why are we here? What is this for?

He is out of my reach.

We go as far as the rickshaw can go: the end of a dirt track. The driver points up, and we can see the dark caves in the side of the mountain.

Stone steps lead the way. 'You want something to eat?' I ask Liam, but he shakes his head no. 'Not water even?' He shakes his head. I offer him a box of mango juice, which he accepts in silence.

We have to lift our knees high to mount each stair. The sun beats on our bare heads. Halfway up, Liam points out a nearly dry waterfall dripping down the rocks. 'I'd like to climb that.'

'Go ahead,' I say, grateful that he's speaking to me.

'I don't want to lose the path,' he says flatly. 'Maybe on the way down.'

We stop to catch our breath and look out over the patchwork of fields, Bedse village with its haystacks. Near the top a white-clad figure peeks over the edge and calls out to Liam, 'Where you are from?' Liam can't catch his accent, so I reply: 'USA. America.' The man has a metal nametag: 'I work for Archaeological Society. It is duty to show.'

When I address the guide in Marathi, he readily switches over and leads us to the outer edge of the construction. 'See the stupa here – human-sized.' The rough walls show the marks of the hammer and chisel that chipped the rest of the stone away to reveal the stone column. 'See the inscription here, that names the donor.' Sensitive that Liam might be annoyed at not understanding the conversation, I translate the guide's words into English for him. He doesn't respond.

The guide happily points out a cistern – 'ten feet deep,' he says. I ask him about the relative date of Bedse, and he says these caves are older than Karla. Liam had seen the Karla caves on his last trip, so I translate this bit of news. He nods, silent. I can't tell if he cares or not.

Next the guide leads us to a small meditation room, about five feet cubed, where stone platforms line three walls. It is cool in the shade, in a place that has never seen sunlight. We each take a seat, the guide sitting cross-legged like an old monk, and the three of us take in the echoing acoustics. 'Buddham saranam gaccami,' the guide pipes up, chanting in Pali, and before he can finish the line I join him in this age-old intoning:

Dhammam saranam gaccami.
Sangham saranam gaccami.
[I take refuge in the Buddha.

The Guide

I take refuge in the Dharma.

I take refuge in the Sangha.]

We smile at each other. Liam just listens. Our voices fill the place, bounding off the walls, as if picking up the traces left by the monks who stayed here two millennia earlier.

We head towards the main hall. Pillars line the entrance, each one topped by a voluptuous couple. 'See these,' the man says, pointing to them. 'These were added later,' he says, and they do look very different from the austere architecture of an earlier age, which relied mostly on symbols like the lotus and the stupa. 'Buddhism changed a lot as it developed,' I tell Liam.

We make our way slowly into the assembly hall, where 26 identical pillars cut from one rock line the sides. A fat stupa cut of the same rock stands at the innermost part of the hall; 20 feet high, it's shaped like an overturned bowl atop a wide pillar. 'In early Buddhism,' I tell him, 'they didn't represent the Buddha. This was it.' I reach a hand out to the stupa and then go around it. From the shadows behind the pillars, the guide chants 'Om' and his slightest hum picks up notes and harmonies from the rocks, which seem to go on singing long after the singer has stopped. Liam goes off into the dark. The guide sings a Hindi film song and it overlaps on its own echoes. Worshippers from 2000 years before seem to be tucked in the shadows too; you can hear them, you can feel them.

We move on to the vihara, the rooms where the monks – perhaps 30 in all, the guide says – lived in single, double and triple rooms. Liam stretches out on a sleeping platform, but he is far too long to fit comfortably. I sit in a tiny room and try to imagine myself back in time. When we are ready, the guide leads us to the monks' bathing place; in the stone floor a hole opens down to a 2000-year-old cistern, still full of water.

Now that we've seen it all, we are reluctant to go. I look out again at the fields below, and Liam leans against a wall, quiet, calm. The guide asks how old Liam is. 'Sixteen,' I say, and the guide says to me in Marathi, 'He's very peaceful.'

'Yes. He is.' We both gaze over at him.

'He's very good,' the man says. Liam leans against the wall, utterly contained, present. '*Kiti shanta ahe*,' the man says again. 'How peaceful he is.'

The guide and I compare the number of children we have: two for me, four for him. He climbs up to a tree growing beside the wall and pulls down four fragrant flowers, handing them to me. 'Champa,' I say. 'I've always loved their scents.'

We finally say goodbye to the guide and start back down the stairs. 'I don't want to leave,' Liam says.

'I don't either.'

But down we go.

'I'd love to sleep here overnight,' Liam says.

'Wouldn't that be cool?' I agree. 'I don't think they'd let you.'

On the way back down we miss the waterfall that Liam had wanted to climb. Looking ahead, we can't see the rickshaw, and Liam says, 'He left us.'

'He won't leave,' I say, hoping I'm right. 'I haven't paid him yet.' Down we go, past stray cows and cacti. Down we go, past a rice field adorned with scarecrows, past a sleeping dog who hasn't moved since we passed the first time. And finally at the bottom, we can see that the rickshaw is still there – 'See?' Our driver is talking to a little girl in the shade of a huge mango tree. I had planned to give him a champa flower, but he already has one of the blossoms in his hand; he has carefully turned its petals under to make a kind of jewel and put it between his fingers. 'See my ring?' he asks, holding it out for me to admire. We climb in the rickshaw, and he just lets it roll, without the engine. 'It's very peaceful here,' I say to him. We pass a farmer plowing with two oxen as he cranks the engine. Down we go, past road workers on their break for lunch, past old ladies and waving children. Our driver asks, 'Have you seen the other caves? Bhaja? Karla?'

'Yes,' I say, 'and I really like Bedse. There's almost nobody there, very quiet.' Two men on a bicycle go by, the one in the rear holding a

The Guide

12-foot-long steel beam.

On the paved road, women are breaking rocks while their children squat around a plate of food. Near the main highway, brassy loudspeakers celebrating something assail us; trucks loom over us, horns blaring. I remember my money pouch again and clutch it toward me. Down through the clogged streets we go, back into the world of day laborers under heavy loads, sugar-cane crushers, and tea drinkers. Near the station, the driver calls out to a woman who leans into the rickshaw to have a word. 'Mummy,' he explains to us over his shoulder. 'She's buying vegetables,' he says. He weaves us expertly through the crowd, dropping us where he left us, and doesn't ask for a penny more than his original quote. 'You are a good person,' I tell him, pressing the notes into his hand.

'Thank you, madam,' he says, and we head down to wait for the train.

On a bench, we eat our chips and nuts, self-conscious: We're being stared at again. 'I think we're the only ones who use the garbage can here,' Liam says, tossing our wrappers. Empty plastic bottles roll on the platform. Plastic bags wrap around weeds.

At last, the train trudges up, and we push on with others. I pull out an old magazine, and we read about Stephen Colbert to escape the eyes for a while. When, after a time, I ask a man across from us, in Marathi, 'What village is this?' he stares back at me while his friend laughs: Look, it is a talking monkey! Another man who has overheard my question kindly leans forward. 'Kadki,' he says, naming the town. Getting back to Pune is slow, and we are hungry and want the refuge of our hotel room.

Night is falling as our station nears; Liam and I get up to push our way out. But just within Pune city limits, the train stops. We wait, poised. Nothing. Now that I'm standing, I see that I am the only woman on board. Faces all around gaze up and down at Liam's tall frame, his head towering over everyone else by a good six inches. I know how it feels to be stared at so; indeed, it's only Liam's presence that deflects their eyes from me. And realizing that, I feel how closely

Liam and I are related, how much we look alike, how much we are allied, how deeply connected, my mother's love trying to throw a protective cloak around him. And it hits me then, what we've seen that day: this is the world, this is what the Buddha spoke of. The struggles of this life: hunger, dreams, sickness, age, lust, hate. It's all right here.

And I think of Bedse, the stupas, ensconced in the mountain, silent.

Finally, the train lurches forward on to our station. There's a crush at the door – yelling and commotion. I touch my money under my clothes, and as crowds line the platform, we make a plan for disembarking: 'You go first,' I say. 'I'll hold on to you.'

RUNNING THE SUBANSIRI
BY BRIDGET CROCKER

I'd just stepped in human shit when I noticed Arun and Tilak praying next to the river's put-in. I wanted to join them, but by the time I had scraped the squished feces from my sandal-clad toes, the young men were finished.

'We made the offering, but the eggs were not rotten. It wasn't so good,' Tilak tells me later as he and Arun stack dry bags on the bow of the raft for me to rig.

'Rotten eggs are better?' I look at my two students, who are along on this exploratory trip as training river guides. Our small team has come to India's remote Subansiri River to see if it can be developed as a commercial trip.

'The Ones on the other side like everything backwards from us,' Arun explains. 'We eat fresh eggs. They eat rotten ones. This is the Donyi-Polo way.' Donyi-Polo is the local religion in Arunachal Pradesh, and is focused on nature worship.

It's not a stretch to see nature as divine here. For several days, we have lived with the Subansiri – we've paddled hypalon rafts downriver, passing fishermen in wooden canoes returning to villages upstream with abundant catches of golden masheer, and awakened on luminescent beaches touched only by delicate civet tracks. We've had our ankles gnawed into swollen lumps by shrewd dam dum flies, and we don't even care; the palpable magic of the wilderness we're in is so captivating, it's an actual balm to physical pain.

Our first night on the Subansiri it rained, and I was kept awake not by thundering cracks in the clouds as I expected, but by silent bursts of lightning moving through the air around my tent, flashing close to the ground.

But today, it's clear skies as we go from rigging boats to scouting and running rapids that, until now, have been known only to the river's fishermen. Our team navigates nine river miles before stopping just above the gorge. We're treated to a near-full moon rising above the canyon wall as we put away the dinner dishes. I walk to my tent, noticing mica flecks glittering in the moonlight like stars beneath my feet. I wonder if that's how the Ones on the other side feel walking above us on constellations of light. Maybe each of us picks up the sun's reflection, appearing on the opposite side as stars. This is the sort of wisdom the Subansiri imparts.

I awake feeling out-of-sorts, and get to work early pulling buckets of water from the river, tuned into my iPod. The Indigo Girls' heartbroken rendition of 'Down by the River' shuffles into play, and it hits me that it's the day before my mother's birthday. Whenever I'm reminded of my mom and our turbulent relationship, I'm flooded with an overwhelming mix of sadness, rage, shock and powerlessness. Usually, I blink it back and run into another part of myself or find a distraction to sidestep the pain. Over the years, drugs, black-out drinking, snorting men and hurling myself down remote whitewater rivers have been my main methods of distraction. As a sober woman in recovery, the usual check-out strategies don't work for me anymore (except occasionally escaping to remote whitewater rivers).

She could drag me over the rainbow – the Indigo Girls are singing about my mom and me. The grief is so jagged, it pulls me far away from this river's shore, to a place where I can't swallow the pain – instead, I am eaten alive by it. This grief has crippled me since the

Easter Sunday when Mama split from herself, simply woke up as someone who was the opposite of who she'd been. On the outside, she looked the same, but inside she was – and still is – unrecognizable to me. The grief comes from having a mother who has died, yet is still alive. I scan the beach to see if anyone is watching me before turning with a shaking chest to face the Subansiri.

She is watching me, as She has since I first put my hand into Her malachite water and admitted to Her that I didn't have the answers. Over these last few days, the Subansiri has pushed my guiding to a deeper level, getting me to do things like line up for the biggest rapid of the trip while closing my eyes. Above the river-wide, stomping ledge hole, I realized I could feel the current better than I could see it. I used my oars as long extensions of my arms, swirling them to grasp the current She wanted to lead me toward. When the tension on my oar blades released, I knew I was centered on the line: I shipped my oars in, like a bird folding its wings, and braced for the drop. I opened my eyes as the raft arched over the ledge smoothly with hardly a splash, then sailed past the house-sized rock at the bottom.

This push/pull dance is not an isolated incident: it has been like this between the Subansiri and me since the put-in outside Daporijo, which is why She knows the exact nature of my strength. She perceives me as I really am. As I struggle on shore to navigate the blinding pain I've had since girlhood, the Subansiri holds up a mirror, and I see that to sidestep this feeling is to quit being the woman She knows me as. But how do I stop chasing the illusion that I can outrun the pain?

Stand in it, She says to me. Try to stand in it.

But how? The anguish is crushing.

You are strong enough – it won't harm you.

I trust Her. Focusing on Her pulsing current, I stop squirming and stand square in the pain. It rocks through my whole body all at once, like water flash-flooding a side canyon.

It will pass and you will still be standing. She shushes me, holds my gaze. You are this strong; no pain can match your strength and endurance.

Running the Subansiri

I believe Her. I let myself feel the aching wound all the way - the complete storm. My body jolts with electricity as old toxins zing through my cells. I weather on, through the tears, knowing my freedom is in my strength, that if I can bear the full weight of this sorrow, I can step into the answer and find peace.

I'm in the vortex of it for two, maybe three minutes and then it's without energy. The force of it peters out and I am still standing, just like the Subansiri knew I'd be.

It's a defining moment in my long jag of running: standing still. I walk upstream from camp and immerse my whole body in Her, offering my transformed tears of freedom and gratitude as I float in Her bosom.

The next day, on my mother's birthday, we float through emerald mun zala rainforest, watching these 'deep forest' monkeys gleefully chase each other in the canopy above stretched-out, shimmering beaches. Then we notice them: unnatural, concentric waves pulsing upstream.

'What is this?' Kevin asks from his kayak, perplexed by the vibrating, curved lines forcing their way against the river's gradient, against gravity. In all our combined decades of running rivers around the globe, no member of our exploratory team has seen anything like this. We stare at the water, then each other; the reversed flow of water eludes logic.

We see it and hear it at the same time. The entire forest on the river's right bank has been stripped away and replaced with cement that's been applied scalding hot, burning the earth's oozing wound into an enormous gray scab.

There's a pounding that grows stronger with the pulsing waves, a spiritless drone that underlies the nails-on-a-chalkboard screeching of metal scraping river rock. Jackhammers and scores of grinding bulldozers throb inside my chest.

It's a dam site.

Our rafts float into it haplessly; behind us a trickling, moss-lined waterfall gently carves its way through elfin forest to join the river.

Before us is hell itself.

Hundreds of workers in yellow hard hats are lined up on the road above us, waving and cheering delightedly as they see our rafts emerge from the forested canyon.

Upriver, our flotilla was similarly greeted by Apatani villagers who lobbed oranges from shore in case we were hungry. I had excitedly waved to the river-dwellers and returned their blown kisses. Floating through the dam site now, no one in our group waves to these dam workers or returns their whistles and cheers.

Our 18-foot boats are tiny specks next to the dam's mammoth foundation; the pipe-fittings have all been secured. The walls supporting the structure are built with river rocks. The Subansiri is being killed with Her own bones.

To know that a river is being dammed is one thing – to feel it vibrating inside your chest is another. Horror, rage, shock and powerlessness force their way up from my stomach, stinging my eyes with tears. It's the pain over one of my greatest teachers dying. This much madness is too much sorrow, the line in the song goes.

I look at Arun, whose face mirrors mine: shock, tears, helplessness. I want to run from the pain. I want to save Arun, Tilak, the fishermen and the sweet, orange-tossing villagers – somehow rescue them from this madness and this sorrow. The Subansiri taught me that the only way out of the pain is through it. I look at Arun square on, without blinking, and surrender to tears. I don't know how to fix this, only that I was made strong enough to witness and survive pain of this magnitude, without being defined by it.

We pass under the dam site's bridge and I notice that someone has painted on the piling in yellow the word 'peace' with the silhouette of a dove underneath.

I dip my hand into the Subansiri's water and whisper, 'My strength is Your strength, my voice is Your voice. Let me use them to honor You.'

I anoint water on the back of my neck, grateful that in the face of anguish, I've been rendered strong enough to bear the weight of Her story. Perhaps in the offering of such a rotten, festering tale, a way toward peace for the river will appear on the opposite side of grief.

We take out just below the dam site, accessing the road that's facilitated Her demise. As I step onto shore, headed for my home on the other side of the world, I have no illusions that I can outrun or distract myself from what I've witnessed. I say a final goodbye, and surrender to keeping the Subansiri alive by reflecting, honoring, celebrating – immersing myself in Her memory, over and over again – the nature of Her strength.

Postscript: Nine years after that exploratory trip, construction of the dam on the Subansiri River has still not been completed, in part due to sustained public outcry and protests along Her shores. As India and China fight over the power that She could generate for a nation, those who fish from Her waters and wash their babies in Her eddies – and those who have studied her currents and found healing in Her teachings – have taken a stand for the Subansiri, that She remain forever free flowing.

203

AT HOME IN GIZA
BY MAGGIE DOWNS

Egyptian traffic is loud, fast-moving and nonstop, separating me from the market where I can get food. I whip my head around, searching for a crosswalk, a traffic light, a traffic cop, even a traffic sign. Anything that will help me move from one side of the street to the other. But I'm staring down vehicular anarchy in a swollen city, where 22 million people stretch the limits of streets built for four million.

Somehow other people manage to navigate this mess. Men wearing airy *galabeyas*, women in hijabs, students sporting smart grey suits, even children brave the road. They find a kind of harmony in the chaos, establishing eye contact with the drivers, walking at a steady pace – moving *shway shway*, slowly slowly, across one lane at a time – until they are absorbed into the traffic flow.

Just when I'm about to give up, I meet Rami.

'There is trick,' he says, standing along my right elbow. He is shaped like a stout lightbulb, with a shiny, bald head and wide smile.

'Really?'

He giggles. 'Close your eyes and pray to Allah.'

With that, he takes my arm and pulls me into the current.

Afterward, we sit together at a street cafe, sipping mint tea in mugs the size of shot glasses and smoking apple-flavored tobacco in a hookah.

At Home in Giza

Rami asks about my family, but I can't summon the words to explain my story – that when my mom began dying, I decided to quit my job, travel the world, and complete the bucket list she'll never finish. It's six months into my travels, and I've already hiked the Inca Trail to Machu Picchu. I tackled the Nile River rapids in Uganda aboard a flimsy yellow raft. I went on a safari and saw breathtaking animals. Now I'm in Egypt to see the pyramids from the back of a camel before heading to India. But I don't tell Rami any of this; I just say I'm backpacking.

When Rami invites me to stay at his family's house in Giza, I say yes. I'm overwhelmed by his generosity – literally opening his door for a stranger on the street – but more than that, in a world that is infinite and strange and beautiful, I'm still searching for some semblance of home. Here is someone willing to embrace me as one of his own, and I'm touched.

I also don't have anywhere else to go. New Year's Eve is approaching, the hostels are booked, and my budget is too meager for the city's pricier options. Just that morning a hostel owner said he was going to kick me out to make room for someone with a reservation.

After Rami and I pick up my backpack, we are met by Rami's uncle, Sabar, a wiry thirtysomething. He pulls up in a beat-up sedan and barely stops moving long enough to let us climb inside.

In a particularly congested part of the city, Sabar rolls down the window with a hand-crank and plops a fake, magnetic police light on the roof. He presses a couple buttons, launching an assault of sirens and flashing lights.

'Makes cars go away!' Sabar laughs.

With traffic, the drive from Cairo to Giza is 50 minutes. We get there in ten. Underneath a bridge, Sabar pulls over, and Rami and I continue navigating the maze to his house. There is a lurching public bus, which takes us just a few blocks. Then we hop into a sputtering rickshaw and weave through traffic – this time scooters and donkey carts – down shadowed alleyways, behind rows of identical concrete buildings. Finally, Rami and I walk a little over a mile on roads too narrow for the rickshaw to negotiate.

The paths are made of compacted dirt, raised slightly above chunky sewage and stagnant water. Garbage clogs the canals, and dead animal carcasses rot on the piles of trash. Rami and I press on through clouds of bloated flies, past unmarked stores and cafes, through the smoke of burning rubber. I never see any street signs.

'Is ok?' Rami says.

'Is fine, is fine,' I say, keeping my doubts to myself. I have no phone. I doubt there's an internet connection for my laptop computer. Nobody knows where I am. I don't even know.

From the outside, Rami's three-story house looks abandoned. Stalks of rebar jut out from the top. Windows are broken. The front door is raised a couple feet from the ground, but there are no steps to get there. I'm tall, and it requires a mighty stretch and Rami's assistance to get in the door. We kick off our shoes and make two neat piles at the foot of the staircase.

The family lives on the second level. The concrete floor of the living room is draped with a rug so thin, it looks like a whisper. There is little furniture.

Rami's mother has been expecting us. She greets me with two sheets of newspaper rolled into a cone. Inside are hot, fried falafel the size of flattened ice cream scoops, wrapped in warm pita bread. Oil soaks through the paper and makes my hands hot and greasy. The crust of each falafel is slightly burnt, which heightens the texture of the soft, warm middle. Flecks of parsley are so fresh, they actually taste like the color green.

'Best chef in Egypt!' Rami beams, and I agree. It is the best I've ever had, and I've eaten a lot of falafel.

When I'm finished, Rami rolls the oily newspapers from our meal into a ball, along with some food waste, wilted vegetables and bones. We carry it to the roof, where the goats live, and feed our scraps to the animals. Whatever the goats can't eat – like an empty potato chip bag – is tossed off the roof, where it joins the other trash blowing through the streets.

It is dusk, and the street below is illuminated with few lights. A boy walks by with a burlap sack that squirms and whines. Puppies.

'Where is he taking them?' I ask. I feel my voice rise with notes of panic.

'They will drown,' Rami says. 'But do not worry. Better to be dead than live in Giza.'

As much as I don't want the puppies to die, I've grown to understand that ending life can be more merciful than letting it continue. My mom has spent ten years dying of Alzheimer's disease, and I've witnessed her slow, backward plunge into dementia. She forgot how to speak, forgot how to walk, forgot me.

Many times I wondered why my mom continued to survive, why her body pressed on without her in it, why we couldn't let this vibrant, beautiful woman go with dignity instead of acting as bystanders to her decline. But our culture is not necessarily one of compassion. We champion those who suffer, even while we don't want to suffer ourselves.

The morning before I met Rami, my mom was moved into hospice care. Her body no longer remembered how to swallow, which meant she wasn't receiving any sustenance. My family decided a long time ago that we wouldn't put my mother on a feeding tube, so it was only a matter of time before she succumbed to starvation. My dad sent me an e-mail that said she wouldn't last long.

Now my mom's impending death feels like the traffic in Cairo. I am unable to weave my way through the lanes, so far from finding footing on the other side.

Rami abruptly leaves to meet friends, and his sister, Raina, is on the phone with her boyfriend. That leaves me with the matriarch, her three sisters and an in-law, and none of them speaks English. Rami's mother turns on the TV and adjusts the rabbit-ear antennas until a show appears. Based on the dramatic expressions and swelling music, I assume this is an Arabic soap opera.

I watch the TV show this way, five women forming almost a complete circle around me, and still I feel alone. What I wouldn't give to watch a dumb soap opera with my mom again. I choke back a sob. One woman shoots me a stern look, raises a finger to her lips and spits as she shushes. They scoot away from me, and there's a hollow, lonely space where these women used to be.

––––––––––––

We sleep that night on the living room floor, all of us jumbled together like a cluttered drawer of cutlery: Rami, his mother, her sisters, the daughters, some friends of the family, and the one in-law. We wrap itchy wool blankets around our bodies, burrito style. I smash one of my sweaters into a ball, and that serves as my pillow. Raina, next to me, curls under a tented blanket to talk on the phone with her boyfriend. Still.

Mosquitoes hum near my ears, and bigger swarms swish the air around my head. I tighten the blanket around my face. Mosquitoes land on my cheeks. I pull the blanket tighter again, until only my mouth and nostrils are bare, and I inhale insects. They fly into my mouth and sting my lips. I pull the blanket over my head until I can barely breathe.

In the morning, my skin is swollen. My face, arms and legs are covered with bites. I point to the hot, pink welts that line my limbs. The family shrugs. The mosquitoes did not touch them. Raina jokes, 'Is because you are so sweet.'

I don't have any lotions or creams to offer relief, and I don't know where to buy any. The only medicine in my backpack is a small vial of sangre de grado, dragon's blood, that I received from a shaman in the Amazon rainforest six months earlier. The dragon's blood is the dark, red resin of a tree, said to be therapeutic for skin ailments and infection.

That morning, while my mother is taking some of her last, ragged breaths on earth, I smear dragon's blood on my body, staining my skin a menstrual red-brown. There are twenty-seven spots on my face, including three on my lips, seventeen on my left arm, twelve on my right. My legs are even worse, so gnawed that I lose count of the welts. Later I catch sight of my reflection in a decorative urn. I look bloody and beaten. I don't even recognize myself.

Raina looks at me with dismay. She is a devout Muslim teen who dresses modestly in turtlenecks and floor-length skirts. But she is also very stylish, donning a lacy tank top over her turtleneck, pulling bright tights underneath her skirt, draping a decorative scarf over her plain, black hijab. And because Raina thinks everything is better with a little sparkle, she drapes layers of necklaces around her neck and slips stacks of glittery bracelets over her wrists. It looks like she purchases rhinestones in bulk.

Finally Raina says, 'My mother is mad at you.'

'Why? What have I done?'

'You blame us for bites on your skin,' she says. 'You think we are dirty. You hate staying with us.'

'No, I don't blame you, and I don't think you are dirty,' I say. 'These bites hurt very much. I am in pain.'

'You hate us.'

'No, I don't,' I insist. 'I'm just sad.'

Raina suggests a shower to feel better, and those are magic words. It has been months since I've had the kind of shower I was accustomed to in the United States. Backpacking around Africa, I took a lot of bucket baths, which are exactly what they sound like – standing over a drain or on a dirt floor with a bucket of water, running a bar of soap over my skin, using a small cup to dump the water all over my body.

While eco-friendly and efficient, bucket baths are not very enjoyable. Not the way I enjoy showers at home. I imagined the slap of hot water on my sore skin. Lathering my hair with shampoo. Letting the water stream over my head and face and shoulders, washing all the dirt and hurt away.

Raina tells me to be patient. The shower will be ready soon. The rest of the family has disappeared, Raina leaves the room, and I wait alone. After about an hour, Raina leads me by the hand into the bathroom.

The bathroom has a toilet, though it can only be flushed by pouring a bucket of water into the tank. There is also a bathtub, though it is filled with plastic chairs, boxes and assorted dishes.

'Where is the shower?' I ask.

'Stand here,' Raina says, positioning me near the toilet. The floor is tile, slanted toward a single drain. Raina leaves the room and returns carrying a fat, metal pot of water. She places the pot on the floor, shuts the door, and instructs me to remove my clothes.

'But shower ...?' I say.

'Here is shower.'

She balances on top of the toilet seat, holding a measuring cup with a long handle. One cup at a time, water is poured on my head. Each tiny cascade is near boiling, hot enough to make my flesh sting. All the while, Raina sings in Arabic. The tune is sweet and mournful.

'My mother is dying,' I say.

'Everybody dies,' Raina says, then continues to sing.

'No, I mean my mother is dying. Right now,' I say. 'She is in a hospital in Ohio. She might already be dead.'

'Everybody dies,' Raina says again. 'Life is to suffer.'

'I thought I already lost her,' I continue. 'But I was wrong.'

Raina dribbles shampoo on my head and combs her fingers through the ropes of my curly hair. Then, with a firm hand, she runs a bar of heavily perfumed soap over my body and rubs my skin until it lathers. When she rinses me, I am pink as a newborn puppy.

I have never been so naked. I have never been so clean.

After the shower, I towel off and dress. Raina takes me by the hand and leads me to her room, where I sit on a cardboard box. She combs the tangles of my hair and pulls it back into a taut, low-slung ponytail, then covers my head with a grey hijab. On top of that, she winds a purple, silky scarf and secures the ends with a rhinestone broach.

'Oh my, very nice,' she says, nodding in approval.

At Home in Giza

She applies concealer to the mosquito bites on my face and slathers on several layers of foundation meant for olive complexions, a stark contrast to my pale skin. The rest of the makeover looks like the kind of make-up I applied at my mother's vanity as a small girl. Penciled eyebrows. Streaks of magenta blush. Layers of shiny, blue eyeshadow that rain sparkly dust onto my cheeks. Lips fat and pink. I am Raina's life-sized American girl doll.

'Now you look so pretty,' she says. 'Ah, yes. Very good.'

For the final touch, she decorates me with costume jewelry. Purple-studded bracelets. Necklaces of green plastic beads, cut to look like diamonds. A tarnished metal ring with a stone like a ping-pong ball.

Raina steps back and appraises her work. 'I cannot take you outside,' she decides. 'All the mens will be looking.'

By now, the rest of the family has returned to the house. I hear a symphony of sounds from the kitchen, the next room over, where the mother is working with the other women. The thud of a knife against wood. A rattle from a heavy, boiling pot. The scrape of pestle against mortar. A strange man arrives and hands paper-wrapped packages to the mother, who disappears into the kitchen once again.

When it is time to eat, there is no table. Instead Raina shows me how to spread a layer of newspapers on the floor. The entire family gathers and squats around the paper. The mother – one plump, bare foot bent under her body, the other sticking straight out, resting against a platter of salad – nods with approval at my makeover.

They fill my plate until it is heavy, heaped with white rice, fava beans, chopped cucumber salad and the bitter, soupy greens of *mulukhiyah*. In the center of it all is a thick ball of grilled meat, bigger than my hand, slick with hot, hissing juice. I realize I never told them I am a vegetarian.

I politely nibble around the meat. 'Oh, I am not so hungry. I cannot eat all this,' I say and rub my belly with one hand. I offer it to Rami. 'Maybe you would like my meat?'

But this is New Year's Eve. Even though this Bedouin family doesn't celebrate the holiday, they know it is a special day for my culture, and I am their guest.

'Very special for you,' Rami says.

He says the family slaughtered their uncle's camel and saved the liver for me. It's a delicacy.

'Eat, eat,' the mother urges.

This family offers me sustenance on a platter, even as the woman who nourished me lies starving. At this moment it is my decision to devour the food or to deny it, but I realize my mom has no choice. Later the cause of death on her certificate will say 'failure to thrive.'

All eyes look to me with anticipation. I take a bite. I close my eyes. I chew. The camel tastes like a punch in the face. Dark and heavy, metal and blood. It is both primal and complex. Something like life itself.

A CREMATION IN BANARAS
BY BISHWANATH GHOSH

A dozen pyres burned at the Manikarnika Ghat. Under the canopy of dark clouds the flames looked their colourful best, violent yellows and volatile oranges leaping from the womb of death to touch the sky of liberation.

The Ganga, swollen and muddied by the monsoon, watched the spectacle like an elderly and indulgent maid who knew that she would have to clear the ashes once the flames had stopped dancing.

Manikarnika Ghat, dating back to the time when gods and goddesses supposedly walked the earth, makes Banaras the most favoured destination for the dead. Devout Hindus believe that if you are cremated at the Manikarnika, you go straight to heaven, with no stopovers in the form of rebirths.

One of the burning pyres was that of my mother. She had not come to Banaras to die, unlike many others who do once they realise their end is near. My mother was only fifty-nine. She did have a heart condition that was slowly deteriorating, but death was the last thing on her mind when she and my father set out from Kanpur, about 200 miles away, to visit my younger brother, who was posted in Banaras. One afternoon, as the three of them were having lunch, she suddenly arched back and died. When the news travelled 1100 miles south to reach me in Chennai, it suddenly struck me that Banaras had been thrust on me.

Thirty-nine years before, when I was still in my mother's womb, my maternal grandfather happened to visit Banaras, and while praying at the Vishwanath temple there, he decided that if his daughter gave birth to a boy, the child would be named after the presiding deity: Vishwanath, the Master of the Universe, another name for Lord Shiva, and spelt by Bengalis as Bishwanath. That's how I got my name, which I have always considered old-fashioned and which I once even hated. But when you find people loving you in spite of your name, you learn to live with it.

And now I was to rush to the very place where my name had been decided when I was still in the womb, to cremate the owner of that womb – my mother. The distance of 1100 miles needed to be covered as soon as possible.

I was surprisingly calm when I saw my mother on a bed of ice. My body continued to have its natural cravings, such as the urge to smoke. A total of eight people, many of them acquaintances of my brother who had moved to Banaras only recently, were present in the house when I arrived. That was how big the funeral procession was going to be.

One of them, an influential journalist, had arranged for the cremation at Manikarnika Ghat. I asked him if the ghat had an electric crematorium. He said Manikarnika did not have one, though Harish Chandra Ghat did have the facility. I suggested that we go to Harish Chandra Ghat instead, because I did not want to watch my mother slowly melting into ashes on a pyre.

A small argument broke out. The majority opinion was that only the fortunate got to be cremated at Manikarnika Ghat and that I would be committing a grave sin by denying my mother her ticket to heaven. I looked at my father: he did not oppose me, but I could sense he was on their side.

The body was placed on a string cot and we set out for Manikarnika Ghat on a mini-truck. The truck dropped us at the mouth of a narrow street, and from there we had to walk up to the ghat, with the cot carried on four shoulders. My brother and I refused to let go of the weight, while others took turns in lending their shoulders.

One narrow street led to another. So narrow were they that my free shoulder often brushed past sachets of shampoo and mouth-fresheners dangling in shops. At one point I stepped on a cavity in the brick path and twisted my ankle. But I walked on despite the sharp pain because my feet had to be in tandem with the three other pairs walking with the cot.

The overcast sky finally came into view and so did the river. We had arrived at the kingdom of the dead, though at first glance it resembled a timber store: we were surrounded by logs of wood piled up high enough to reach the roof of a two-storey building.

Manikarnika Ghat is indeed a kingdom. Since time immemorial, cremations are conducted exclusively by members of the *doam* caste, who are governed by the *doam* raja, or the king of *doams*. He is considered far more powerful than the king of Banaras and not without reason. The influence and fortunes of a political ruler can change with times, but the ruler of *doams* need not worry about the vicissitudes of life: death is always certain.

An elderly Bengali priest met us at the ghat. He asked me to remove my clothes and handed me two white sheets to wear: one was to be tied around the waist and the other thrown over the shoulders. As I carried out his instructions, a friendly *doam* appeared and said the pyre was ready on the terrace of the ghat.

While the others carried the cot to the terrace, I stayed back with the priest for a certain ritual that I – as the elder son – was required to perform before lighting the pyre. The two of us sat on our haunches in a corner of the ghat where the priest made a paste by mashing rice grains, curd, milk, sweets and banana. He then asked me to draw lines on the floor with the paste. The lines I drew under his direction resembled a square puzzle. Were they meant to demystify life?

After the ritual I made my way to the terrace, where I found my mother's pyre placed on the far end. Reaching it was like walking through a furnace because six bodies were already burning on the terrace. On seeing me, the *doam* handed me a flaming sheaf of holy grass and asked me to touch the fire to my mother's lips. Barely had I done that – her lips instantly blackened – when he took away the burning grass from my hand and placed it between the logs for them to catch fire. 'Please leave now, all of you,' he told us firmly, 'and wait downstairs. I will call you when it is all done.'

So I had just performed something I always dreaded: *mukhagni*, touching the fire to the mouth of the dead before it is consigned to flames. Electric crematoriums automatically spare you of this ritual, and even in traditional crematoriums in bigger cities, families can take liberties with the tradition. But this was Manikarnika Ghat, the mother of all cremation grounds, where tampering with tradition is not allowed. I felt a sense of accomplishment as I walked through the furnace once again – now I had the courage to look at the other burning pyres – and climbed down the terrace.

I also felt free. The one question that had been nagging me for several years – what if mother died? – was now out of the way. I finally began to take notice of Manikarnika Ghat. Twelve bodies were burning in all, six on the terrace and six on the steps leading to the river. More bodies were coming in. They would keep on coming. The fire never dies at Manikarnika Ghat, which is as old as the city of Banaras – and no one knows exactly how old Banaras is.

We found places to sit at the ghat and made ourselves comfortable. As luck would have it, the funeral procession of eight people included our long-time neighbour from Kanpur: he happened to be visiting his ancestral village near Banaras when he got the news and had come over right away. His presence at the ghat was comforting. It made us, especially my father, less unfamiliar with the surroundings.

One of my brother's acquaintances got tea for all of us, and soon we were chatting like friends who met every evening at the neighbourhood tea stall. Goats and cows walked past, looking for garlands and flowers to munch on. Dogs hovered around, attracted by the inescapable smell of burning flesh. Other mourners had also found their own corners. Death was a business here, not a tragedy. The loss of a loved one ceased to be a personal loss the moment you emerged from the narrow streets onto the ghat, where you found many other bodies awaiting cremation – and many others already burning.

From time to time, a speck of ash, originating from some pyre or other, would land on our tea. Those who noticed the ash on their tea drank it anyway. For the superstitious – and my mother was superstitious – drinking ash-laced tea would amount to drinking death, but the wise would see that as accepting death.

I felt like smoking and I walked up to the tea stall and bought a cigarette. I stood on the steps, away from my father's view, and lit it up. He knows I smoke but I do not smoke in front of him. I surveyed the river. I had known the Ganga all my life – I grew up by it, in Kanpur – but today, for the first time, I stood on its banks bound by duty.

I looked at the boats floating past. Countless boats. Their occupants looked at me curiously. Actually they were looking at the kingdom of death – the living museum that makes Banaras famous world over. I was merely one of the many displays. What they didn't realise was that I, too, like them, was a spectator. And unlike them, even though I was in a mourner's robes, I was constantly taking mental notes, something I could use in a future book. The thought of a few thousand people reading that book and sharing my sorrow had presently divided my sorrow into so many minute pieces that there was hardly any sorrow left for me to feel. Far from being a grieving son, I felt like a writer who had lucked into rich material.

Soon the *doam* sent word that the cremation was over. The priest asked me and my brother to accompany him to the terrace. The pyre, which had stood at about three feet until three hours ago, was now reduced to a bed of smouldering ashes.

The priest handed me a clay pitcher and asked me to fill it up with water from the river. When I returned with the filled pitcher, he asked me to empty it over the cinder. I heard a hissing sound as I poured the water and then nothing remained of my mother – even the smoulder in her ashes had died. But something did remain, which the priest could spot, a tiny piece of burnt flesh. He asked the doam to hand it to us on a clay bowl.

'This is your mother's navel,' the priest explained. 'Fire is able to burn the entire body into ashes, but not the navel. It remains indestructible. Now immerse it in the Ganga and with that we are done for the day.'

My brother and I walked down the steps of Manikarnika Ghat and together we flung the navel into the river and freed our mother from the cycle of birth and death.

Six years later: I am back in Banaras, roaming its ghats and narrow streets because I finally have the contract for the book that was only a remote possibility back then, but whose imaginary success had anaesthetised me against my mother's cremation.

'Nothing is permanent,' the waiter is telling an Italian couple as I come to the terrace of the riverside lodge for breakfast. 'Everything must come to an end.' I have arrived late to catch the context, but I can see the couple listening to him wide-eyed.

'What is there today,' he continues, 'will not be there tomorrow. That is the truth.' The waiter is a boy barely eighteen.

The people of Banaras – and I mean the families settled on its ghats for generations – are one of the happiest people on earth. Unhurried and unworried and unambitious, living and letting live, helping themselves to a cannabis-laced sweet or drink every evening to celebrate the extension of their existence on this planet by one more day, they come across as sages who have answers to life's square puzzles.

After a few days in the city, it is not difficult to see why they are the way they are.

Banaras – called Kashi during the ancient times, Benares during British rule, and officially Varanasi now – is essentially a string of eighty-four ghats that follow the bend in the river. The centrepiece of this string is the Dashashwamedha Ghat, occupied during the day by priests conducting business with pilgrims, boatmen calling out to tourists, and fake sadhus obliging amateur photographers for a small fee, and during the night by locals who come in small groups to wind down after they have had their daily dose of *bhang*, or cannabis.

It's a happy ghat, where lamps are waved at the river – Goddess Ganga – shortly after sunset. But hardly fifteen ghats away, to its east, lies the Harish Chandra Ghat. And hardly fifteen ghats away, to its west, lies the Manikarnika Ghat. Since cremation in these two ghats is a public spectacle, it is almost impossible to miss the burning pyres, whether you are a visitor or a resident. The images, while they fade for visitors once they return home, serve a daily reminder to the people of Banaras: no matter who you are, you too will end up in either of these two places, Harish Chandra Ghat or Manikarnika Ghat.

And so in Banaras, where thousands come each day to seek answers to life's square puzzles, you realise that life isn't a puzzle after all: It's pretty much a straight line, starting with birth and ending with death.

THE FOOL
BY JEFF GREENWALD

When I was 24, I was confused about what to do with my life. Though I'd just graduated with a degree in clinical psychology – 'You are what you need,' my brother quipped – it was hard to imagine myself as a shrink. What inspired me most were the fine arts: writing, photography, sculpture. But after four years sitting in classrooms, the first two seemed too cerebral. I wanted to work with my hands.

I'd already been doing some sculpture, assemblage mostly, in a 'studio' awkwardly located in my Santa Cruz living room. The shag carpet was suffused with sawdust, bent nails and bits of artificial fur. The one material I hadn't played with was stone – and having just read *The Agony and the Ecstasy*, I was of course obsessed with Michelangelo. So I bought a set of chisels, a two-pound iron mallet, and a ticket to Greece. The plan: to spend ten weeks on the island of Paros, famed for its white marble.

———————

Right after reaching Athens, I visited the National Archeological Museum. The artworks thrilled me, but none more than the Early Cycladic sculptures. Carved more than 4000 years ago, the abstract

The Fool

marble forms presaged the modern works of Brancusi, or Henry Moore.

I was sketching one of them – a harp-playing musician – when a woman entered the gallery. An American, I guessed. She was tall, with straight chestnut hair and the calmest, most beautiful eyes I'd ever seen. A camera was slung around her shoulder. She stood next to me for an instant, and every ion in my body pulled toward her. When she wandered off, the world deflated.

A voice I'd never heard before echoed in my brain. The rest of your life, it said, depends on that woman. What could I do? I followed her, my heart pounding, into the Mycenean room. And stood beside her. She looked at me quizzically, and half-smiled. I had to say something.

'Hi. Are you a photographer?'

'What? Me?'

'That's a pretty fancy camera.'

She glanced downward.'It is? I guess. Are you a photographer?'

'A sculptor.'

She swept her arm. 'You're right in your element.'

We continued through the galleries together, talking art and travel. She agreed to have a coffee with me at the museum's café. Her name was Alice; she'd just earned her MD and was visiting Greece with her sister before flying onward, alone.

'So where are you heading next?'

'To Nepal. Do you know it? Kathmandu. I'll be doing a residency in ayurveda: traditional Indian medicine. Then home, for my internship.'

'I mean tomorrow.'

She laughed. 'My sister and I are heading to Naxos. We'll catch the first ferry from Piraeus in the morning.'

I showed up at the docks at seven, and found them in line. 'Naxos sounds like fun,' I shrugged. 'They have pretty good marble, too.'

Alice's sister was a blast, lanky and fearless, a perfect complement to her sister's quiet radiance. They took me in. We traveled together for two weeks, from lemon-scented Naxos to rustic Santorini, where we celebrated my 25th birthday. After retsina and candlelit pastries in my room, Alice nodded at her sister, who grinned and stood up. 'I'll see you guys in the morning,' she said.

All the ambiguity in my life seemed to end that night. There was only one place to be, and one person to be there with. Alice felt the same way – but her course was set.

Which meant that mine would have to change.

———————

When Alice and I parted in mid-March, we didn't know for certain we'd see each other again. Where the fuck was Nepal? It was an abstraction, a fantasy, practically an impossiblity. My entire knowledge of the place came from Tintin, Hergé's famous comic about a young reporter and his dog. But I had vowed to raise the cash for airfare, and join her in Kathmandu. No mission in my life had ever seemed more urgent.

And so I traveled by overnight ferry to Heraklion, hoping to find work.

Crete was a rough but sylvan island, covered with fruit trees and carved by canyons. Job-seeking travelers were as common as squashed olives. My first gig, loading crated tomatoes onto trucks, was a disaster: US$25 a day for back-breaking labor. A fellow traveler told me about a construction site in Ierapetra, a town on the northeast coast. So I made my way there, and was hired – the irony not lost on me – to chisel excess cement from pre-cast hotel rooms. It was miserable work, but it paid okay. If I lived on Greek salads for three months, I might save enough money for a ticket.

There was an early morning bus from my pensione to the job site. I took a seat beside a shapely, weary-eyed woman named Caitlin. She knew the guy building the hotel: a local millionaire who'd made his fortune writing English/Greek textbooks. Caitlin was his 'masseuse'. I told her about my own weird mission – and the artistic pretentions that had brought me to Greece in the first place.

The Fool

My second Thursday in Ierapetra, I was working in one of the hotel's newly cast rooms – wearing a particle mask, and covered head to toe in cement dust – when someone barked my name. Turning around, I was astonished to see a tall, pepper-haired man in an immaculate suit, waving his hand in front of his face.

'You are Greenwald?'

I nodded hesitantly.

'Caitlin told me you are an artist. A sculptor. Is this correct?'

This was no time to be coy. 'Yes, sir.'

The man grunted. 'I need a person to design my hotel's discotheque,' he said, 'and build a playground near the seaside. Can you do it?'

I had no idea how either might be accomplished. 'Yes, sir. I can.'

'*Kala.*' He nodded. 'Come with me.'

Hercules Anoptis was an arrogant, insufferable ass, but he quadrupled my salary. I hired an engineering assistant who knew something about materials. Within two months the 'Moonspinner' disco was designed, and three cement animals – a seal, a turtle and a snake – stood in the hotel's play area. 'Future Greek ruins' my assistant said, half-jokingly.

In mid-May I took the ferry back to Piraeus, visited a travel agency in the Plaka, and bought an 'around the world' ticket. It would get me to Bombay (from where I'd travel overland to Nepal) and eventually carry me home: first to Bangkok, and onward to Los Angeles. The ticket was good for six months.

On the eve of my departure I stopped at American Express, where travelers picked up snail mail in the pre-web epoch. Though she'd written almost daily, it was always a thrill to get a letter from Alice. I tore the envelope open and unfolded the sheet of rice paper.

'Forgive me,' she wrote. 'I've fallen in love with another man.'

Broken-hearted I boarded the plane, blind momentum carrying me onward. But could that have been all? I don't think so. There was another force at play. Like the Fool in the Tarot deck, my journey was decided. Inner and outer influences had braided themselves together, forming a cable with irresistible pull.

After a shell-shocked week in the manic kaleidescope of Bombay, I boarded a train to Patna and made the short flight to Kathmandu. I arrived the morning of 7 June, 1979, during a brief thunderstorm, and made my way into Thamel.

Nepal was the antithesis of crowded, oppressive India. Kathmandu was cool and kind, ringed by vivid green hills. Incense filled the air, and bicycle bells rang everywhere. Cows and kids shared the streets with rickshaws and pariah dogs. People were laughing, and looking me in the eye. The whole place seemed like a chaotic movie set, between takes. I couldn't guess what film was being shot, or what the story was – but I knew I wanted a role. I checked in to the Kathmandu Guest House, pulled out my journal, and wrote two words: 'Welcome home.'

226

———

Though I'd shipped my hammer and chisels home from Greece, the gig on Ierapetra had rekindled the spark beneath my trip. During my first week in Kathmandu, noticing the lack of places for kids to play, I lit on a scheme to build playgrounds. There were potential materials everywhere: bricks, ropes, pipes, tires. So I drew up some plans and took them to the UNICEF headquarters in Patan, just over the river.

It was early evening by the time I got back to the Kathmandu Guest House. Soon the fruit bats would drop from the trees surrounding the Royal Palace; I'd watch from the high rooftop. The clerk stopped me as I strode toward the stairs.

'A note for you, sir.'

I unfolded a sheet of rice paper: *I'm in the garden, in the moonlight – Alice*

She stood up as I came through the back doors, toward the sitting

Buddha. Our hands came up, intertwining instantly. She looked at me, calm and wondering. 'I made a mistake,' she said. 'A really bad mistake.'

Her backpack and medical books were at the man's house, a short rickshaw ride past the Royal Palace. Alice asked me to come with her.

'He told me he'd stay away, but his best friend is there,' she told me. 'A guy named Rick. He's in Nepal on a Fulbright, studying Tibetan rituals.'

We arrived at the house, a white and modern single-story structure in a garden compound across from a soccer field. Roses bloomed in the garden. Alice knocked at the door. The housemate answered. He had an intelligent, squarish face and short black hair, and regarded us with narrowed eyes through pop-bottle glasses.

'Hi, Rick,' said Alice. 'This is my friend…'

'You,' he cut her off, 'come get your things. And you – ' he jabbed a finger at me ' – can wait right there.'

He stood at the doorway like one of the guardian lions in front of the New York Public Library, wilting me with a look of disdain. We more or less held that pose until Alice reappeared. She threw her gear into our rickshaw, and we rattled away.

I'll fast-forward through the five months that followed. Alice and I stayed in Nepal through the monsoon and fall festival season, sharing adventures. We traveled to India, celebrated Diwali in Kathmandu, then trekked in the Annapurnas, sleeping in stables and eating a lot of chapatis with jam. Nepal was an endless tapestry of stories, mysteries and surprises. I fell in love with the place. But the romance with Alice was withering. By the time we left Nepal, our future together was doubtful.

In mid-November, we were sharing a beach hut in Thailand when news of the Cambodian civil war reached us. Tens of thousands of Cambodians were fleeing to the Thai border, seeking refuge from Pol Pot's genocidal regime.

'I can't lie on the beach when people are desperate for medical help,' Alice announced. I agreed. We returned to Bangkok, and volunteered with the UN High Commissioner for Refugees. They stuck us on a bus, and shipped us to the dry plains of Aranyaprathet. Our last days together were spent at the Khao-I-Dang refugee camp – she as a medic and me, with my sketchy building experience, as a water engineer.

We'd reached the point where our polarities had shifted completely; the qualities that had drawn us together – her unflagging optimism and my sardonic humor – repelled us. I flew back to North America on my own, discovering that culture shock is far more powerful in reverse.

With nowhere to live in the States, I crashed with friends in Santa Barbara. During the Christmas holidays, bored and alone, I wrote a story about my experiences on the Thai–Cambodian border. It was published in the town's independent weekly paper. Two weeks later, I was offered the position of Features Editor. It was an invitation to belong someplace, and I accepted.

But Nepal was where I belonged. Kathmandu had kept me in a continual state of surprise, which had translated into pure inspiration. I'd found myself creating more than visual art – I was writing. Not just scribbling self-absorbed words, but describing things that fascinated me: the mysterious rituals with drums and fire, the savage, erotic gods and goddesses, the serene eyes of the Buddha.

And I was still under their spell. Clouds massing behind the Santa Barbara hills, peaked like white meringue, tricked my eyes and made my heart ache with memories of the Himalaya. I had to get back, by any means necessary. In 1983, I applied for – and won – a Rotary Journalism Fellowship to the Kingdom.

It's funny how bad vibes stick around. Though I lived in Kathmandu for a year on that gig, that guy Rick – who was part of the expat inner circle – held a grudge against me. I'd 'stolen' his buddy's girlfriend; I was not to be trusted.

It wasn't until 1985, when I came back to Nepal a third time, that Rick and I found ourselves sharing a table at a reception, and were compelled to make conversation. I'd just seen *The Killing Fields*, and my experiences in Cambodia intrigued him. We found we had interests in common: Kubrick films, jazz piano, vintage cameras. Rick himself was a filmmaker; he'd recently directed *Lord of the Dance*, a documentary about a mysterious Tibetan Buddhist ritual in Nepal's middle hills (narrated, impressively, by Richard Gere).

Two years later, I was back in Kathmandu yet again. This time Rick and I saw a lot of each other – and when our paths later converged in the Bay Area, our friendship deepened. We became nearly inseparable – so it seemed almost fated that, when my book *Shopping for Buddhas* brought me to Nepal once more in 1989, I ended up living in the very house he had blocked me from entering ten years earlier.

Rick was married when we first met. By 1988 he'd been separated from his wife for several years. That's when he met Marianne – a brilliant and beautiful student of Buddhism, and a successful info tech architect.

Those were good years. San Francisco's Asian Art Museum staged a blockbuster show called Wisdom and Compassion: The Sacred Art of Tibet. The Dalai Lama attended the opening; Rick, now a PhD in Tibetan Studies, was co-curator. And with *Shopping for Buddhas* recently in print, my own star was slowly rising. I began writing for national magazines, and worked on a proposal for another book: *The Size of the World*.

Rick married Marianne in 1990, twice: in both the Buddhist and Universal Life traditions. She was pregnant during the ceremonies. In June of 1991, their son Jonathan – to be known as Jack – was born. I joyfully accepted the role of godfather.

———————

There was some question, early on, about the symptoms. Rick had been in a fender-bender on his way home from work; this was the likely cause, the doctor guessed, of the blood in his urine. But the bleeding continued. By the time Rick was diagnosed with bladder cancer, his options were limited.

Jack was three when Rick first got sick. I don't want to say much about the illness. It was long and painful and the Tibetan remedies Rick requested, hoping to avoid a debilitating surgery, didn't work. It took a while to find that out. When he started getting worse, the decline moved fairly quickly.

I remember pushing Rick in his wheelchair along the Inspiration Point trail in Berkeley's Tilden park, in March of 2000, with the lupines in bloom. He spent most of April in the oncology unit of Alta Bates hospital. We moved him home in May, and into an adjustable bed in his upstair bedroom several weeks later. He protested violently, knowing – despite the morphine – what it meant. My beloved friend died on 28 May, holding Marianne's hand as she sang to him.

He had asked me in the hospital to take care of his son, now eight years old. Help Marianne guide him through life. To love Jack, as he knew I loved him. I promised I would. Having no children of my own, it was a welcome role. It has been a privilege.

———————

Sixteen years have passed since Rick's death. My godson is nearly 25, a gifted artist, now traveling in Japan with his sweet, vivacious girlfriend. He's the same age I was when I first visited Athens.

As for Alice, we haven't communicated for more than 30 years. I know, through some online sleuthing, that she's in private practice and doing well, with a family of her own.

I wish her every blessing. Our chance encounter in the archeology museum, so long ago, was the most important single moment of my life. Everything changed. It is impossible to imagine where I would be today, who I would be, had I detoured into a different gallery – or ignored that small voice in my head.

It's unlikely I'd have written three books about Nepal – or that I'd be writing this story in Kathmandu, where I've just delivered five digital cameras to the kids at the Camp Hope refugee camp. Their villages were destroyed by the 2015 earthquakes, and I'm helping them document their lives in transition. The budding photographers range in age from ten to 16; some show amazing talent. Their parents were not yet born when I followed Alice to Nepal in 1979.

Though I've given up my dreams of sculpting, I still love a good museum. And I still notice beautiful women in the galleries. But I don't chat them up so much anymore; one trip through the looking glass is enough.

THE MAN WHO TOLD FUTURES

BY PICO IYER

Kristin and I were scuffling around the backstreets of Kathmandu on a lazy November afternoon. We'd already gone to the zoo that day, and been pierced, unsettled to see a brown bear clutching at the bars of his cage, wailing piteously. We'd trudged around the National Museum, where every artifact of the King's life was recorded, with particular reference to 'The Royal Babyhood'. We'd passed an early evening among the spires of Durbar Square, watching bright-eyed boys play carom, while their elder brothers brushed against us in their jackets, muttering, 'Brown sugar, white sugar, coke, smack, dope.'

But now the afternoon was yawning ahead of us and we didn't know what to do. It was a rare opportunity for shared sightseeing: Kristin was accustomed to heading out every night at 10pm, reeling through the pubs and bars of the old city, being chatted up by self-styled mystics before fumbling back to our tiny room in the Hotel Eden as the light was coming through the frosty windows. I'd take off a little later into the heavy mist, notebook in hand, to record the bearded sages who sat along the streets, peddling every brand of cross-cultural wisdom. She was collecting experience, we liked to think; I was collecting evidence.

We'd met in New York City eight months before and, on a wild impulse, had decided that Kristin should join me on the last stop of a four-month tour through Asia that I was planning to take. She had a charming boyfriend back on East 3rd Street, and I was romancing my notebook, so it felt more than safe as we settled into our sixth-floor room on Freak St.

I opened my Lonely Planet guide now – my companion through all the countries I'd visited – and pointed out to her the one item that had long intrigued me. There, tucked among long lists of trekking agencies and meditation centers, explanations of living goddesses and apple-pie emporia, was the single most startling entry I had seen in such a work: 'The Royal Astrologer'. For a price, the write-up said, this mage who consulted with the palace on even its most important decisions – when was the right day to pass some edict, which time boded well for a royal birth – was available to anyone who wished to see him.

How could either of us resist?

I had grown up in England, among little boys who defined ourselves by everything we imagined we could see through. By day we committed to memory the lines of Xenophon and Caesar, by night we proved ourselves 'superior' to everyone around us with cascades of fluency and quasi-sophisticated airs we'd borrowed from our books.

Three times a year, I left my all-male internment camp and flew back to my parents' home in California. There, in a blinding yellow house perched above the clouds, my father was reading the palm of every stranger who visited, and talking of Aquarian precessions and the ascended masters of the Himalayas. His students, graduates of the Summer of Love, were attuned to psychic vibrations, auras and verses from the Gita, but I wasn't sure they'd recognize real life if it punched them in the face.

What better environment for producing someone who loudly announced he believed in nothing?

Kristin, however, had never given up on magic. She was five years younger than I – 23 to my 28 – and she had a powerful belief in herself (or some parts of herself) matched only by her conviction that life would reward that faith.

One time, she'd come to my office on the 25th floor of a high-rise in Rockefeller Center, and I'd pulled out a backgammon set. I was one throw from victory, and the only way she could defeat me was by throwing a double six. She closed her eyes, she shook the dice again and again between her hot palms, she muttered something nonsensical and then she sent the dice clattering across the board. One stopped rolling, and disclosed a six. The other came at last to rest: another six.

Now, though, as we tried to follow the runic instructions to the Astrologer – which true sage would allow himself to be listed in a Lonely Planet guide, I wondered? – we found ourselves passing through empty courtyards, and along a scribble of narrow lanes. We were directed towards a golden temple, and then through another maze of darkened backstreets, and then led out into an open space where a ladder brought us up to a second-floor redoubt.

When the Royal Astrologer greeted us with a business card listing his doctorate and his work for NASA, my every doubt was confirmed.

Still, I was sure I could get a good story out of this, so we agreed on neither the priciest of his readings, nor the cheapest. We padded off, to while away the hours before he could give us his verdicts, and settled into one of the cafes that might have doubled as Ali Baba's cave.

Nepal in those days was budget time-travel to all the revolutions we were just too young to have experienced firsthand. Pillows and cushions were scattered across the floor of this (as of many a) cafe, and a swirl of peasant-skirt bedspreads turned the space into a kind of magic tent. A creaky cassette of 'The Golden Road of Unlimited Devotion' unspooled blearily on the sound system, and any number of mushroom enchiladas and 'secret recipe' lasagnas on the menu promised transport of a more mysterious kind.

Travel, for me, had always been a testing of the waters. Every journey is a leap of faith, of course, a venture, ideally, into the unknown; but for me a large part of the point of encountering the Other was to see what to believe in and how much. Every stranger approaching me with a smile posed a challenge of trust – and asked me, silently, how much I could be trusted, too. Something was at stake in nearly every transaction, I felt, and it was as essential as whether you believed the world made sense or not.

Kristin and I had met when she, a former student of my father's, had read a cover story I'd written on the Colombian drug trade. She dreamed of being a writer, though for now, just out of college, she was working as a temp in a succession of Manhattan offices, deploying her capacity for typing at a furious speed; I had similar dreams even though, for the time being, I was cranking out long articles every week on world affairs for *Time* magazine, drawn from the reports of colleagues in the field. The explosion of demonstrations that was convulsing apartheid-stricken South Africa, the maneuverings preceding the Mexican election, the gas leak in Bhopal: I covered them all with the assurance of one who had never seen the places I was describing.

In the warm summer evenings, the two of us met often in the gardens of tiny cafes in the East Village, and she showed me the story she'd just written about Desiree, an Indonesian bride arriving in America. I told her of the book I was going to write on Asia. We swapped our latest discoveries from James Salter or Don De Lillo, and she told me of her girlhood adventures growing up in India, Japan and Spain (her father a spy under deepest cover).

By the time we headed out into the streets again, dusk was beginning to fall over the Nepali capital, and turn it into fairy-tale enchantment once more. Oil lamps and flickering candles came on in the disheveled storefronts, and faces peered out at us, almost invisible save for their eyes. We slipped and lurched across the uneven, potholed paths, the silhouetted spires of temples all around us. The noise and crowds of the big city seemed to fade away, and we were in a medieval kingdom at its prime.

As we climbed the stairs back to the Royal Astrologer's chamber, we might have been stumbling into an emergency room after an earthquake. Half of Nepal was there, or so it seemed, shivering in the near-dark as everyone waited for their fortune: a family wondering when to take its newborn to the temple, and how to name him; a nervous couple thinking about auspicious marriage dates.

Quite often, a sudden thump at the door announced an urgent messenger – from the palace perhaps? The Royal Astrologer handed out futures as easily as a doctor might, and the people who left his room were seldom the ones who'd come in.

Finally, he summoned us closer and pored over the charts he'd drawn up from our times and places of birth.

'So,' he said, turning to Kristin – she craned forwards, taut with attention – 'generally, I have found that you have a special talent.' She braced herself. 'This gift you have is for social work.'

I'd never seen my friend look so crushed.

'Does it say anything about creative work, an imaginative life?'

He looked again at the circle with all the partitions and said, 'Your talent is for social work.'

She didn't say a word at first. 'Nothing about writing, then?'

He shook his head.

When it came to my turn, I worried it might prove awkward once he confirmed my future as a ground-breaking writer after what he'd said to my friend.

'So,' he said, looking down, 'generally I have found that your strength is dilgence.'

'Diligence?'

He pointed out the calculations and quadrants that confirmed this.

'Diligence in the sense of doing one's duty?'

'Yes,' he said, and began explaining every scribble, but to someone who was no longer listening.

I knew that diligence was the quality that the Buddha had urged on his disciples in his final breath. But the Royal Astrologer wasn't a Buddhist and nor was I. To me the word smacked of Boy Scout badges and 'to do' lists.

'I think,' he went on, perhaps sensing our disappointment, 'that every month, on the day of the full moon, you should meditate for an hour. And eat no food all day.'

This sounded like the kind of thing my father would say. He'd been a vegetarian all his life and was full of talk of the virtues of stilling the mind and fasting so as to access a deeper wisdom.

I negotiated the sage down to fifteen minutes a month and a day without meat, and we filed out.

My four months wandering amid the conundrums of Asia changed my life more irreversibly than I could have imagined. I went to California to write up my adventures, and when my seven-month leave of absence was over, and I returned to New York City, I knew I could never survive in an office now that I had such a rich sense of how the world could stretch my sense of possibility in every direction. While writing up my droll account of the magicians of Kathmandu – and the others I'd met across the continent – I'd remembered to keep an eye out for the full moon and had sat still for a few minutes once a month, restricting myself for one day every thirty to Panang vegetable curries.

It hadn't seemed to hurt.

So now I served notice to my bosses, packed up my things in the elegant office overlooking another 50th Street high-rise, emptied my 11th-floor apartment on Park Avenue South and moved to a small room on the backstreets of Kyoto without toilet or telephone or, truth be told, visible bed.

As I was settling into my cell, my twentieth week in Japan, I found a letter in my mailbox downstairs. It was from Kristin, in New York. Her father had died, suddenly, the previous year, she told me. She'd been distraught, hadn't known where to turn or how to get her longing out, so she'd taken to her desk.

Every night, while everyone around her slept, she'd typed – and typed and typed. When her novel was finished, she'd sent it out to publishers. Within hours, Random House had signed her up for a six-figure sum, and by now rights had been sold in a dozen countries around the world; she and her friends were spinning a globe as the number mounted.

At 26, she seemed assured of a glorious future. She'd rolled a double six again.

A few weeks later, I walked, as I did every Wednesday afternoon, to the little shop across from Kyoto University that stocked a few foreign magazines. It was my one tiny moment of connection with the world I had abandoned; I forked over 700 yen, collected this week's copy of *Time* magazine and consulted it, as I always did, while ambling back through the quiet, sunlit lanes to my tiny room.

As I was paging through the magazine, from the back, something caught the edge of my gaze that looked like a misprint – or, more likely, a projection of an over-eager imagination. There, in the Books pages, was a picture of someone who looked a bit like me – or, rather, like me in my previous life, in button-down shirt and striped tie.

I knew the magazine was eager never to take notice of books written by its staff – or even former members of the staff – but I looked again and there, among the eminences, was a small, friendly review of my book about whirlwinding across Asia, accompanied by a visa-sized picture. I had any number of other projects I'd been chafing to complete, and now, I felt, I could try to be a writer at last.

'Diligence' and 'social work' indeed! The Royal Astrologer didn't know a thing.

———————

That was half a lifetime ago, almost to the day, and more than a hundred seasons have passed. A few years after our visit, the palace in Kathmandu was torn apart by a crazy massacre and I had no doubt that the Royal Astrologer was no longer in service (if only because he would have been in trouble if he had predicted such a bloody coup – or, in fact, if he hadn't; telling futures for the powerful has never been a reliable source of income).

As for Kristin, her path of double sixes had continued, almost impossibly, for quite a while. Her boyfriend in the Village, like so many, was a committed Star Trek fan and like thousands of Trekkies, no doubt, had sent in a script on spec to the program's showrunners in Hollywood.

Unlike most such fans, though, he'd seen his script accepted. He'd been flown out to LA and offered a full-time job with the program. He'd taken up a big house with Kristin in the Hollywood Hills, a chief architect of the universe he'd once worshipped from afar.

Few couples of my acquaintance had found such lustrous futures in their twenties. When I visited, Kristin and her beau seemed to have exceeded anything they might have hoped for, with their Spanish-style villa above the canyons, the red open-top sports car, publishers and TV executives waiting to turn their words into pictures.

But Kristin had always had a restless soul – perhaps the same soul that had brought her to Nepal and sent her out into the streets every evening – and somewhere along the way, in flight from stability, but not sure exactly of what she wanted instead, she'd burned the life she'd found and lost it all. Now, in her early fifties, she lives alone with a beloved cat, tending to every lost animal, still writing, but in a world that doesn't seem very interested in novels, especially from those not so young.

Her strongest quality, though, remains her fierce attachment to her friends. She lives through them and with them, the centers of her universe, and keeps up with pals from high school in Tokyo and Delhi on a sometimes daily basis. She sends me warm and mischievous messages on my birthday and remembers every last detail of 1985. As the years have passed without bringing all the adventures that once seemed inevitable, she tells me that the trip to Kathmandu was one of the highlights of her life.

And me? A couple of years after my first book came out, I sat in a car just under the yellow house above the clouds and watched a wildfire take it apart, every inch of it, so that everything I and my parents owned – not least the notes and outlines I'd drawn up for my next three books – was reduced to ash. In any case, I'd fallen under the spell of Japan and silence by then and decided to take on a wife and two kids, giving up my thoughts of becoming a writer, and simply turning out several articles a week to support an expanding household.

Writing, I'd seen, demands a ferocious, all-consuming commitment, a refusal to be distracted – or, sometimes, even to be responsible – that would never be my gift.

I smile when I hear people say that the young are too credulous, too open, too ready to be transformed. I and my school friends were so much the opposite. It was only travel – being propelled beyond the world we thought we knew and could anticipate – that stripped us of our petty certainties, our flimsy defenses, our boyish confidence. It was only figures such as the Royal Astrologer who showed us that we didn't know a thing.

We sit on opposite sides of the world now – Kristin essentially a model of social work, with the passionate attention she brings to her friends, while I steadily meet my daily deadlines, the very picture of diligence – and see that life has much wiser plans for us than we ever could have come up with. The only one who really was exercising a writer's imagination – the kind that sees the future as easily as the past – was the well-meaning man I had mocked as he tried to nudge us towards a truer understanding of who we really were.

HUNTING WITH THE HADZABE

BY JAMES MICHAEL DORSEY

Mdu squatted on a large bloodstained rock, his chin resting on his knees as he prodded the cooking fire with a small tree branch. His eyes held mine as he stoked the embers, studying me as he had done all day on the hunt. He was somewhat feral but with that same gleam in the eye that betrays deep intelligence.

His kinsmen stood behind me as the bloody baboon meat crackled and sizzled directly on the open flame. They waited respectfully for me to take the first bite, offered by their leader, as my mind raced with the endless mistakes I might commit as a guest in such a situation. Ancient societies live by ceremony and I was learning those of the Hadzabe in real time as I went.

I looked around at those wiry men the color of wet mud with their baggy shorts held up with braided roots and took in the trailways of veins that stood out on their whippet-thin arms and legs. These are men who can drop an elephant with arrows and shoot birds on the wing; they hit their target on the run and can run all day. I was now sitting among them, about to eat seared baboon that two hours prior might have killed me.

When I first arrived, Mdu was standing on an outcropping of granite boulders in front of a cave entrance from which issued the sweet smell of a wet wood fire. The cold granite glistened from its fine coating of rain and the mud tried to suck off my boots. His head was encircled with a halo of baboon hair that I assumed was his mantle of power as none of the others wore such decoration. He pounded his chest twice with a fist and spread his arms wide, as if to say, 'This is my land', implying the vast panorama of the Manyara highlands that enveloped us in western Tanzania. His enormous bow, slung across his thin shoulders, was taller than he was, and I could not help noticing various animal skins spread over rocks to dry in the sun. He was an impressive sight with the Great Rift Wall behind him.

I lowered my head, acknowledging his dominance, and with that he beckoned me inside the entrance where his diminutive kinsmen eyed me warily and where my attention went immediately to the enormous bush knives they were using to slice meat on the open fire. His allowing me to approach was already a personal coup, but I would also be tested. Mdu stamped out the small fire with a leathery foot and walked me through the ceremony of making a new one with two sticks, kindling, and some steel. To record this momentous occasion for prosperity I set my mini-tripod on a rock, set the camera timer, and ran back to make fire.

After three failed attempts, a tiny puff of flame sprang to life. Apparently this was sufficient because after that I was handed a carved bone pipe stuffed with local weed. Mdu lit it for me with a burning twig he took from the fire with a bare hand. I took a short draw before handing it back to him. It was potent and went straight to my head. I did not want to be stoned in this situation but it was necessary if I was to enter their society. They all laughed as I hacked and coughed.

Having no common reference points, I reminded myself that I was among people attuned to the rhythm of the earth. They lived by the cycles of nature. For them there was no division between the spiritual and material worlds and suddenly, there I was, a creature from a different planet. They did not smoke weed to get high but to reach an altered state of consciousness beyond my current comprehension, a state I was unused to entering myself. If I was to penetrate their society, I had to cast aside all preconceived ideas, think on my feet, and react to them in the moment – all of that while being jacked on local ganja.

The Hadzabe are true Bushmen who, like their Saan cousins from Namibia who became unwitting film stars in *The Gods Must Be Crazy*, speak the Khoisan click language. They are not just nomadic but build temporary shelters only in the most dire of weather conditions, preferring to sleep on the ground or in caves, and when they make a significant kill the entire village will relocate to feast upon it. They use iron tools, thanks to their willingness to trade meat with the local Barbaig people who are master blacksmiths, but the Hadzabe themselves have never reached that level of sophisticated toolmaking. They wear beaded jewelry that they have traded for with the Maasai, warriors who surround them in this valley, outnumbering them by 3000 to one. While most of the estimated 3000 existing Hadzabe have assimilated into cities to live on government subsidies, this isolated pocket of hunter-gatherers, estimated to number fewer than 300, is barely removed from the Stone Age, and they have no desire to join the present world.

So while early man and I sat staring at each other, I felt a physical presence creeping upon me like a ground fog. Perhaps it was the collective consciousness of mankind that has permeated the land since Mdu's forefathers sat where he was, or maybe it was just too much history and emotion for this traveler to absorb. Sitting around a fire with a clan of cavemen was not just extremely cool, it was also physically intimidating and emotionally exhausting. I had removed my watch and ring before arriving to prevent them from becoming talismans or being appropriated as unwilling gifts, but Mdu was still fascinated by the buttons and zippers of my clothing. He ran his fingers over both like a blind person seeing through touch. He ran his hands over my arms and through my hair while turning to comment to his clansmen as though delivering a medical lecture about a specimen. He pointed at objects around the fire, naming them in clicks, and seemed amused when I repeated his words as though I were a quick-learning pet. The others seemed to have little or no interest in me; I was simply there and had no bearing on their lives. However, without my knowledge, I was about to play a much larger role.

Suddenly Mdu stood up, so I did too. He grabbed his bow and arrows and we exited the cave, trotting down a muddy trail into thick bush. Mdu would stop and squat, pointing out minute scratches in the soil or bent leaves that I assumed were signs of an animals passing. He watched me intently to make sure I was taking it all in. Sometimes he froze in mid-stride and sniffed the air, and at any little sound his bow was instantly nocked with an arrow.

He melted into the surroundings, silently, as much a part of the forest as the trees or animals, and he pointed at things in branches I could not see until I realized that he was talking to me like a teacher to a small child. Why else would I have approached him if not to learn? I was happy to be his student.

He would squat there in the dirt staring at me, unmoving as I tried to enter his mind. I lost track of time and miles as I walked by his side, conscious of passing through an age before recorded history. Hundreds of generations of Hadzabe had walked that trail but I may very well have been the first white man. Language was not necessary as Mdu passed on to me a sense of complete merging with both the spiritual and natural environments. In his presence I reached a mental state I have rarely achieved on my own. I wondered if I really was the end product that men like him would evolve into over the next thousand years.

He clicked away as we walked, seemingly oblivious to what I may or not have understood. I pointed out a contrail in the overhead sky and wondered if it meant anything to him other than a bird or spirit. At that point he gave a great sigh as though I was just not getting it and began a lengthy oration of clicks mixed with words that I found fascinating. He gestured all about him throughout this grand lesson, then finished with a foot stomp to emphasize all that he had said was final. With that he turned and walked away. I thought perhaps I had just heard the Big Bang Theory from someone whose oral histories began with it.

He would disappear into thick brush then pop back out and beckon me to follow. I always found him crouched, observing a small creature that was unaware of his presence and unworthy of his arrow. One of those times I lost him for several minutes and he did not reappear. It was then that I thought I heard him coming through the undergrowth and was surprised at how much noise he was suddenly making. I froze in place just as a large and very enraged baboon broke cover no more than 20 feet from me. It was shrieking and stomping its foot, its hands balled into tight fists. I knew that baboons are fierce predators who will not hesitate to attack a man. I also knew they are the main diet of the Hadzabe and react accordingly when approached.

The next few seconds are recalled as if in a dream because I froze in the moment and retain only flashes of memory. Before I could move I heard the dull thud as the points of two arrows pierced the animal's neck. Suddenly the baboon that moments before was poised to rip me to shreds, lay before me twitching from the neurotoxin on the arrows that were ending its life. Both were clean kill shots. Mdu stood to one side while one of his men was on my other; both already had another arrow nocked in their bows. I had not heard either one of them nor was I aware they were that close.

Mdu's man had trailed us without me realizing it and Mdu had used me as bait to draw the baboon out. They had me covered the entire time and had demonstrated a perfect example of a coordinated hunt. The realization that he had used me like a tool was slowly being tattooed on my memory.

With adrenalin pulsing, I had no time to be angry at what might have cost me my life. At the same time the writer in me was already thinking, 'What a story! Who will believe this? I WAS THE BAIT!' I watched in stunned silence as Mdu pulled his knife and severed the animal's head, then gutted its innards with deft strokes, while his wingman shouldered the dead beast like a backpack and took off down the trail. Mdu approached and streaked my cheeks with the creature's blood, acknowledging my part in the hunt, then knelt to spread the dirt until no sign of the kill was left in evidence. He handed me his bow to carry on the long walk back to the cave and I considered that an honor. That night the baboon skull would hang in a tree with the bow suspended from it in order to take the animal's power for the next hunt.

I felt tears through the drying blood on my cheeks as emotion took over, not only from the wild animal attack and my dramatic rescue, but from my acceptance by this hunter-gatherer clan. My day had been an avalanche of emotion, from expectation to anxiety, to camaraderie, fear, and pure joy, and after we climbed the small rise back to the cave entrance, I slumped to the ground in a heap, spent in body and spirit. I reached for a notebook to record my thoughts but found my hands shaking too much to write anything.

Sleep took me briefly, but I awoke to the smell of burning meat and the sight of Mdu kneeling before me, holding a sizzling piece of seared baboon. He was about to hand it to me, but first, he leaned in and touched his forehead to mine. At that moment I felt connected to all of human existence.

Since that day I have thought about Mdu often. I imagine him sitting under a silver moon, stoking a fire, smoking his ganja, telling tales of days on the hunt. His life seemed quite simple compared to mine, but then I am sure that even a bushman, unencumbered by material goods, has his own burdens. I have thought long and hard about what my life would be like had I been born an African Bushman because the circumstances of our birth, something that none of us can control, are really all that separate any of us. I believe I would be happy.

It was only after my return home that I came upon a long-term DNA study of the Hadzabe conducted by Stanford University. Their paper declared in 2003 that the Hadzabe are one of three distinct primary genetic groups from which all of mankind has descended. If that is correct, I had met my own ancestors – as the bait on a baboon hunt.

Has this story affected my life? Oh yes.

More than once I have awakened in a cold sweat a second before an angry baboon sank its fangs into my throat, and one time I exited a dream while washing imaginary blood from my face. Other times I simply relive sitting by a fire eating seared meat with cavemen in animal skins, and I smile. The romantic in me has imagined the dinner conversations that my death would have inspired: 'Did you hear? He was torn apart by a wild animal in Africa!' For good or bad, such an experience is never far from recollection. Travel by definition gifts us with unique moments, moments that become memories, memories that turn into stories – and in Africa especially, stories become history.

The Hadzabe gave me this story. And I like to think that somewhere in the Manyara highlands, a man with a halo of baboon hair is captivating an audience around a campfire with the tale of the large white man who unwittingly helped them kill a baboon.

ON DREAM MOUNTAIN
BY TAHIR SHAH

The journey ended in a story.

Not the kind of story you hear any old day.

But a tale conjured from the farthest reaches of fantastic possibility – a kind of sci-fi grimoire....

A tale that slipped out slowly from between the lips of Mustapha Benn.

In the dozen or so years that I have lived in Morocco, I have heard all manner of stories.

Stories of Jinn, afreets, and of princesses locked in enchanted towers.

Stories of honour and chivalry, of lost hope, destiny and enlightenment.

Stories about stories.

Some of them are true or, rather, are presented as a form of truth. Others are clearly fiction. But the ones I hold most dear are those which are a hybrid of the two.

A blend of fact and fantasy.

A factasy.

Through a primitive alchemy of their own, they suck you in. Seep into your bones. Sing to you. Seduce you. Torture you. Enthuse you. Bewitch you.

On Dream Mountain

All the while, they affect the listener – in the most profound way.

Hear the story told in the right conditions, by the right person, and it changes you – from the inside out.

That is how it was with the tale told to me on Dream Mountain by Mustafa Benn.

But, before the tale could begin, a zigzag of raw adventure was necessary.

A journey as unlikely as the tale itself.

It began a little before dusk on a day of heavy winter downpours. The air had been rinsed and rinsed again, the ground beneath it pooled with puddles and mud. There was a stillness, as though the world were locked in limbo between evil and good.

I was standing in the slender lane outside my home in Casablanca, a house said to have once been infested with evil Jinn. I can't quite remember what had lured me out. But the reason was unimportant. What mattered was that my feet were standing there when the dim shadow of a man approached.

In Morocco, people believe that the future is written. You can bob and weave your way through life but, ultimately, fate prevails. There's nothing you can do about it. Indeed, they say that the harder you try to evade what is destined for you, the faster it will grab you.

The strange thing about fate is that you never quite know how or when it will strike. A chance encounter or random phone call can lead to a door opening – one that was invisible only moments before. In the same way, any amount of preparation and planning can lead to a dead end.

The shadow advanced fitfully.

First along the whitewashed wall, then over the mud, which stretched from my front door until the road a good distance away.

I watched it, taking note of the way it moved.

So preoccupied by it was I, that I failed to notice the man to whom it belonged. It was as though the shadow had a presence of its own. As if it were unconnected to anything by itself.

Six strides or more before reaching me, the man gave greeting in a low muffled voice. Before I knew it, I had replied – '*Wa alaikum salam.* And peace be upon you' – affirmation that he had come as a friend and was to be received with hospitality. His face and clothing were as worn out as the voice.

Tired watery eyes.

Skin as tough as elephant hide.

A nose sloping ungraciously to one side.

An old *jeleba* robe patched and patched again.

We stood there for a while in silence.

After all, a man who comes in peace needs no reason to visit.

I was about to say something, when the man held out a clenched fist. Not in anger but in friendship. The fingers were curled up, as though gripping something – a gift.

Squinting in the approaching darkness, I leaned forward.

The fist slackened and the fingers drew back, revealing a dark leathery palm.

An inch across, a round object was sitting upon it, like an island surrounded by a flat furrowed sea.

A seed.

About the size of a walnut, but oval in form, it was red on one side and black on the other.

'Take it,' said the muffled voice. 'It is for you.'

As anyone who has made their home in Morocco knows, a favour may not be asked until a gift has been presented and received. The gift may materialise in the shape of an object or an introduction, or even a fulsome line of praise. What matters is that the act of giving is completed before a request is made.

It was for this reason that I had become weary of receiving unsolicited favours or gifts – especially from strangers. In more usual circumstances I would have politely declined. But there was nothing usual about that evening, or the guest who had arrived.

This was made clear a moment after the seed had been revealed.

On Dream Mountain

Our guardian happened to be brushing past just as the large oval seed was being offered.

Never one to be given to emotion of any kind, he clasped a hand to each unshaven cheek, his lower jaw hanging down, mouth wide open in stupefaction, and eyes wide.

'An honour,' said the guardian, choking for breath.

'A seed,' I said.

'A special seed,' corrected the muffled voice.

We repaired to the garden and sat on damp stools.

Many pots of sweet mint tea followed, poured into glasses little bigger than thimbles. There was much conversation, most of it garbled and indistinct. My ancestors were praised, as was my health, and that of my family and friends. The visitor's hand threw a few grains of incense onto the embers burning in the brazier. Pungent smoke took me back to travels far away.

Now clenched in my own fist, the seed seemed to tingle as the tea was drunk, and the conversation made.

Occidental training urged me to ask whether the object had a purpose. The old man grinned at the question, his mouth an uneven chequerboard of black and faded white.

'You will know its use when you have found it,' he said.

'But shall I plant it?'

'If you wish.'

'What will it grow into?'

'It is not that kind of seed.'

'Not a plant?'

'No.'

'I don't understand.'

The fingers that had first placed the object into my own, blurred as they waved left, right, left.

'This is the seed of a journey,' said the muffled voice.

'A journey to where?'

The visitor shrugged.

'The destination is not important.'

'But how would I know when I have reached if I don't know where I am going?'

Again, the grin came and went.

'By trusting,' said the man.

'Trusting in what?'

'Trusting in the seed.'

Since earliest childhood I was raised not to think too much. My father used to say that deliberation stifled possibility, just as it slayed the chance of real adventure.

Instead, he would reward me for sipping from the cup of spontaneity, and for following my gut.

Even though my desk was piled high with writing work, and my diary packed with obligations, I felt a calling – the kind that can't be explained, except to those who have felt it themselves.

It was deep in my bones.

The frenzied gnaw of anticipation.

The desperate urge to travel.

The need to set off without delay.

So, next morning, I packed a small bag, stuffed the red and black seed into my pocket, and found myself in the lane outside my home. Our guardian was sweeping the mud with a dried palm frond. He said that the visitor had stayed up late swapping stories for hospitality. When I asked where he had gone, the guardian looked me square in the eye.

'He will be waiting for you,' he said.

'You mean, here at home … when I get back?'

The guardian cocked his head to the side.

'No, not here.'

'Then where?'

'At your destination.'

I rolled my eyes and, pining for a world that was black and white, I set off.

A journey without planning followed.

Not once did I ask directions or pull out a map. Nor did I give any thought to why I was travelling, or where I was going. From time to time I would remove the seed from my pocket, weigh in it in hand and close my eyes.

It may seem far-fetched, but it was as though the little object had a presence. As if it knew that I was on a journey – that it was both my travelling companion and my guide.

Whenever I wondered which fork in the road to take, I would grasp the seed, close my eyes, and would feel the answer seeping in through my skin.

Through days and then weeks I roamed the kingdom.

During that time, I encountered people and places that changed me in a deep down way.

At a grim cafe in the backstreets of Tétouan, I met a musician who was missing three fingers and a foot. He played a crude violin that he himself had made. As he played, he sang, a deep guttural lament of lost love and forgotten hope.

Once finished with his performance, he hobbled over, sat down beside me, sipped a café noir, and explained he had always dreamed of going away to sea. He longed to witness the sunset with nothing but water all around.

'We are close to the Mediterranean,' I said, 'and so your dream is surely an easy one to arrange.'

The musician seemed glum.

'I will tell you a secret,' he said.

'What?'

'My fear.'

'What fear?'

'The fear that prevents me from ever getting in a boat.'

'Are you afraid of drowning?' I asked.

The musician shook his head from side to side.

'No. Something much worse than that.'

'Tell me.'

'Do you promise to tell no one?' he said. 'For if it is spoken, a Jinn will surely hear it and taunt me.'

I promised.

Leaning over the scuffled tabletop, the musician winced.

'I'm very fearful of fish,' he whispered.

'Fish?'

'Yes, fish.'

The musician drained his glass and drifted away.

When he was gone, I took a bus southward, into the Rif, the thought of ocean sunsets and fish in my mind.

After zigzagging through small towns and villages, I came to a hamlet perched on the side of a cliff.

At a tea stall there, I found a farmer with sad mournful eyes and a great shock of white hair. He was bemoaning the loss of his favourite donkey. Having strayed down a steep hillside, the creature had missed its footing – and had tumbled to its death. The farmer said his life would never be the same, that the donkey had been his closest friend.

In a village beyond, I came across an American woman called Joanie. She walked barefoot and was utterly broke, had a knotted mane of dreadlocks down her back, and the kind of glazed look of someone on a spiritual quest. She had difficulty in remembering the basic details of her past, as though the quest had forced her to shun her own history – like a snake sloughing its skin. The only thing she wanted to speak about was a glade deep in the Moss Forest.

When describing it, Joanie's face was illuminated as if touched by angelic light. Her breathing deepening, she recounted how it was the most enchanted spot in the entire world. Despite my asking over and over, she wouldn't reveal the location of the forest. All she would say was that a traveller ripened by adventure made discoveries to which raw eyes were blind.

My own journey continued.

Through days and nights I travelled, the red and black seed never far from my thoughts or my hand.

North.

East.

South.

West.

No plan or map to steer me.

Nothing but my gut as guide to a journey of unending possibility.

At the edge of a desert track, I met a lean lopsided shepherd wearing a talisman crafted from a nugget of amber. The size and shape of an apricot, it was etched with the ninety-nine names of God.

In a grove of wizened olive trees, a throng of schoolboys mobbed me, begging for chocolate and for pens.

At a truck stop on the margin of a lake of uncertain name, a man tried to sell me a wooden box. It was half full of dry sand. He promised that each grain would make a wish come true.

Leaving the box for another traveller, I kept going.

In Marrakech, I met medicine men and magicians, street-side dentists who doubled as barbers, and on the flat pink plain beyond, a clutch of little boys swinging squirrels around and around on strings.

I saw villages fringed in palms, and camels chewing their cud in the shade. And goats in trees, feasting on argan nuts. And skeins of freshly dyed wool, hanging to dry in the blinding winter light. And mounds of dampened mint destined for thimble-sized glasses of tea. And children skipping along craggy paths on their way back home from class. And ferocious guard dogs with crazed maniacal eyes. And towering cork oaks harvested for their bark. And neat rows of fossils laid out for sale on twisting mountain roads. And chameleons sunning themselves on boulders as old as time.

Some nights I slept in ramshackle hostels – or rather tried to sleep – tossing and turning against the riotous din of young men buoyed by drink and lust. On other evenings, I lay on flat roofs, or beside streams, or on desert sands – and watched the heavens as they turned.

A canvas of galaxies and stars.

Like a handful of salt cast over a black tiled floor.

There is nothing so wondrous as lying out undisturbed on the side of a small spinning planet, as it races through space and time.

Nothing, that is, except for the kind of surprise that only unplanned travel can bring.

The kind of surprise that changes the way you see what you think you know.

Bordered by an ocean and a sea, Morocco is a land of endless deserts and forests, of snow-capped mountains, ancient walled cities and open fields. It's a realm united by extraordinary beauty, by hope and by possibility.

The jewel of jewels in the treasure trove is the High Atlas.

They rise up from the baked sand plain like the arched backbone of a prehistoric creature poised for attack. A mass of crags and secret valleys, of high pastures and oblique precipices, there's nowhere that comes close in sheer magnificence.

Little by little I ascended.

Shafts of platinum light and freezing shade.

One blind bend after the next.

Boulders the size of houses.

Rivulets gushing down mountainsides.

The young walking on stout legs.

The old perched on donkeys, cheeks chapped and eyes lost in wrinkles.

Sometimes I took a ride in the back of a pickup. Or squeezed between others in a clapped out Mercedes as it slalomed heavenward, the gears grinding, the driver high on kif.

At other times, I walked.

Eventually, I reached a knot of low mud-built homes clustered in the shade of a little mosque and minaret. For once, the dogs were too old or too tired to bark. So, I slumped down on the ground and caught my breath.

Within a minute or two, greetings had been showered on me by the imam. Half a pomegranate had been forced into one hand and a cup of water into the other. God was praised. More salutations were proclaimed. Neighbours were called. Mouths smiled. People streamed from their homes. Laughter mixed with cries of surprise.

And God was praised again.

Once the pomegranate was in my stomach and the water had quenched my thirst, I did something which I had not done before on the journey.

I took out the seed and held it for all to see.

The villagers peered at the object, taking in the red and the black.

All of a sudden, they started to talk.

Urgently, the imam held up a hand.

'It's not here,' he said. 'But in the next village.'

'What is?'

'The place you are looking for.'

Not for the first time since setting off from home, I didn't quite understand. But, having given thanks, I took to the road again.

After more steep twists and turns, giant boulders, rivulets, blinding light and ice-cold shadow, I reached another village.

More hands were shaken, salutations given, refreshments, and thanks to God. Once the pleasantries were over, I took out the seed.

Again, the villagers huddled forward.

'He lives up there,' said a young man, pointing to a shack encircled by cacti.

'Who does?'

'Mustapha Benn.'

On my travels I have come to learn that it is sometimes better not to try and make sense of things. Like a bubble of air rising up through water, an explanation usually arrives.

That is, if an explanation is supposed to come.

So that is how I reached the battered old door and found a familiar face.

The face of the visitor who had presented me with the seed.

'Peace be upon you,' he said, seemingly unsurprised at my arrival.

'What are the chances of meeting you here?' I said, flustered and confused.

Mustapha Benn ushered me into the two-room home where he lived alone, and set about boiling water for tea.

'If you believe in possibility,' he replied, 'then anything is possible.'

'Even the impossible?'

'Yes, of course. Especially the impossible.'

After tea, a simple meal was served, then more tea, some conversation, silence, and bed.

I woke early, my head aching, my body cupped round the embers of the fire.

Mustapha Benn was sitting in a chair near the window.

'You slept well,' he said.

'Yes. But…'

'But your head feels like a hammer has struck it.'

'How did you know?'

Rubbing his watery eyes with his thumbs, Mustapha Benn let out a chuckle.

'There is a reason for everything,' he said.

'And what is the reason for my headache?'

'A story.'

'I don't understand.'

Leaning back in the chair, Mustapha Benn slowly recounted a tale – a tale as outlandish as it was familiar.

It was the story of a princess called Yasmine, whose veins ran with music, and who was terrified of the ocean and its waves. She was protected from drowning by an amulet made from amber, sold into slavery by a blind magician, then transformed into a lizard and back again, by a Jinn. A herd of donkeys befriended her, taught her the language of the peacocks, and were slain in a battle with albino dwarfs. She was married to a hunchback king, tricked into slavery once again, before escaping into an enchanted forest – carpeted in the softest emerald moss. At the end of a long life, Princess Yasmine drank from a goblet of silver water and floated up into the heavens, where she glints each night as a star.

At the end of the tale, I applauded.

'I don't know how you did it,' I said, 'but your story is as magical as the black and red seed.'

My host rubbed his eyes again.

'It's not my story,' he said cryptically. 'It's yours.'

Slipping me a smile, an uneven chequerboard of black and faded white, Mustapha Benn put a log on the fire, and brewed a pot of tea.

As he stirred the water, I took out the seed and looked at it hard.

'What should I do with this now?' I asked.

My host let out a grunt.

'Take it home,' he said. 'Put it in a box and let it wait.'

'Wait for what?'

'Wait for the day when you are ready for an adventure once again.'

Authors

DON GEORGE

Is the author of *Lonely Planet's Guide to Travel Writing* and *The Way of Wanderlust: The Best Travel Writing of Don George*. Don has edited ten Lonely Planet literary anthologies, including *The Kindness of Strangers*, *A Moveable Feast*, *Better Than Fiction* and *An Innocent Abroad*. Don is Editor at Large for *National Geographic Traveler* and Special Features Editor for BBC Travel. He also edits GeoEx's blog, Wanderlust: Literary Journeys for the Discerning Traveler. Don was previously Global Travel Editor at Lonely Planet, as well as Travel Editor for the *San Francisco Examiner & Chronicle* and the founder and editor of Salon's Wanderlust website. He has received dozens of awards for his writing and editing, including eleven Lowell Thomas Awards from the Society of American Travel Writers. He teaches writing workshops and speaks about the transformational power of travel at conferences, corporations, and colleges around the world. He is co-founder and host of the Weekday Wanderlust reading series in San Francisco, and co-founder and chairman of the annual Book Passage Travel Writers & Photographers Conference. His website is www.don-george.com.

TORRE DEROCHE

Is the author of *Love with a Chance of Drowning*. Her second book, *The Worrier's Guide to the End of the World*, is due out in early 2017. Her writing has appeared in the *Atlantic*, the *Guardian*, *Open Skies* and the *Sydney Morning Herald*, and she blogs at www.fearfuladventurer.com. In her spare time she writes horror stories.

BLANE BACHELOR

Is a former newspaper sportswriter. Blane covers travel, outdoor adventure, and culture for outlets including *New York* magazine, the *Washington Post*, *Outside* magazine, *Runner's World*, *Hemispheres*, *Men's Journal*, *Marie Claire*, *Fodors* and many others. Her career in journalism has included covering breaking news, spending a year abroad in Barcelona, writing a popular dating column, and countless (mis)adventures all over the world. A Florida native and graduate of the University of Florida, Blane now resides in San Francisco. She still never misses the chance to leave the airport on a long layover.

Authors

REBECCA DINERSTEIN

Is the author of the novel *The Sunlit Night* and the bilingual English-Norwegian collection of poems *Lofoten*. Her nonfiction has appeared in the *New York Times*, the *Guardian* and the *New Yorker* online, among others. She received her BA from Yale and her MFA in Fiction from New York University, where she was a Rona Jaffe Graduate Fellow. She lives in Brooklyn.

JAN MORRIS

Is Welsh and 90, has written 40-odd books of history, travel, fiction, biography, memoir and collected essays. She lives in Wales with her partner of 60 years, Elizabeth Morris, in an 18th-century stable block between the mountains and the sea, and is an Honorary Fellow of her old Oxford college, Christ Church.

ELIZABETH GEORGE

Is the *New York Times* and international bestselling author of a British crime series that feature a large cast of characters reflecting the spectrum of social class in England. She's been twice nominated for an Edgar Award, and has received the Anthony Award, France's Grand Prix de Littérature Policière, and Germany's MIMI. She's received an honorary doctorate in humane letters from California State University Fullerton, an honorary MFA from Northwest Institute of Literary Art, the Distinguished Alumnus Award from University of California Riverside, the Barnes and Noble Writers for Writers Award from *Poets and Writers Magazine*, the Distinguished Alumnus Award from California State University Fullerton, and the Ohioana Book Award. She is also the force behind the Elizabeth George Foundation, which gives yearly grants to poets, emerging playwrights, unpublished novelists, students attending MFA programs, and organizations serving disadvantaged youth in the area of the creative arts. She teaches creative writing around the world and online. In her spare time, she gardens and pets her dog.

JANE HAMILTON

Is the author of novels that have won literary prizes, been made into films, and become international bestsellers. Two of them, *The Book of Ruth* and *A Map of the World*, were selections of Oprah's Book Club. Her nonfiction has appeared in the

Authors

New York Times, *Washington Post*, *Allure*, *O: The Oprah Magazine*, *Elle* and various anthologies. She's married to an apple farmer and lives in Wisconsin.

ALEXANDER MCCALL SMITH

Is the author of the *No. 1 Ladies' Detective Agency* series, the *Isabel Dalhousie* series, the *Portuguese Irregular Verbs* series, the *44 Scotland Street* series and the *Corduroy Mansions* series. He is professor emeritus of medical law at the University of Edinburgh in Scotland and has served with many national and international organizations concerned with bioethics. He was born in what is now known as Zimbabwe and was a law professor at the University of Botswana.

KEIJA PARSSINEN

Keija Parssinen is the author of *The Ruins of Us*, which won a Michener-Copernicus award and was long-listed for the Chautauqua Prize; and *The Unraveling of Mercy Louis*, which won an Alex Award from the American Library Association and was chosen as Book of the Month by Emily St. John Mandel. Her writing has appeared in *Salon*, *FiveChapters*, *The Brooklyn Quarterly*, the *New Delta Review*, *This Land Magazine*, *Marie Claire*, and elsewhere. A graduate of Princeton University and the Iowa Writers' Workshop, where she was a Truman Capote fellow, she is an Assistant Professor of English at the University of Tulsa. Raised in Saudi Arabia and Texas, she now lives in Oklahoma with her husband and son.

MRIDU KHULLAR RELPH

Was born and grew up in New Delhi, India, and now lives just outside of London, UK. Her writing has been published in the *New York Times*, *Time*, the *Independent*, *CNN*, *ABC News*, the *Christian Science Monitor*, *Ms* and others. In 2010, she was named Development Journalist of the Year by the Asian Development Bank Institute. She is currently working on her first novel.

YULIA DENISYUK

Is a passionate writer and photographer specializing in uncovering shared human truths everywhere she goes. An ethnic Russian-Chuvash, she was born in Kazakhstan, grew up in Estonia, and now lives in the United States. Yulia started traveling solo at the age of five because her family was scattered across the four corners of the former USSR. Her mixed identity and a confusing family geography have inspired her to travel ever since. A four-year stint with the US Navy brought her to the arid fields of Afghanistan and Iraq, while an MBA program took her to the skyscrapers of Japan and rural homes of Northern India. Yulia eventually quit her corporate lifestyle to turn to adventure, travel, and storytelling full-time. Her work has appeared in various publications, including *Upward* magazine and Turkish Airlines' *Skylife*. She is currently working on a photo poetry book based on her recent four-month trip around the world and planning a 2017 Mongol Rally adventure. When not traveling, Yulia can be found in New York or Chicago reading Mikhail Bulgakov's *Master and Margarita* with her goldendoodle Misha by her side. Learn more about Yulia at www.yulia-denisyuk.com.

EMILY KOCH

Is a journalist living in Bristol, UK. Her awards include being named Young Journalist of the Year in the 2012 Regional Press Awards. She has had flash fiction published in the 2015 National Flash Fiction Day Anthology, and is currently finishing her first novel.

CARISSA KASPER

Is a Saskatchewan transplant born in Newfoundland and now rooted in Vancouver with her bulldog, Truman. Like the achene of a dandelion, she has grown, taken, and left hairs of herself in the 24 countries she's visited throughout the Americas, Europe and Africa, as a creative writing graduate from Kwantlen Polytechnic University, Fundraising Coordinator for BC Book Prizes and WORD Vancouver, and as a consultant for community and individual food gardens. Her work hovers around what it means to 'be home', and in this publication, her work has found its first home.

JESSICA SILBER

Grew up in Connecticut. She had the great good fortune to study in Paris during college, to move to Tanzania after college, and to relocate to California after she left Tanzania. With all respect to San Francisco and its wonderful cafes, she still misses croissants from France, chai from East Africa and, yes, Dunkin' Donuts from the Northeast.

CANDACE ROSE RARDON

Is a writer, sketch artist, and illustrator with a passion for telling stories about the world – through words and watercolors. Her work has appeared on National Geographic's Intelligent Travel site, BBC Travel, and World Hum, among others, and her travel blog, The Great Affair, has been featured in the *New York Times*. After seven years of traveling and living overseas, she now calls San Francisco home.

MARILYN ABILDSKOV

Is the author of *The Men in My Country*. Her work has been published in *AGNI*, the *Sun*, the *Pinch*, the *Rumpus*, *Black Warrior Review*, *Alaska Quarterly Review* and elsewhere. The recipient of fellowships from the Rona Jaffe Writers' Foundation, the Corporation of Yaddo and the Utah Arts Council, she lives in the San Francisco Bay Area where she teaches creative nonfiction in the MFA Program at Saint Mary's College of California.

SHANNON LEONE FOWLER

Is a marine biologist, writer, and single mother of three young children, currently living in London. Since her doctorate on Australian sea lions, she's taught marine ecology in the Bahamas and Galápagos, led a university course on killer whales in the San Juan Islands, spent seasons as the Marine Mammal Biologist onboard ships in both the Arctic and Antarctic, taught graduate students field techniques while studying Weddell seals on the Ross Ice Shelf, and worked as a science writer at National Public Radio in Washington DC. Her memoir, *Traveling with Ghosts*, will be published by Simon & Schuster in 2017.

ANN PATCHETT

Is the author of three books of nonfiction and seven books of fiction, including her latest novel, *Commonwealth*. Her work has won numerous awards and been translated to more than thirty languages. She is the co-owner of Parnassus Books in Nashville, Tennessee, where she lives with her husband Karl and their dog Sparky.

Authors

FRANCINE PROSE

Is the author of *Mister Monkey*, her most recent novel. She is Distinguished Visiting Writer at Bard.

TC BOYLE

Is the author of 26 books of fiction, including most recently, *T.C. Boyle Stories II*; *The Harder They Come*; and *The Terranauts*. He lives in Santa Barbara, California.

KAREN JOY FOWLER

Is the author of six novels and three short story collections. She's written literary, contemporary, historical, and science fiction. Her most recent novel, *We are all completely beside ourselves*, won the 2013 PEN/Faulkner, the California Book Award, and was shortlisted for the Man Booker in 2014. She lives in Santa Cruz, California.

ROBIN CHERRY

Robin Cherry is a Cleveland-raised, Hudson Valley-based writer with a passion for Eastern Europe, undiscovered wine regions and garlic. She has written for many publications including *National Geographic Traveler*, *Afar*, the *Atlantic*, *Saveur*, and *Wine Enthusiast*. She is the author of *Catalog: The History of Mail Order Shopping* and *Garlic: An Edible Biography*. After majoring in Russian history at Carlton College, she almost joined the CIA but she can't keep a secret.

ROBERT TWIGGER

Is a writer and photographer specialising in adventurous travel. He has crossed the Rockies in a homemade birch bark canoe, caught the world's longest snake for a *National Geographic* documentary, made numerous desert journeys in the Sahara and written eleven books. His latest is *Red Nile*, a biography of the world's greatest river. He has written a self-help book called *Walk*, a guide to happiness, and is writing another for Penguin called *Micromastery*.

Authors

POROCHISTA KHAKPOUR

Was born in Tehran, raised in Los Angeles and lives in New York City. She is the author of the novels *The Last Illusion* – a 2014 'Best Book of the Year' according to NPR, Kirkus, Buzzfeed, Popmatters, Electric Literature, and more – and *Sons and Other Flammable Objects*, the 2007 California Book Award winner in 'First Fiction,' one of the *Chicago Tribune*'s 'Fall's Best,' and a *New York Times* 'Editor's Choice.' Her writing has appeared in *Harper's*, the *New York Times*, the *Los Angeles Times*, the *Wall Street Journal*, *Al Jazeera America*, *Bookforum*, *Slate*, *Salon*, *Spin*, the *Daily Beast*, *Elle*, and many other publications around the world. She is currently writer-in-residence at Bard College.

NATALIE BASZILE'S

Debut novel, *Queen Sugar*, is soon to be adapted into a TV series by writer/director Ava DuVernay, of Selma fame, and co-produced by Oprah Winfrey for OWN, Winfrey's cable network. *Queen Sugar* was named one of the *San Francisco Chronicle*'s Best Books of 2014, was longlisted for the Crooks Corner Southern Book Prize, and was nominated for an NAACP Image Award. Natalie has a MA in Afro-American Studies from UCLA, and holds an MFA from Warren Wilson College's MFA Program for Writers. Her non-fiction work has appeared in The *Rumpus.net*, *Mission at Tenth*, *The Best Women's Travel Writing Volume 9*, and *O, The Oprah Magazine*. She is a member of the San Francisco Writers' Grotto

SUZANNE JOINSON

Is an award-winning writer of fiction and nonfiction whose work has appeared in, among other places, the *New York Times*, British *Vogue*, *Aeon*, Lonely Planet collections of travel writing, and the *Independent on Sunday*. Her first novel, *A Lady Cyclist's Guide to Kashgar*, was translated into sixteen languages and was a national bestseller in the US. She lives in Sussex, England. Her website is www. suzannejoinson.com.

ANTHONY SATTIN

Is a journalist, broadcaster and the author of several highly acclaimed books of history and travel that focus on the Middle East and North Africa. These include

Authors

The Pharaoh's Shadow: Travels in Ancient and Modern Egypt, an account of his search for Egypt's surviving ancient culture; *The Gates of Africa*, which tells of the 18th-century search for Timbuktu; and *Lifting the Veil*, a history of travellers in Egypt from 1768 to 1956. *A Winter on the Nile* tells of the parallel journeys made by Florence Nightingale and Gustave Flaubert. Anthony's most recent book, *Young Lawrence*, was inspired by the journey he recounts in 'I Would Go' and looks at the formative years Lawrence of Arabia spent in the Middle East before WW1. His award-winning journalism on travel and books has appeared in many publications, including the *Wall Street Journal*, the *Observer*, *Daily Telegraph* and the *Sunday Times*, where he contributed a weekly book column for many years. A fellow of the Royal Geographical Society, editorial advisor on *Geographical Magazine* and contributing editor to *Conde Nast Traveller*, Anthony has been described as one of the key influences on travel writing today.

LAURIE HOVELL MCMILLIN

Has traveled among Buddhist communities in South Asia since 1982; she has lived and studied with Ambedkar Buddhists and in Tibetan communities. Interested in both nonfiction and scholarly writing, she teaches writing at Oberlin College in Ohio. She is currently working on a book about encounters with Buddhists in contemporary South Asia. Her first book, *English in Tibet, Tibet in English: Self-Presentation in Tibet and the Diaspora*, explores British accounts of travel to Tibet during the colonial era as well as Tibetan self-presentations in English. Her book of memoir and history, *Buried Indians: Digging up the Past in a Midwestern Town*, focuses on Native American memory in her Wisconsin hometown. Her travel writing has appeared in *Travel Writing and Ethics: Theory and Practice*, and in the journal *ISLE: Interdisciplinary Studies in Literature and the Environment*. She also created and edits the online journal *Away: Experiments in Travel and Telling*, with the aim of including new forms and voices in writing about travel.

BRIDGET CROCKER

Is an outdoor travel writer and river guide. She has guided remote expeditions down many of the world's greatest river canyons in far-flung regions of Zambia, Ethiopia, the Philippines, Peru, Chile, Costa Rica, India and the Western United

States, and has led several international exploratory trips. She is a contributing author to Lonely Planet guidebooks and *The Best Women's Travel Writing* series from Travelers' Tales. Her work has been featured in many magazines, including *Men's Journal*, *National Geographic Adventure*, *Trail Runner*, *Paddler*, *Outside*, and *Vela*. Bridget lives on the edge of the continent in Southern California with her husband and two daughters, and chronicles the family's travels on her blog, The Adventures of Little Mama. Visit her at www.bridgetcrocker.com.

MAGGIE DOWNS

Is a columnist, essayist, and journalist based in Palm Springs, California, who has worked in print and online media for more than 15 years. Her work has appeared in the *New York Times*, the *Washington Post*, the *Los Angeles Times*, *Roads & Kingdoms*, Smithsonian.com, *Eating Well*, and the *Rumpus*, among other publications. She holds a BSJ in magazine journalism from Ohio University and an MFA in creative nonfiction from the University of California Riverside-Palm Desert. She has one son, Everest.

BISHWANATH GHOSH

Is a journalist and writer. He was born in December 1970 in the north Indian city of Kanpur and currently resides in Chennai (formerly Madras), where he works as an Associate Editor with *The Hindu*, one of India's largest and most-respected newspapers. He is the author of the hugely popular *Chai, Chai: Travels in Places Where You Stop but Never Get Off*, which was his first book; *Tamarind City: Where Modern India Began*; and *Longing, Belonging: An Outsider at Home in Calcutta*. His forthcoming works include *On Radcliffe's Trail: Travels on the Line That Partitioned India*, and a travelogue about the ancient city of Banaras, provisionally titled *Life in Death*.

JEFF GREENWALD

Is the author of six travel books, three set in Nepal. He divides his time between Oakland and Kathmandu. Jeff is also the director of a non-profit organization, www.ethicaltraveler.org.

Authors

PICO IYER

Has been based in a two-room apartment in suburban Japan since 1992, and since 1982 has been writing up to 100 articles a year, for the *New York Review of Books*, *Harper's*, *Granta*, *Vanity Fair* and more than 200 other periodicals across the globe. His most recent books are *The Art of Stillness* and *The Man Within My Head*.

JAMES MICHAEL DORSEY

Is an award-winning author, explorer, photographer, and lecturer who has traveled extensively in 46 countries. He has spent the past two decades researching remote cultures around the world. He is a contributing editor at *Transitions Abroad* and a frequent contributor to *Perceptive Travel* and United Airlines' *Hemispheres* magazine. He has also written for *Colliers*, the *Christian Science Monitor*, the *Los Angeles Times*, *BBC Wildlife*, *Wend* and *Natural History*. His most recent book, *Vanishing Tales from Ancient Trails*, is available on all major bookseller sites. His stories have appeared in ten travel anthologies. He is a thirteen-time Solas Award category winner from Travelers' Tales, and a contributor to their *Best Travel Writing, Volume Ten*. He is a fellow of the Explorers Club and former director of the Adventurers Club.

TAHIR SHAH

Is the author of some twenty books and has spent two decades showing the world to itself in a way that is often surprising, and sometimes quite magical. Tahir is fascinated by considering the ordinary in new and different ways, and his published works have appeared in dozens of languages, the world over. A great many of his books chart the unusual quests that are his hallmark – from studying magic with the godmen of India, to his search through the upper Amazon for the birdmen of Peru, to the zigzag adventure through Ethiopia for the fabled goldmines of King Solomon. Tahir Shah has made documentary films as well, has published numerous novels, and is a regular contributor to *Lonely Planet* magazine. It is the lure of raw adventure – journeys without maps and planning – that gets him salivating. As for his favourite motto, it is this: 'A life without steep learning curves is no life at all.' For more about him, visit www.tahirshah.com.